Patriots, Politics, and the Oklahoma City Bombing

This book explores new ground in social movements by analyzing an escalating spiral of tension between the Patriot movement and the state centered on the mutual framing of conflict as "warfare." By examining the social construction of "warfare" as a principal script or frame defining the movement-state dynamic, Stuart A. Wright explains how this highly charged confluence of a war narrative engendered a kind of symbiosis leading to the escalation of a mutual threat that culminated in the Oklahoma City bombing. Wright offers a unique perspective on the events leading up to the bombing because he served as a consultant to Timothy McVeigh's defense team and draws on primary data based on face-to-face interviews with McVeigh. The book contends that McVeigh was firmly entrenched in the Patriot movement and was part of a network of "warrior cells" that planned and implemented the bombing. As such, the bombing must be viewed through the lens of a social movement framework in order to fully understand the incident and the role played by McVeigh.

Stuart A. Wright is professor of sociology and Assistant Director for the Office of Research and Sponsored Programs at Lamar University (Beaumont, TX). Dr. Wright received his Ph.D. from the University of Connecticut in 1983. He is the author of *Leaving Cults: The Dynamics of Defection* and editor of *Armageddon in Waco*. He has published more than thirty articles or book chapters in scholarly venues and has become a widely recognized expert and legal consultant. Dr. Wright worked with U.S. congressional subcommittees in 1995 investigating the government's role in the Waco siege and testified in House hearings. Following the highly publicized hearings, he was retained as a consultant by defense attorneys in the Oklahoma City bombing trial of Timothy McVeigh. Dr. Wright has received numerous grants and research awards.

Cambridge Studies in Contentious Politics

Editors

Jack A. Goldstone *George Mason University*
Doug McAdam *Stanford University and Center for Advanced Study in the Behavioral Sciences*
Sidney Tarrow *Cornell University*
Charles Tilly *Columbia University*
Elisabeth J. Wood *Yale University*

Ronald Aminzade et al., *Silence and Voice in the Study of Contentious Politics*
Javier Auyero, *Routine Politics and Violence in Argentina: The Gray Zone of State Power*
Clifford Bob, *The Marketing of Rebellion: Insurgents, Media, and International Activism*
Charles Brockett, *Political Movements and Violence in Central America*
Gerald F. Davis, Doug McAdam, W. Richard Scott, and Mayer N. Zald, *Social Movements and Organization Theory*
Jack A. Goldstone, editor, *States, Parties, and Social Movements*
Doug McAdam, Sidney Tarrow, and Charles Tilly, *Dynamics of Contention*
Kevin J. O'Brien and Lianjiang Li, *Rightful Resistance in Rural China*
Sidney Tarrow, *The New Transnational Activism*
Charles Tilly, *Contention and Democracy in Europe, 1650–2000*
Charles Tilly, *The Politics of Collective Violence*
Deborah Yashar, *Contesting Citizenship in Latin America: The Rise of Indigenous Movements and the Postliberal Challenge*

Patriots, Politics, and the Oklahoma City Bombing

STUART A. WRIGHT
Lamar University

CAMBRIDGE
UNIVERSITY PRESS

CAMBRIDGE UNIVERSITY PRESS
Cambridge, New York, Melbourne, Madrid, Cape Town, Singapore, São Paulo

Cambridge University Press
32 Avenue of the Americas, New York, NY 10013-2473, USA

www.cambridge.org
Information on this title: www.cambridge.org/9780521872645

First published 2007

Printed in the United States of America

A catalog record for this publication is available from the British Library.

Library of Congress Cataloging in Publication Data
Wright, Stuart A.
Patriots, politics, and the Oklahoma City bombing / Stuart A. Wright.
   p.   cm. – (Cambridge studies in contentious politics)
Includes bibliographical references and index.
ISBN 978-0-521-87264-5 (hardback) – ISBN 978-0-521-69419-3 (pbk.)
1. Oklahoma City Federal Building Bombing, Oklahoma City, Okla., 1995.
2. Militia movements – United States.   3. Government, Resistance to – United States.
4. Radicalism – United States.   I. Title.   II. Series.
HV6432.6.W75   2007
322.4′20973–dc22   2006038153

ISBN   978-0-521-87264-5 hardback
ISBN   978-0-521-69419-3 paperback

Dedicated to the loving memory of Jenna Wright, 1976–2006

Contents

List of Figures and Tables

Preface and Acknowledgments

As this book entered the copyediting stage, the November 2006 mid-term elections saw Democrats take back both houses of Congress. Opposition to the war in Iraq was thought to have been the swing issue for voters. The Bush administration's misguided "war on terror" mired in the military occupation of Iraq has created a number of critical problems for the nation that will likely reverberate for years to come, including the staggering economic costs of the war, the incitement of new waves of anti-Americanism generating more recruits to groups like al Qaeda, the alarming assault on civil liberties at home, and the damage done to U.S. relations among allies abroad. Opinion polls now show that a majority of Americans oppose the war in Iraq. The Bush administration is facing deepening divisions in its own party over the war and Democrats have seized the opportunity to push for change. The oversight responsibility of the new Congress, through hearings and investigations, should shed more light on some of the ill-effects of the war just mentioned. However, even as policy analysts turn toward the future and sort through the myriad problems, one concern likely to be overlooked is the potential impact on domestic terrorism.

After the 9/11 attacks on the World Trade Center and the Pentagon, the threat of a new external enemy quelled much of the antigovernment activity among far-right movement organizations and actors. But a recent report released by the Southern Poverty Law Center (Holthouse, 2006) reveals that Patriot warriors have been strategically preparing for the next insurgent episode, exploiting the state's surge in militarism. Capitalizing on opportunities afforded them by the war in Iraq, large numbers of white supremacists and far-right militants have enlisted in the armed services, giving them access to sophisticated weaponry, explosives, combat tactics, and training, as well as contact with other military personnel. A Department of

Defense investigator told the Southern Poverty Law Center that Aryan soldiers stretched across all branches of service. The investigator reportedly found evidence on 320 extremists at the Fort Lewis, Washington, military base alone. According to the DOD source, the numbers of far-right extremists in the Army are well into the thousands.

In 2005, the military failed to meet its recruiting goals for the war and was forced to widen the net. The Pentagon has been under increasing pressure to maintain enlistment numbers, resulting in a lowering of standards. One investigative report by the *Chicago Sun-Times* cited in the SPLC study found that the percentage of recruits granted "moral waivers" for previously committed crimes had more than doubled since 2001. Recruiters are consciously permitting neo-Nazis and white supremacists to enlist. Far-right activists, keenly aware of recruiting shortages in the military, have promoted enlistment as a means to become battle-ready for future violent conflicts. One National Alliance leader explicitly encouraged racist skinheads to enlist in the infantry because light infantry operations, such as patrolling, ambush, raids, cordon and search, and search and destroy, would be invaluable training for "the coming race war" (Holthouse, 2006).

The growth of state militarism, the power grab by the executive branch claiming wartime powers, and the disturbing erosion of civil liberties under the Bush administration's war on terror, fostered by the Patriot Act, may well spawn new threats and opportunities for mobilization of a nascent network of movement actors on the far-right. Specifically, a number of provisions of the Patriot Act expand powers of the state that far-right movement actors and organizations already perceived as threatening. Should the United States withdraw from Iraq and work with the international community to stabilize the threat of global terrorism, it may well find that it faces a growing problem of antigovernment sentiment at home. This is more likely to be the case if the state demonstrates reticence to relinquish these expanded powers acquired under wartime conditions. If Patriot movement actors were threatened by the perception that the U.S. government was "at war" with them before 9/11, the prospect for another round of movement-state contention, given these contingencies, is a real possibility to consider.

The far-right has demonstrated enough of an historical resilience in this country so that one would expect it to find new threats and opportunities to exploit in the future. Indeed, the increased public concerns over illegal immigration and undocumented workers seem well-suited to far-right threat attribution and claims making. Controversial debates over gay marriage and equal rights for gay families also play to deep social divisions and reactionary elements. Perhaps these issues or others will provide far-right actors with the opportunities to manufacture new enemies, fuel public apprehensions and fears, and broker new ties to like-minded groups. Should legislators or the courts play an aggressive role in safeguarding the rights of undocumented residents or gay families, far-right movement entrepreneurs may well be able to capitalize on new grievances toward government, construct new frames, and mobilize for a new round of collective action. As with the Patriot movement, the new frames will have to mask the racism and bigotry that impel movement leaders in order to appeal to a wider public and build a broad base of support. Scholars of social movements will be challenged to locate and explore new forms of contention arising on the far-right as movement actors look to reinvent themselves and the issues in a shifting political climate.

When I set out to write this book I never imagined it would take me eight years to complete. For a number of reasons, both good and bad, the project seemed to grow and take on a life of its own. There were countless times I had to resist the temptation to set this manuscript aside and move on to other projects. A critical turning point for me was the Rockefeller Scholar-in-Residence grant I received in the fall of 2005. My brief residency at the Bellagio center in northern Italy provided me with uninterrupted time to write, and I was very fortunate to have this opportunity. I want to express my deepest gratitude to the Rockefeller Foundation for its recognition of my work and the extraordinary program that it has created in Bellagio. I was inspired by the breathtaking beauty of Lake Como and encouraged by the collegiality I found among the other scholars at the center. I was able to rediscover the passion and vision I had initially for the book, which made its completion a deeply gratifying experience.

Of course, the book would never have gotten off the ground had I not been approached to be a consultant in *United States of America v. Timothy James McVeigh*. The telephone call I received in August 1995 from Stephen Jones, the lead defense attorney in the Oklahoma City bombing case, provided an extraordinary window into the world of Tim McVeigh and the invaluable resources made available to the defense. I am most appreciative to Jones for the opportunity to work on this historic legal case and for the access to McVeigh. I am confident I helped the defense team better comprehend McVeigh's rage over the Waco debacle and the emergent ideology of the Patriot movement. Curiously, when some of the attorneys in the case were made aware that I planned to write this book, they pressed Jones to

xiii

remove me from the case. Jones resisted the pressure and defended me in this regard. Since I was bound by a confidentiality agreement, he said, the book would not violate the client's rights. Ironically, McVeigh expressed no objections about my book and even seemed to take an interest. During the trial in Denver in 1997, McVeigh asked to speak to me over a lunch recess. I was taken to his holding cell above the courtroom and we talked about the book. He was aware of the grumbling by some of the attorneys and dismissed it. He said he wanted to make it clear to me he had no qualms about my intentions to write the book. Indeed, three years later he would give a full account of his involvement in the bombing to two Buffalo news journalists. Obviously, McVeigh knew something the attorneys didn't.

In between McVeigh's execution in 2001 and my Rockefeller grant in 2005, a number of new facts surfaced about McVeigh and the bombing (these are discussed in Chapter 8). As this information came to light, a more complete picture of the bombing plan began to congeal. This information, together with my own research, shows that McVeigh was part of a network of Patriot insurgents who planned and carried out the bombing. The lone-wolf theory posited by the government has steadily disintegrated with each new revelation. As fate would have it, my protracted project turned into a distinct advantage because I was able to include the new data and assess the goodness of fit with the theoretical models. I hope anyone who continues to think McVeigh acted alone will read this book. The evidence against such an argument is compelling, and the degree to which McVeigh and the Patriot insurgency network overlapped in the months leading up to the bombing is disturbing and inescapable. Nonetheless, the reader can decide if I have made my case in convincing fashion.

I would like to thank my institution for its support in allowing me the time away from my duties at Lamar. At the time of my residency in Bellagio, I was Assistant Dean in the College of Graduate Studies and Research. Several individuals were willing to step into the breach and keep my office operating efficiently. I want to especially thank Dean Jerry Bradley, Carmen Breaux, and Jim Westgate for their assistance and support. The Provost, Steve Doblin, provided travel funds from his office, as did the Dean of Arts and Sciences, Brenda Nichols, and my department chair, Li-Chen Ma. I received some additional travel support from the Jack Shand fund through the Society for the Scientific Study of Religion. It goes without saying that the book would not have been completed without this generous support.

I am also indebted to the assistance of graduate students who helped make contacts with militia and Patriot groups, attended gun shows and Patriot meetings, gathered leaflets and printed materials, and helped with online searches and graphics. These individuals include Dean Peet, Paul Gregory, Quenton Sheffield, Joe Pace, and Daniella Medley. Several colleagues and friends provided critical feedback and constructive conversation along the way; especially Terri Davis, James J. Love, Jean Rosenfeld, Cathy Wessinger, and Don Lighty. I am most grateful for their input and friendship.

I received very constructive criticism and suggestions from the anonymous reviewers at Cambridge University Press. I found their comments extremely helpful, and I am most appreciative of the careful reading they gave to earlier versions of the manuscript. I also want to thank Lew Bateman, the senior editor at Cambridge. Lew recognized the potential of the first draft and gave me the chance to make the manuscript much stronger. He was encouraging in the early stages when it was most important. My production editor, Louise Calabro, and my copy editor, Stephen Calvert, gave the manuscript a meticulous reading and exhibited impeccable professionalism.

Finally, I am saddened that my oldest daughter Jenna is not here to read this book and give me her thoughtful and insightful comments. Jenna died suddenly and unexpectedly in February 2006. I am going to miss having that conversation with her and all the other discussions we would have had in the future about politics and culture. This work is dedicated to her memory.

1

Codicil to a Patriot Profile

I first met Timothy McVeigh in the federal correctional facility in El Reno, Oklahoma, in November 1995, about seven months after the Oklahoma City bombing. The lead attorney for McVeigh's defense team, Stephen Jones, phoned me in early September after reading a book I published on the Branch Davidian tragedy that same year. I surmised that he had purchased a copy of the book in Kansas City and read it on the plane while flying back to Oklahoma City the day before. Jones wanted to gain a better understanding of the Waco incident because the government was claiming that McVeigh engineered the bombing of the Alfred P. Murrah Building in retaliation for the federal assault on the Branch Davidians two years earlier. Initially, I had some reservations about taking on any kind of role that would cast me as an apologist for the alleged perpetrator of such a heinous crime. A few weeks after my telephone conversation with Jones, one of the attorneys assigned to the case, Dick Burr, a death penalty specialist, drove over from Houston, and we met for about an hour in my office. I remember thinking he was dressed very casually for an attorney: He showed up wearing an old pair of corduroys and a shirt badly in need of ironing, and his hair was uncombed. But he had a demeanor that was disarming and genuine. As I later learned, Dick Burr was a '60s political activist and labor organizer before attending law school at Vanderbilt. We hit if off from the start, sharing similar political views and common interests. He told me that his involvement in capital punishment cases developed after taking his first case in 1979. After that, he said, he decided to specialize in death penalty practice, largely because of his personal opposition to capital punishment. I was aware of the difficulty in this area of legal specialization: Attorneys lose about 90 percent of their cases. This one had an even smaller chance to succeed. Nonetheless, I felt comfortable after my meeting with Dick Burr

1

and tentatively agreed to become involved in the case as a consultant. I think my fascination with the case outweighed any reservations. After all, I told myself, Timothy McVeigh was entitled to his Sixth Amendment right to defense counsel. Jones and Burr were appointed by the court as public defenders to represent McVeigh. In a curious twist of irony, I would find myself in the employ of the federal government.

Like many other Americans, I was disturbed by the government's handling of the Branch Davidian siege and standoff, not to mention the evasive machinations by partisan politicians in the House hearings on Waco in 1995. I had testified in the congressional hearings that year, and I was still bothered by the government's lack of accountability. I published an edited volume on the incident, *Armageddon in Waco* (Wright, 1995a), which pulled together nineteen scholars from various fields of study, including sociology, law, history, and religion. The book was very critical of the Waco debacle, and that gave us some common ground. I was confident that I could help the defense team piece together a poorly understood tragedy by the general public. The opportunity to serve in a consultant's capacity also meant that I could devote more time to study new documents and reports that were not available earlier. I also welcomed the chance to meet with McVeigh because it would give me an insider's look at this historic legal case, and I was already planning to write another book about the emergence of the militant right.

My first meeting with McVeigh, on November 29, 1995, was preceded by a half-day conference with key members of the defense. I recall that it was bitterly cold in Oklahoma at that time. Dick Burr and I had flown to Oklahoma City the day before and then driven to Enid in preparation for a meeting with Stephen Jones and another defense attorney, Rob Nigh, the next morning. I didn't know it at the time, but Rob would later take over the lead in the appeals process following the criminal trial. The meeting was very instructive as I got my first glimpse of Stephen Jones. Stephen was a puzzling sort. He was a lifelong conservative Republican, but with libertarian leanings. In the mid-sixties, he worked on Richard Nixon's legal staff in New York as a researcher, and he talked openly of his admiration for the former president, much to my chagrin. Richard Nixon hardly evoked fond memories for my generation. But there was another side to Stephen. He had also taken several unpopular civil liberties cases during the sixties. He once represented a dissident college student who had been arrested for carrying a Vietcong flag into an ROTC gathering at the University of Oklahoma. Jones's insistence on representing the student cost him his position with an Enid law firm. He also represented Abbie Hoffman when Oklahoma State

2

University refused to let the political activist speak on campus. No doubt the civil liberties cases came back to haunt Jones. He ran for public office four times in Oklahoma, all resulting in defeats, including an unsuccessful run for the U.S. Senate. Nonetheless, by most standards, he had achieved a distinguished practice in law. The walls in his office were embellished with photographs of Jones with prominent national and international political figures. Despite characterizations of him as a "country lawyer" (which he didn't disavow), Stephen Jones was a forceful, intense, and charismatic individual who liked to be in control. He had an exceptional wit and a dry sense of humor that helped to cut the tension in lengthy meetings where the gravity of the task weighed heavily on everyone. There was a lot of verbal sparring, usually initiated by Jones. He was fond of bashing "liberals," a ritual that provoked considerable bantering and repartée. But he was always courteous, professional, and appreciative of my work on Waco. I looked forward to working with him, ideological differences notwithstanding.

The meeting moved along rapidly that morning, and we broke for lunch around noon. Dick, Rob, and I grabbed a sandwich at the café on the first floor of the East Broadway office building. While we ate, the attorneys traded assessments of McVeigh and talked about legal strategies in building a defense. After lunch, Dick and I drove from Enid to the small town of El Reno.

The federal prison in El Reno is a venerable, intimidating, fortresslike structure, probably built in the 1930s. It looked like something out of an old Edward G. Robinson movie. McVeigh was being held in maximum security, and the procedures involved in the visit were elaborate and painstaking. After clearing security, we were escorted down a long corridor through several sets of double doors, each locked and heavily fortified. As we approached the third set of doors, two armed guards met us. McVeigh was being held in an isolated cell. We were ushered into a small room containing a table and two chairs while the guards retrieved their most famous prisoner. In the days leading up to this encounter, I wasn't quite sure what to expect; I had only seen brief clips of McVeigh on the news. Meeting him face to face would allow me to form my own opinion rather than try to muddle through the endless speculations of broadcast journalists and hastily compiled news reports. In truth, the public didn't know very much about this young man at all, though that would change over the next few years. After a few minutes, McVeigh was escorted into the room by a prison guard, and we were introduced. McVeigh had become aware of me through my book, which I learned he had read cover to cover. He said that he had a lot of time to

3

read, revealing a slight grin as he spoke. My first impressions of the accused bomber put me at ease. McVeigh didn't strike me as a "terrorist." He was soft-spoken, friendly, and inquisitive, with a boyish quality that defied the stereotypical image of an embittered radical. In fact, he didn't seem all that different from thousands of students I have had in the classroom over the years. During the initial meeting, which lasted about four hours, I found him to be articulate, demonstrating above-average reasoning and analytical skills. He expounded on portions of my book, indicating good comprehension of complex issues. While he had only attended college for a semester, he appeared to be a bright young man. He was introspective and curious – good qualities to have as a student. As likeable as he was, though, I had to make a concerted effort to remind myself that he was accused of what the press liked to say was "the worst act of domestic terrorism ever on American soil."

To my dismay, McVeigh talked openly of his role in the Oklahoma City bombing. He was willing, even eager, to discuss the evolution of his thinking and the series of events leading up to that dreadful day. I can say this now, because McVeigh's public confession to two Buffalo news journalists in the months before his execution essentially voided the confidentiality agreement to which I was bound. I was asked to sign an attorney–client privilege statement agreeing not to divulge any information that I learned in my capacity as a consultant. I intended to honor that agreement in the writing of this book. But six years later, it became moot. Much of what appears in the book *American Terrorist*, by Lou Michel and Dan Herbeck, was also told to me during the time I got to know McVeigh, save the sundry details of his childhood and adolescence.

McVeigh was a true believer, in his mind a combatant in the resistance movement or underground army battling the New World Order, a global conspiracy by wealthy elites designed to subjugate the United States and other nations under the control of the United Nations. He was a self-made patriot and freedom fighter, defending his country against the alleged forces of tyranny and treason. McVeigh likened his mission to blow up the Murrah Building to a special-operations assignment. The challenge of this stealth mission was both formidable and dangerous, requiring undaunted self-discipline, efficiency, and skill. He was steeled to the task and said that he expected to be caught in an FBI manhunt and die in a shootout with federal agents, a fate that befell several other patriots before him, including Robert Mathews and Gordon Kahl. McVeigh believed that his mission was successfully completed – a *fait accompli*. In his mind, he inflicted a lethal blow on the enemy and sent a message that the Patriot underground, however small in number, would not stand silently by while, as he put it, "a war was waged by the government against its own people."

The Oklahoma City bombing was first and foremost an act of retaliation for the 1993 federal assault on the Branch Davidian settlement at Mt. Carmel outside Waco. But there were other factors as well, such as the federal standoff with Randy Weaver in Ruby Ridge, Idaho, and the passage of tighter gun laws. As we will discover, McVeigh saw all these forces as part of a single conspiracy leading to an inevitable outcome. McVeigh believed that the siege at Waco was a *military* operation carried out illegally against American citizens. The charges of weapons violations made in the affidavit accompanying the search-and-arrest warrant for David Koresh signified, in his eyes, an expanding campaign of disarmament by the federal government. The resistance of the Davidians to the federal siege was justified, McVeigh believed, and it proved how far the government was willing to go to achieve its objective. McVeigh was enraged by the events at Waco, and he spoke with great passion and intensity in condemning the government raid and standoff. While not condoning McVeigh's actions, I understood the "insurgent consciousness" (McAdam, 1982) that he displayed. But I was confounded by some of his choices in the planning of the bombing. Why blow up the building during the daytime, when all those people were there, I asked. What purpose did that serve? The bulk of victims were not federal agents, but rather were clerical staff and office workers with no direct responsibility or culpability. Why not wait until evening and destroy the building when it was unoccupied? That way, you could make an effective political statement, if you were so inclined, without the mass deaths and injuries. His answer stunned me: "Because in order to really get the attention of the government," he said, "there has to be a *body count*." He said it so matter-of-factly, it took me a moment to process the statement. "A body count?" I replied. "Yes," he insisted. He then explained to me that the government could easily sweep under the rug the destruction of a building. Replacing a building was just "a temporary inconvenience." On the other hand, the deaths of government workers inside the federal building, particularly their own agents, could not be ignored. McVeigh's explanation had a certain martial logic, allowing for the presumption that he was in a "war." But the statement about the body count chilled me. I have never forgotten it. I would later learn, however, that neither the idea of bombing the Murrah Building nor the "body count" statement originated with McVeigh. They could be traced to James Ellison, the founder and leader of the Covenant, Sword and Arm of the Lord (CSA), part of the vanguard of

5

the Patriot movement in Arkansas, eleven years earlier. (I will have more to say about this later.)

By the time of this first meeting, everyone in the country was aware of the details of the Oklahoma City bombing. The deadly blast was caused by a homemade bomb using a mixture of ammonium nitrate and nitromethane fuel contained in 55-gallon drums resting in the back of a Ryder rental truck. The truck was parked in front of the Alfred P. Murrah Federal Building on the morning of April 19, 1995, the second anniversary of the fatal FBI assault on the Branch Davidian sect that killed seventy-six people, including twenty-one children. The Oklahoma City bombing killed 168 people, including 19 children, and injured more than 500 others. The outrageous act of violence shocked the nation and became headline news for months. In the immediate aftermath of the incident, many observers speculated that the bombing was an act of foreign terrorists. Truck bombs had been used in Mideast terrorist attacks in the past and were the method deployed in the World Trade Center bombing only two years earlier. But within a few days of the bombing, federal authorities announced that the alleged perpetrator was not a foreign enemy, but a "domestic terrorist."

Only an hour and fifteen minutes after the bombing, Oklahoma state trooper Charles Hanger pulled over the accused about seventy-five miles north of Oklahoma City on Interstate 35 for not having a license plate on his yellow Mercury Marquis. The officer found a loaded weapon in the car and booked McVeigh on a gun violation and took him to the local courthouse in Perry, Oklahoma, where he was detained for a routine procedure. A check of his criminal record alerted the FBI, which soon determined that McVeigh matched the description of the bombing suspect. Federal agents tracked the identification number on the axle of the Ryder truck to a Kansas rental facility where McVeigh had obtained the truck. The FBI arrested McVeigh in Oklahoma. He was found to have a pair of earplugs in his possession. In the car, which was searched two days after it was impounded following McVeigh's arrest, police found an envelope full of antigovernment literature. Among the papers stuffed in an envelope was a page from the popular far-right novel *The Turner Diaries*, with a passage about government bureaucrats that stated, "We can still find them and kill them." The sealed envelope was labeled with a handwritten message: "Obey the Constitution of the United States and we won't shoot you." Inside the envelope also were quotations from Samuel Adams and John Locke about the dangers of overzealous governments. The circumstantial evidence was incriminating, and the federal agents believed they had their man. The searing visual image of McVeigh in handcuffs, exiting the Noble County jail accompanied by FBI agents, wearing prison orange issue and facing the angry threats and jeers of a hostile crowd was splashed across every television screen in the United States and is one that most people will always remember. The revelation was doubly shocking. The alleged bomber was one of our own: a clean-cut 27-year-old white male with no previous criminal record and a decorated Gulf War veteran. How could this be?

In the following months, the public learned that Timothy McVeigh was a disgruntled ex-soldier who held strong antigovernment views, moved in and among the gun show subculture, visited the scene of the government standoff with the Branch Davidians, and was reportedly angered by the federal government's use of military tactics and weapons against the sect. McVeigh easily recognized the Bradley tanks at Waco – they were identical to the tank he manned as a gunner in Desert Storm. The Waco operation looked all too familiar to him, like a *war* exercise. But this broadside was being waged against American citizens, not Iraqis. When the CS (tear) gas assault erupted in a fiery holocaust on April 19, 1993, McVeigh was visiting brothers Terry and James Nichols at their farm in Decker, Michigan. The three men were horrified as they watched on TV the Davidian settlement burn to the ground. According to federal prosecutors, the men vowed to retaliate. The government charged that McVeigh, along with Terry Nichols, bombed the federal building in Oklahoma City to avenge the siege at Mt. Carmel. McVeigh was charged with an eleven-count indictment; one count of conspiring to use a weapon of mass destruction, one count of using a weapon of mass destruction, one count of destruction by explosives, and eight counts of first-degree murder for the deaths of eight federal agents. McVeigh's defense counsel entered a plea of not guilty. The stage was set for the largest criminal investigation in U.S. history. U.S. District Judge Richard Matsch, an ex-prosecutor appointed to the bench by former President Nixon, was assigned to the case by the Tenth U.S. Circuit Court of Appeals. It is worth noting that Matsch was the same judge who presided over the trial of members of Robert Mathews's group, The Order, who were charged in the slaying of Jewish talk show host Alan Berg in 1985. (The importance of this connection will acquire added meaning in later portions of the book.) Matsch replaced U.S. District Judge Wayne Alley, whose chambers were damaged in the Oklahoma City blast. After vigorously contested requests by defense attorneys for severance and a change of venue, the motions were granted and the trial was moved to Denver. The trial date was set for March 31, 1997.

7

As we left the El Reno federal facility that cold November day, I was numb from the hours of intense listening and note taking. I wasn't allowed to record the interview, so I endeavored to write down everything I possibly could at a furious pace. As often happens in such situations, more questions arose than could be answered. I departed with some frustration, knowing I would need to regroup and formulate a new battery of questions. We walked back through the sequence of security checks, thanked the prison officials, and got into Dick's rental car. Dick and I didn't speak much on the drive back to Oklahoma City, but he asked me what I thought of McVeigh. I responded by saying I thought he seemed awfully young to be in this much trouble. I know we talked further about McVeigh's family background and history, his military training, his friendship with Terry Nichols, and other matters, but I was trying to digest what I had learned and to make sense of it all. I had pages full of notes, and I was anxious to get back to the hotel room to organize them in a more manageable fashion. When we arrived back in Enid, Dick dropped me off at the front of the hotel. He had a rented apartment in Enid because he was spending so much time in the city. He said that he would pick me up in the morning and we would drive to the airport. I worked on my notes until about 2 A.M., but despite being exhausted I didn't sleep well that night.

I would make another visit to El Reno the following February for a half-day visit and interview with McVeigh. I had formulated a new list of questions for him that we covered methodically. He was very patient and engaging, often volunteering painstaking details in response to inquiries. There is no doubt that he savored the reprieve from solitary confinement and the company of an empathetic listener. The constant surveillance and strict supervision in the maximum-security unit was starting to wear on him. He complained that prison guards were eavesdropping on his meetings with defense lawyers. On one occasion, he stopped talking after we heard a noise and pointed to the outside wall of the room. He leaned over and whispered to us that the guards were trying to listen in on his conversation. He continued to talk softly to avoid being heard. I dismissed his suspicions out of hand. Ironically, however, four weeks before the case went to trial, incriminating and confidential details about McVeigh's activities leading up to the bombing were leaked to the press.

On March 1, 1997, the *Dallas Morning News* ran a story that essentially documented McVeigh's every move in planning the bombing. ABC and CNN produced news specials based on this damning information, walking the viewer through a detailed chronology of the alleged bomber's actions prior to April 19, 1995. Stephen Jones denied the stories were credible and threatened to sue the newspaper. He insisted that the events were fabricated in an attempt to flush out another suspect. But everyone involved with the defense team knew that the information was accurate. Even the statement about the "body count" appeared in the news reports. McVeigh's paranoia now seemed justified. More troubling, the source of the leak was allegedly a staff person on the defense counsel. The *Dallas Morning News* reporter, Pete Slover, said the story was based on statements made by McVeigh to his defense team between July and December 1995. The period of time covered by the leaked story corresponded to my initial interview with McVeigh. I knew I had not spoken with anyone about these details, but the coincidence was unsettling. It was later discovered that somebody in Jones's office was responsible for leaking the confidential material. After that, the attorneys took extensive measures to heighten security and protect any further mishaps. I had a personal file of McVeigh's letters and documents, all of which were photocopied in Jones's office, for my use in assisting the attorneys in the case. A few weeks after the leak, Dick Burr called me and asked me to return the contents of the file. I took copious notes from the materials over the next few days and returned the files, as requested. The attorneys were visibly shaken by this embarrassing turn of events. It was evident to me that things were not quite the same among the members of the legal team from that time on. A cloud of suspicion enveloped us, and the tensions played out in various ways. At one point during the trial in Denver, for example, I was waiting outside Dick Burr's office before a meeting perusing the contents of a stack of binders resting on top of a filing cabinet. To my surprise, I was abruptly accused by Dick's wife and fellow law partner, Mandy Welch, of secretly garnering evidence for the opposition, perhaps to sell or leak to the media – I'm not sure which. It was a surreal episode. Welch was obviously feeling the stress of a high-stakes court battle and was transferring her anxiety by venting at me. I left the building with my research assistant when it became apparent that we were not going to have the meeting.

For nine weeks – between March 31 and June 14, 1997 – the McVeigh trial was the focus of widespread national media attention. The grounds in front of the Denver courthouse were jammed with news crews from major broadcast and print media outlets. Live news coverage was maintained around the clock. News analysts detailed every argument and speculated about the effects on the outcome of the trial. At each break in the trial, journalists descended on prosecutors, witnesses, defense attorneys,

9

and experts as they entered or left the courthouse. I attended the trial in early June, sitting with defense counsel in the crowded courtroom in the first row reserved for the legal team. It was a spectacle to behold. Lines formed in front of the building before dawn each day for those wanting to secure a seat for the proceedings. Inside the courtroom, families of the bombing victims and media representatives were the most visible attendees. Prominent news reporters whose faces I recognized – Jeffrey Toobin (ABC), Dick Gregory (NBC), Tim Sullivan (Court TV) – were seated just behind me. The courtroom was quite small, designed to hold only about one hundred people, but the numbers clearly exceeded this figure. The atmosphere was tense and emotionally charged. Everyone in the courtroom was keenly aware of the historic significance of the case. It was like nothing I had ever witnessed.

Some legal experts were predicting that the trial might take six months, given the enormity of the case. But the Denver trial proceeded rapidly. The prosecution called 137 witnesses during a stretch of eighteen days. The government introduced evidence that McVeigh had planned the bombing, had purchased bombing materials, and had traces of an explosive substance, penta erythrite tetral nitrate (PETN), on his T-shirt. With the leaked chronology of McVeigh's movements before the bombing and phone records from a calling card, the government was able to piece together a compelling argument about McVeigh's day-to-day activities. Key pieces of evidence included an axle from the Ryder truck combined with eyewitnesses who rented the vehicle to McVeigh. Government attorneys also called as witnesses Lori and Michael Fortier, friends with whom McVeigh had stayed in Arizona during the planning of the bombing. McVeigh knew Michael Fortier from his Army days, and Fortier shared some of McVeigh's antigovernment beliefs. Fortier was well aware of McVeigh's intentions; he helped store bomb materials and stolen goods and even accompanied McVeigh to Oklahoma City at one point to case the Murrah Building. The Fortiers turned state's evidence in exchange for more lenient sentences. The government agreed not to file charges against Lori and asked the court to consider Michael's cooperation with prosecutors in the sentencing phase.

Prosecutors also called McVeigh's sister, Jennifer. Tim and Jennifer were very close, and he had written to his sister a number of times during his metamorphosis, sending her a copy of *The Turner Diaries*, Patriot newsletters, and other reading materials, often highlighting portions he thought were important. During her trial testimony, Jennifer told the jury that her brother wrote to say "something big is going to happen in the month of the Bull," an astrological reference to April or May. She also testified that Tim grew increasingly angry after the Waco raid and began stockpiling explosives. "He was very angry about the events that resulted in the deaths of 81 [*sic*] people, including women and children, at the end of the FBI siege at Waco," she said. At one point, McVeigh indicated that he was no longer in the "propaganda stage," that he was moving into the "action stage." In the fall of 1994, McVeigh visited his sister at their home in Lockport, New York, using her computer to write a letter to the American Legion that referred to federal law enforcement agencies as "power-hungry storm troopers" and advocated citizen militias as a solution to ensure government compliance with the Constitution. He wrote in parentheses: "Many believe the Waco incident was first blood." The FBI retrieved the letter from Jennifer's computer and asked her to identify it for the jury. She also described an incident in which Tim told her that once while hauling a thousand pounds of explosives in the trunk of his car, he was nearly involved in an accident. It was the cruelest of ironies that Jennifer's testimony was perhaps the most damning. The Fortiers' testimony could conceivably be dismissed by the jurors as self-serving. But Jennifer clearly loved her brother, and it was obvious to everyone in the courtroom that she was pained to have to testify against him. This made her a very credible witness.

Because much of the evidence was circumstantial, prosecutors took some liberties in relying on emotional testimonies of victims and survivors accentuating a mood of vindication. Though it was technically irrelevant to the evidence of McVeigh's guilt or innocence, prosecutors persisted in the strategy. Defense attorneys strenuously objected, and Judge Matsch warned the prosecutors on a number of occasions to halt the tactics of emotional incitement. The judge also instructed jurors not to base their decisions on the impulse to remediate the pain of victims, but clearly the jurors struggled with this charge. Comments by jurors after the trial indicated a strong psychological identification with the victims and their families. Several jurors wept during anguished statements from survivors and relatives of victims, and according to one juror, "There were a lot of tears in the jury room" (Richardson, 1997: A5).

Perhaps the most difficult impediments to the defense came from pre-trial rulings by Judge Matsch. Hampered by rulings limiting or excluding evidence that could be introduced, the defense called only twenty-five witnesses in three-and-a-half days of testimony. It was expected that the defense would extend the trial several more months. What was the evidence excluded in the trial? A key ruling to exclude the testimony of an ATF informant, Carol Howe, who would connect McVeigh to a Christian Identity and survivalist encampment in southeastern Oklahoma, Elohim City, handcuffed the defense. ATF informant Howe told her superiors in late 1994 that she overheard two men, Andreas Strassmeir, a German national, and Dennis Mahon, a leader in the White Aryan Resistance (WAR), discuss bombing the Murrah Building while at Elohim City. This discussion took place on more than one occasion, and one of the men participating in a conversation fit the profile of McVeigh and used the name "Tim Tuttle," an alias McVeigh was known to use. An ATF memorandum obtained by the defense confirmed that Strassmeir and Mahon had connections to the neo-Nazi movement in Germany and other European countries. This exculpatory evidence was withheld from the defense but discovered later during its own investigation (Jones and Israel, 1998). The residents at Elohim City were angered by the Waco assault and discussed retaliation against the federal government by means of bombings in Oklahoma City, Tulsa, and Little Rock. Some of the men also expressed fears that they might be the "next Waco," according to Howe (*Final Report on the Bombing of the Alfred P. Murrah Building*, 2001: 305). Connections between McVeigh and Elohim City could be established, and the defense wanted to argue that McVeigh was only a pawn in the bomb plot. Mahon and Strassmeir were believed to be the masterminds behind the bombing. Howe succeeded in filming Strassmeir making hand grenades, and the ATF was planning a raid on Elohim City to arrest him. But on February 22, 1995, Howe's immediate superior, agent Angela Finley, was notified by the Oklahoma Highway Patrol that the FBI had an ongoing investigation at Elohim City, preventing the arrest. The next day, the Tulsa office of the ATF was told that Bob Ricks, chief of the FBI regional office, wanted a meeting to discuss the investigation at Elohim City. Ricks was also the agent in charge of the FBI press briefings during the Waco standoff. Shortly after, Agent Finley filed a request for removal of Howe from Elohim City. No arrests were ever made. Strassmeir left the country for Germany, and – according to Joseph Hartzler, lead prosecutor in the McVeigh case – the FBI never considered him a suspect in the case, even though according to telephone records McVeigh placed a call to Elohim City asking for "Andy the German" a few weeks before the blast. The day after the Oklahoma City bombing, Howe was called by agent Finley and asked if she could identify the sketches of the suspects. Howe eventually became distraught that the government had prior knowledge of the bombing and had failed to prevent it. Evidently seeing Ms. Howe as a liability in the Oklahoma City bombing case, the FBI arrested her in March 1997 – just before the beginning of the trial in Denver – on charges of conspiracy, making a bomb threat, and possession of a nonregistered destructive device. Curiously, the charges against Howe ignored the fact that she was working undercover as a federal informant. Stephen Jones filed a writ of mandamus to the Tenth Circuit Court of Appeals accusing the government of trying to silence a witness the defense intended to use. The Appeals Court denied the writ, and Judge Matsch ruled that Carol Howe could not be called as a witness. Howe was later acquitted of all charges, but it was too late to help McVeigh's defense.

The defense also wanted to introduce into evidence the Inspector General's FBI Crime Lab Report. The report, based on an eighteen-month investigation, found widespread mishandling of forensic evidence, including posed or manufactured evidence, unscientific speculation favorable to the prosecution, inappropriate techniques of analysis, use of degraded or unchecked equipment, biased and false testimony, and, generally, persistent violations of standard operating procedures at the crime lab that directly impacted the Oklahoma City bombing case (Kelly and Wearne, 1998). One of the attorneys on the defense team, Chris Tritico, was prepared to attack the government's evidence based on the Inspector General's report. But Judge Matsch confined the defense to using only a small part of one chapter in the report. Matsch made a similar ruling regarding the testimony of Frederic Whitehurst, the FBI chemist and whistleblower whose allegations led to the investigation of the crime lab.

These rulings dealt crippling blows to the defense and explain in some measure the brevity of the defense portion of the trial. On June 2, after deliberating twenty-three hours, the jury delivered a guilty verdict on all eleven counts. Following the verdict, the trial moved to the penalty or mitigation phase. The jury was asked to decide if Timothy McVeigh should receive the death penalty, weighing aggravating and mitigating factors. Arguments for both sides lasted only a week. Defense attorneys argued that McVeigh was incensed by the FBI's actions at Waco and carried out the bombing as an act of retaliation. However, the evidence regarding Waco was restricted by Judge Matsch to what McVeigh "believed" happened at Waco. Matsch informed the court that he would not allow "the government to be put on trial." It was certain that McVeigh's perceptions or beliefs would be discounted by the prosecution and the jurors as groundless. Lead prosecutor Joseph Hartzler echoed Judge Matsch's view, stating to the jury during closing arguments that "Waco is not on trial here." On Friday the 13th,

13

after two-and-a-half days of deliberation, the jury returned a death penalty verdict.

It might be instructive here to say just a word about the quality of McVeigh's defense, which was later called into question by some critics. During the guilt phase of the trial, the defense attorneys argued that their client was innocent. But after the jury found the accused guilty of the charges, the defense basically conceded that McVeigh was responsible and argued that his motivation – the federal assault on Waco – should be a mitigating factor in considering whether to give McVeigh the death penalty. The strategy seemed convoluted and counterproductive. What was the rationale behind this ill-fated strategy?

McVeigh had wanted the attorneys to use a "necessity defense," one that would allow the self-declared patriot to confess to the bombing and argue that it was necessary because he was in imminent danger from the threat of federal government tyranny and abuse. Indeed, McVeigh wanted to stand up in court and openly admit to the act, offering a lengthy discourse on the dangers of a federal government out of control. McVeigh was insistent, and apparently Jones was willing to entertain this possibility for a while, perhaps simply to placate McVeigh. The defense counsel was divided into two teams, A and B. Team A was assigned the task of attacking the government's evidence and finding holes in its case. Team B was assigned the task of exploring aspects of the necessity defense, focusing on the killings and cover-ups at Waco and Ruby Ridge, the increasing militarization and violence of law enforcement, and the expanding control and intrusiveness of government. Stephen Jones would eventually decide that the necessity defense was untenable. But in all likelihood, the puzzling tactic employed during the mitigation phase was a reluctant concession to McVeigh, once the guilty verdict was returned.

Timothy McVeigh was sentenced to die by lethal injection in Judge Richard Matsch's court on August 14, 1997. The convicted bomber was given the opportunity to address the court in a final statement prior to sentencing. McVeigh stood up, not making eye contact with the judge or jury, walked slowly to the microphone atop a podium, and read a very succinct prepared statement, only four sentences in length. The statement said: "If the court please, I wish to use the words of Justice Brandeis dissenting in *Olmstead* to speak for me. He wrote: 'Our government is the potent, omnipresent teacher. For good or for ill, it teaches the whole people by its example.' That's all I have." And with that, McVeigh returned to his seat and sat in silence. Reporters, jurors, survivors, and family members of victims were disappointed and perplexed by the truncated remarks. There was an air of expectation in the courtroom that the young Gulf War veteran would shed more light on his motives, perhaps even articulate his antigovernment beliefs at this opportune moment, or at least offer an apology to the survivors and their kin. They received nothing of the kind. I overheard one news reporter outside the courtroom say that McVeigh's remarks were so cryptic that families of the bombing victims were not sure what he meant. Some were offended by McVeigh's expropriation of the esteemed jurist's writings. Prosecutor Joseph Hartzler told reporters: "Do me a favor. Don't interpret his words as those from a spokesperson or statesman" (Thomas, 1997: 1A). Others said they wished McVeigh had used his own words rather than quoting someone else. Generally, the consensus inside and outside the courtroom was that the Brandeis quote was abstruse and irrelevant. What did he intend to say?

Judging from the reactions, the underlying message was missed. The text of the quote was taken from the 1928 decision *Olmstead v. United States*, in which Justice Brandeis lashed out at government abuse of civil liberties when the court upheld evidence obtained from wiretaps in a bootlegging probe. The meaning of the statement is better understood if taken in context. The following excerpt includes the whole portion of the text from which the quote derives. It states:

Decency, security and liberty alike demand that government officials be subjected to the same rules of conduct that are commands to the citizen. In a government of laws, existence of the government will be imperiled if it fails to observe the law scrupulously. Our Government is the potent, omnipresent teacher. For good or ill, it teaches the whole people by its example. Crime is contagious. If government becomes the lawbreaker, it breeds contempt for the law; it invites every man to become a law unto himself, it invites anarchy. (*Olmstead v. United States*, 277 U.S. 438 [1928])

The full text of the selected quote reveals a broader meaning. McVeigh believed that the federal actions at Waco and Ruby Ridge, as well as other military-like raids targeting gun owners, were evidence of a growing pattern of government tyranny and served to breed contempt for the law and invite anarchy. In particular, the lack of accountability by government for the carnage at Waco demanded justice and fomented vigilante reactions culminating in the deadly bombing. However misguided the bombing of the federal building in Oklahoma City, McVeigh did not leave us without an explanation of motive.

In late December 2000, McVeigh formally ended his appeals, against the advice of his attorneys, and asked for an execution date. McVeigh was scheduled to be executed on May 16, 2001, by lethal injection at the federal facility in Terre Haute, Indiana. Six days before the execution date, however, the FBI revealed that it had failed to disclose 3,135 pages of documents as "Brady material" (that is, documents to which the defense was entitled and that might help prove the innocence of the accused) to McVeigh's defense team. It was a colossal blunder on the part of the FBI, which claimed that the material was discovered during a routine archiving of records. But failure to disclose evidence was grounds for a mistrial if it could be shown that the materials would have altered the outcome of the verdict. Attorney General John Ashcroft announced a thirty-day stay of execution to give McVeigh's attorneys time to look over the newly discovered evidence and determine the possibility of a challenge to the conviction and death sentence. The new date of execution was moved to June 11. By the end of May, the FBI had uncovered an additional 1,314 pages of undisclosed documents, bringing the total to 4,449. Most of the materials were "lead sheets," or what the FBI calls "302s" – interviews with witnesses who may have information about a crime.

Curiously, most of the 302s pertained to witnesses who said they saw John Doe 2, an unidentified coconspirator. Defense attorneys for McVeigh filed a motion on May 31 claiming that the federal government had "perpetrated a fraud upon the court" by deliberately withholding the documents and argued that the government continued to withhold evidence from the defense. In a three-hundred-page brief, they cited an FBI interview report by former special agent Ricardo Ojeda, who worked on the Oklahoma City bombing case. Ojeda stated that he believed that the FBI withheld exculpatory evidence from the defense. McVeigh was amused by the government's chicanery and gave his attorneys permission to fight for a stay of execution. Judge Matsch ordered federal prosecutors to respond by June 5 to the defense's motion. However, Matsch wasted no time in ruling on June 6 that the FBI documents did not mitigate McVeigh's guilt or invalidate the sentence. According to the court transcript, Judge Matsch said there was a difference between "alternative" perpetrators and "additional" perpetrators, and the culpability of additional conspirators did not assuage the evidence used to convict McVeigh. An appeal to a three-judge panel of the Tenth Circuit Court of Appeals produced the same result the following day. McVeigh instructed his attorneys to abandon the appeals. The execution date ordered by Attorney General Ashcroft would stand.

McVeigh's death marked another milestone in history: It was the first federal execution in 38 years. Like the criminal trial, the execution of Timothy McVeigh was a mix of drama and carnival. The lethal injection was transmitted over closed-circuit television to an audience of 232 bombing survivors and victims' families back in Oklahoma City. More than fourteen hundred media representatives from all over the world congregated outside the Terre Haute federal prison. The networks and the 24-hour news channels devoted exclusive coverage to the event, giving millions of Americans endless details of what could be called the closest thing to a public execution in modern times. Hordes of reporters and camera crews staked out the victims memorial site in Oklahoma City to film survivors and family members paying respects to deceased loved ones. ABC's *Good Morning America* refused to cover the execution from Terre Haute in deference to the victims, claiming a higher moral ground for its telecast. A group of bombing victims, whose faces were now familiar to many, were interviewed and asked for reactions to the events of the day. Most were relieved that the execution date had finally arrived. The majority of victims selected their words carefully, expressing sympathy for McVeigh's family, but supporting the death sentence. "This proves that the legal system works in our country," one bombing victim proclaimed.

Strangely, McVeigh reveled in the fact that his execution had become an international news event. He had even suggested at one point that the execution be broadcast for the general public, but the offer was nixed by the U.S. Attorney General. McVeigh's response mystified people and offended others, but the logic was not too difficult to decipher; McVeigh wanted to draw attention to his cause. He wanted people to ask themselves how and why. And they did. "What turned an all-American boy into America's worst nightmare?" the *Today Show*'s Matt Lauer asked. Variations on the question were posed countless times among print and broadcast media on this day, which only seemed to add to McVeigh's mystique. Certainly, in McVeigh's mind, he had cast himself as a martyr. According to a prison diary kept by a fellow inmate, McVeigh had been dieting in the months before the execution so that he would look like a "concentration camp victim" (Borger, 2001). McVeigh chose to embark on a strict vegetarian diet in order to lose weight and appear emaciated for the witnesses to the execution and possibly for postmortem photos. Several news accounts of the execution reported that McVeigh looked cadaverous. Linda Cavenaugh, a media witness who spoke to a press conference after the execution, stated, "The last time I saw Timothy McVeigh was in a court room in Oklahoma

City. He had changed markedly, he was paler, he was thinner...." The *Washington Post* described McVeigh as "pale and gaunt" (Romano, 2001: A1). The message was sent as intended: Tim McVeigh believed he was "at war" with the federal government, so he thought of himself as a prisoner of war (POW). Taken captive, he was to be executed by the enemy, but he would die defiant and unwavering in his convictions.

McVeigh chose the inspired words of a Victorian poet to express his final thoughts. He asked that a hand-printed copy of "Invictus" be distributed to witnesses. The poem was composed in 1875 by William Ernest Henly, who suffered from tuberculosis. Translated from Latin, the title means "invincible" or "unconquerable." It reads:

> Out of the night that covers me,
> Black as the Pit from pole to pole,
> I thank whatever gods may be
> For my unconquerable soul.
> In the fell clutch of circumstance
> I have not winced nor cried aloud,
> Under the bludgeonings of chance
> My head is bloody, but unbowed.
> Beyond this place of wrath and tears
> Looms but the Horror of the shade,
> And yet the menace of the years
> Finds, and shall find, me unafraid
> It matters not how strait the gate,
> How charged with punishments the scroll,
> I am the master of my fate:
> I am the captain of my soul

Having failed to ignite a revolution with a violent act of insurgence, McVeigh intended to leverage his image as a martyred patriot in hopes that it might seed the ground for a future revolt. But in the final analysis, McVeigh miscalculated the response of antigovernment warriors and soldiers to the bombing of the Murrah Federal Building. The horror and scope of the political crime in Oklahoma City had an adverse effect on the Patriot movement as a whole. According to one watchdog organization, in the five years following the Oklahoma City bombing, from 1996 to 2000, the number of active Patriot groups in the United States dropped from 858 to 194 (Southern Poverty Law Center, 2001). Some of the remaining active groups were driven underground, while others desperately tried to dissociate themselves from McVeigh by condemning the bombing. McVeigh was keenly aware of this misreckoning by the time of our first meeting, but he never abandoned his belief that the act was the moral equivalent of the government's actions at Waco, and he remained steadfast in his convictions to his last breath.

Plan of the Book

On June 11, 2001, the enigmatic life of Timothy James McVeigh came to an end, but the issues raised by the Oklahoma City bombing did not end with McVeigh's execution. Using the Oklahoma City bombing as a focal point, I would like to explore larger questions about the growth of the Patriot movement, a loose coalition of militant-right groups to which McVeigh was linked. The pivotal question in this inquiry concerns the pervasive conviction among Patriot groups that the government was waging war against its own citizens. How did this shared perception of a state campaign of war arise? And what role, if any, did this play in fueling an antigovernment movement that ignited the militancy of McVeigh and others? I intend to show that the Patriot movement was transformed from a small, disenfranchised, and poorly organized network of disparate groups to a significant social force, in part by the state's increased efforts to define and frame social control in terms of "warfare," predicated on claims of an increasing threat posed by crime and drugs. The "war model" or "military model" of crime control (Kraska, 1993, 1994, 1996, 2001b; Kraska and Kappeler, 1996; Skolnick and Fyfe, 1993: 113–24), fueled by claims of a widening threat, had a transmogrifying effect on police culture, policies, and practices, fostering a process of militarization. Militarization has been facilitated most acutely through the war on drugs as the state has permitted an expanded role for the military in interdiction. Easing legal prohibitions separating civilian police and the military, the state found new roles for the military, guided in part by the U.S. Department of Defense's (DOD's) low-intensity conflict (LIC) model of warfare and augmented by the need to redefine the military's mission in the post–Cold War era. Ironically, at the same time that conservative political officials and organizations were trumpeting the downsizing of the federal government throughout the Reagan–Bush years, federal crime and drug control programs mushroomed and became increasingly integrated with the military.

In a highly polarized political and cultural climate during the 1980s and early 1990s, aptly captured in the phrase "culture wars," key leaders within the emergent Patriot movement responded to new threats and opportunities by reconfiguring old conflicts and hostilities with the state that drew from wider currents of discontent. By linking social problems to perceived threats of domination posed by state actors allied with international elites, far-right ideologues adeptly deflected racist and anti-Semitic concerns and repositioned themselves as "Patriots" and freedom fighters, using coded nationalistic speech and giving the movement a more broadly acceptable language and image. Consequently, the reconstructed Patriots were shielded from having to confront their traditional prejudices and found success in recruiting new adherents to their movement.

One important development in the political environment that helped far-right movement actors and organizations mobilize arose with the 1980s "farm crisis," involving the largest displacement of farm families since the Great Depression. By capturing cultural symbols, identifying culpable agents, frame bridging, and eventually appropriating social networks, movement entrepreneurs made significant inroads into farm communities, engaging in grassroots recruitment and offering a means of addressing grievances. Using radio broadcasts and small-town meetings in church basements, sale barns, school auditoriums, and American Legion halls throughout the Farm Belt, far-right leaders like Jim Wickstrom, Rick Elliot, and Willam Potter Gale promoted the blended anti-Semitic message of "Christian Identity" and Posse Comitatus while telling farmers that the torrent of farm foreclosures was part of a government scheme to destroy the small farmer. Some violent confrontations with the state ensued, involving bankrupt farmers who became adherents and either faced property foreclosures or became embroiled in bitter tax protests. In at least two cases (Gordon Kahl and Arthur Kirk), these confrontations involved standoffs and deadly shootouts with state paramilitary police units or SWAT teams. Posse Comitatus and Christian Identity leaders were able to parlay these violent encounters into enhanced antigovernment sentiment and movement mobilization among farmers in rural America. Episodes of insurgency in the early to mid-1980s followed but were short-lived, sporadic, and effectively quelled by the state. After 1986, the movement quietly settled into a state of abeyance, where it continued to exist largely in the form of informal networks and loosely aligned organizations.

With the end of the Cold War, changes in the political environment created new perceptions of threat and revived old ones. The framing of disputes with government as "warfare" assumed new levels of resonance with heightened enforcement of gun laws by paramilitary police units. The escalation of warfare rhetoric and actions produced an upward spiral of conflict that came to a head at Ruby Ridge and Waco. In the wake of these deadly military-like sieges, Patriot rhetoric and ideology about "warfare" assumed a prophetic status and helped to mobilize and legitimate a more militant antistatist movement. The extension of the war model of crime control to redoubled efforts at gun control through the 1993 Brady Bill and 1994 Federal Crime Bill shortly after the deadly sieges spawned widespread and exaggerated fears of a disarmament campaign by the state, the central theme of the movement's most important tome: *The Turner Diaries*. By 1995, significant numbers of Patriots believed they were engaged in a war with the government. In this context, the plan to bomb the federal building in Oklahoma City was resurrected and revised from the ashes of an earlier plot by members of the defunct Covenant, Sword and Arm of the Lord, which itself was the target of a federal siege exactly ten years to the day before the Oklahoma City bombing: April 19, 1985.

In this manner, McVeigh and other members of the Patriot movement intended to lead an insurgency against what they perceived was a police state. This perception reveals much about the freighted meanings that shaped and defined the movement's collective identity as "warriors." The destruction of the Murrah Federal Building in Oklahoma City was flush with Patriot signification and meaning. It used *The Turner Diaries* as a blueprint by (1) emulating the fertilizer truck bomb tactic to destroy a federal building, even timing the blast to occur within a few minutes of the time recorded in the fictional narrative; (2) using underground cells to organize insurgent activities; and (3) defining the final catalyst for the revolution as the "Gun Raids," seen by Patriots as part of a state disarmament campaign. On the first page of *The Turner Diaries*, the story's protagonist declares, "We are at war with the System." The blurb on the back cover poses the query "What will you do when they come to take your guns?" It resumes, "Earl Turner and his fellow patriots face this question and are forced underground when the U.S. government bans the private possession of firearms and stages mass Gun Raids to round up suspected gun owners." McVeigh envisioned himself as an Earl Turner prototype, a heroic protagonist in the Patriot subculture. The date of the bombing was equally fraught with meaning, occurring on the second anniversary of the federal assault on the Branch Davidians and the tenth anniversary of the federal siege of the CSA in Arkansas. No one in the Patriot movement, and no one familiar with the ideology of the movement, had any trouble interpreting the symbolism of this event.

By examining how the social construction of "warfare" became the principal script or "frame" defining the dynamic between the state and the burgeoning Patriot movement, I hope to show that this highly charged confluence of a war narrative engendered a kind of symbiosis and led to an escalation of mutual threat that eventually culminated in the plan to bomb the Oklahoma City federal building. Both parties to this conflict constructed warfare scripts that defined the other as "enemy." Ironically, the rhetoric of warfare served to affirm and fuel each other's perception of threat, giving way to an upward spiral of violence.

2

Patriots, Political Process, and Social Movements

Too little attention has been paid to right-wing movements among social movement scholars. Indeed, the considerable body of sociological research in social movements over the last forty years has focused on progressive and left-wing movements. This trend continues today, even though conservative or right-wing politics has achieved a degree of hegemony in the American political system. While some critics might take issue with this characterization of social movement scholarship, there is ample support for the argument. An examination of the only specialized journal devoted exclusively to social movement theory and research, *Mobilization*, illustrates the disproportionality problem. A survey of published articles from the inception of the journal in 1996 through 2005 identified a total of 141 articles covering ten volumes. Of the total number of published articles, only 4 percent ($N = 5$) focused research activity on conservative or right-wing movements. On the other hand, 67 percent of the articles ($N = 95$) focused on progressive/left/liberal movements while 2 percent of the articles ($N = 3$) examined both left- and right-wing movements. Twenty percent ($N = 28$) addressed theoretical, conceptual, or methodological issues with no specific movement as their focus and 7 percent ($N = 10$) defied the left–right classification scheme. These numbers convey a pattern that I would contend is generally consistent with the larger body of research on social movements. There is no reason to think that this reputable journal or the scholars who publish in it are atypical.

This peculiar intellectual pedigree has a logical explanation. The academic interest in social movements exploded in the turbulence and political unrest of the 1960s. Not surprisingly, many students of social movements were born of this period, developed and held ideological affinities with liberal and left-wing movements, and in some cases became activists (see

23

Gitlin, 1993: 2–3; McAdam, 2004: 281; Meyer, 2002: 7). Universities served as incubators of political dissent and protest throughout the United States, as well as in Western Europe. Concomitantly, the popularity of sociology on university campuses swelled, and social movement courses became routinely entrenched in the curriculum. Universities burgeoned as both laboratories for studying social movements and venues for campus activists. Civil rights, feminism, the environment, gay and lesbian rights, and opposition to the Vietnam War emerged as powerful issues galvanizing collective action, and university faculty and students were front and center in "movement" activism. Though right-wing movement activity was certainly vigorous during this same period (Bennett, 1988; Hofstadter, 1965; Lipset and Raab, 1973), it did not dictate political discourse on college campuses in the same way that left-oriented liberation movements did. Hence, the bulk of social movement attention and scholarship concentrated on progressive actors and organizations.

While the grounding of social movement scholarship in the progressive tradition can be understood in cultural and historical terms, it does raise a curious question: How reliable is the current array of concepts, models, and theories when applied to right-wing movements? Do these analytic constructs have equal utility and merit? Are the same dynamics of contention operative in the same way, or are there distinctive differences? In setting out to study the Patriot movement a few years ago, I began with a loosely held, tacit assumption that right-wing insurgency simply mirrors left-wing insurgency. Yet there was little substantive or empirical basis to merit such an assumption. As I conducted a literature review, I found a rich body of research on right-wing and far-right political organization and activity, including studies of the Ku Klux Klan, racist and segregationist politics, nativism, totalitarianism, fascism, Nazism, neo-Nazism, nationalism, and the Religious Right, but not often from a social movement perspective. These studies tend to be lodged in the domain of political sociology, comparative politics, or historical studies. While there are some notable exceptions to this pattern (for example, Diamond, 1995; Gallaher, 2003; Giugni et al., 2005; Koopmans, 1997), generally, I believe, this constitutes a deficit in an otherwise impressive stock of knowledge that has to be addressed. I raise this issue not merely as a criticism but as an opportunity to test critical ideas. What adjustments, modifications, or accommodations might be involved in the broadening of a research program to include more right-wing movements? To what degree can we expect to find mirrored results? Perhaps a greater focus on right-wing movements will yield new insights

24

or new answers to some old questions. It remains to be seen whether our arsenal of conceptual and analytical tools is as compelling in its explanatory value. The present inquiry makes a modest contribution to that end.

Political Process

This work is undertaken as a social movement analysis informed by political process theory (McAdam, 1982, 1999; Tarrow, 1983, 1994; Tilly, 1978), but with an eye toward the rapidly evolving analytic program of contentious politics focusing on dynamic and intermediate-level mechanisms and processes (McAdam, Tarrow, and Tilly, 2001). With varying degrees of emphasis, social movement theorists have generally identified three broad sets of factors in movement formation and growth: (1) the attribution of opportunities or threats confronting challengers and state (or nonstate) elites in the development of innovative collective action; (2) social appropriation of a social/organizational base or "site" for initial mobilization, sometimes called "mobilizing structures"; and (3) framing or other interpretive/social construction processes that mediate between opportunity and action. As an essential foundation of any analysis of social movements, researchers must at least account for these factors in explaining how aggrieved groups construct meaning and opportunities and how they organize and engage in contentious politics.

In addition to the three broad sets of factors in movement formation and growth identified here, an effort is made to integrate intermediate, or "meso-level," dynamics (McAdam, 2003: 284) into the analysis, the most important of which for this study concerns "trajectories" of contention (McAdam, Tarrow, and Tilly, 2001: 34). Trajectories may take many paths. Some episodes of contention are brief, while others are protracted; some end in demobilization, while others expand into revolt or revolution. Trajectories are difficult to predict because the driving force in their progression involves the *interaction* of the parties in contention. Social movement scholars must take into account patterns of moves and countermoves between state actors and challengers, third parties, and countermovements when assessing trajectories. States, of course, have a pivotal role because they can lay claim to the legitimate use of force against challengers. Repressive state actions can stall protest campaigns by making the costs of participation too high. Yet research shows increased state repression does not necessarily mitigate or quell protest and may actually lead to heightened protest and mobilization (DeNardo, 1985; Goldstone and Tilly, 2001; White, 1989).

25

In this study, I am concerned with the relationship between state repression and far-right movement radicalization and insurgency. By focusing on intermediate mechanisms and dynamics, I hope to explain how Patriot movement insurgency evolved over time and through an ongoing stream of contention between state and movement actors predicated on a mutual framing of conflict as "war." McAdam, Tarrow, and Tilly (2001) employ the concept of an "opportunity/threat spiral" to describe a trajectory of escalating contention in a few historical cases. I want to develop this construct more fully to explain the trajectory of the movement-state dynamic that fueled the development and mobilization of the Patriot movement.

Opportunity/Threat

Political process theory has made a unique contribution to the unfolding development of an analytic framework for contentious politics. According to Tarrow (1994), political process theory developed in response to observed weaknesses of earlier perspectives, such as resource mobilization or grievance-based conceptions of social movements. He notes that "political opportunity" helped to explain why movements do not necessarily arise in direct response to grievances or availability of resources within a group: "For if it is political opportunities that translate the potential for movement mobilization, then even groups with mild grievances and dense resources – but lacking opportunities – may not (Tarrow, 1994: 18). Movement mobilization is linked to "openings" in, "increased access" to, or the "expansion" of political opportunities occasioned by the state or political elites. Social actors typically lack resources and opportunities to marshal power and effect change. But triggered by the incentives generated through shifting or expanding political opportunity, movements may be empowered to overcome obstacles to collective action and sustain their challenge to political or institutional opponents. If mounting, coordinating, and sustaining contentious collective action is the essential task of social movements, there must also be external or environmental conditions that are conducive to this task. Political opportunity pinpoints the vital external resources that can be taken advantage of and commandeered even by weak or disorganized challengers as increased access opens up the possibility of new alliances and shows where elites and authorities are vulnerable. The formation of new alliances among challengers alters the configuration of conflict, broadens the base of opposition and places new pressures on the state or political elites to meet demands for change.

Political opportunity helps to draw people into collective action through known "repertoires of contention" (Tilly, 1978) and by creating innovative forms or strategies around their margins. Known repertoires speak to the fact that forms of collective action are part of the larger public culture, learned conventions that are culturally inscribed and communicated. These may cease to be effective as state agents respond and make adjustments to control them, compelling movement entrepreneurs to carve out new forms. Fundamental changes in forms of contention, in turn, depend on fluctuations of opportunity, as well as interests, resources, and organization. Challengers constantly explore new forms in the search for tactical advantage in making claims against the state or institutional elites. Movement leaders may succeed in creating innovative forms by blending elements of convention with new frames of meaning. But such innovations are more likely to occur when political opportunity arises and affords new openings and incentives for challengers. Improvisation and struggle by claimants must confront and respond to changes in the external political environment that reduce the costs of collective action for themselves and for potential recruits.

An abiding theme in political process theory is the importance attributed to factors and processes external to the movement, or rather how the political environment *interacts* with movement formation and mobilization. This has to be understood in the context of its historical formation. Political process theorists set about to fashion a corrective to the overly psychological explanations of movement participation that invoked individual/personality factors such as isolation, social marginality, deprivation, stress, emotionality, irrationality, or other variations on social and psychological deficits (Hoffer, 1951; Klapp, 1969; Kornhauser, 1959). Herein, potential adherents facing normative uncertainty disrupted by change were drawn into movement activity by "a mix of personal pathology and social disorganization" (McAdam, 2004: 281). The political turmoil of the 1960s challenged this view and made the largely apolitical-psychological view of social movements untenable. If the American political system operated on an entrenched power structure resistant to minority participation, as was made more evident in the sixties, then movements were better viewed as "politics by other means" – essentially, rational efforts to compel inclusion and recognition of demands. Moreover, political process theorists were among the first to demonstrate that it was through established groups or networks (mobilizing structures) that mobilization was most likely to occur, not through the disorganized or isolated segments of society. Ostensibly, this approach would not have great utility in analyzing far-right political activism, a domain

27

frequently dismissed even by conservative critics as the lunatic fringe. But as we shall see, two cycles of effective mobilization enjoyed by the Patriot movement in the 1980s and 1990s entailed precisely that kind of access to, and alliances with, established groups and networks among farm organizations and gun rights organizations, respectively.

Tarrow argues that movements emerge when ordinary citizens, emboldened by leaders, take advantage of changes in the allocation of opportunity that reduce the costs of collective action, expose the vulnerability of elites, and reveal potential allies. McAdam has defined the condition of expanding opportunity as "changes in either the institutional features or informal political alignments of a given system that significantly reduce the power disparity between a given challenging group and the state" (1995: 224). Political process theory posits the notion that political opportunity lowers the costs of contentious action among movement participants while raising the perceived benefits and prospects of a successful challenge to powerful elites. Notwithstanding the earlier and more narrowly structuralist conceptualization of opportunity ("political opportunity structures," or POS) by Tarrow and others, subsequently challenged by culturalists (see Goodwin and Jasper, 2004, for an overview of the debate), political process theory has advanced important new lines of inquiry and research in the field of social movements.

More recent formulations of political process have forged a corrective to the overly rigid distinction between objective conditions and subjective interpretations of opportunity and threat. These formulations have stressed the importance of collective meaning-work in human endeavors, noting that movement actors must respond effectively to changes in the political environment by fashioning viable collective-action frames in order to stimulate movement mobilization. Labeling and imposing meaning are consequential political acts in themselves and are part of what must be explained. Hence, labeling and assigning meaning to opportunities and threats do not comprise objective categories but are subject to *attribution*. In moving toward a more dynamic mobilization model, McAdam, Tarrow, and Tilly (2001: 43) state: "Rather than look upon 'opportunities and threats' as objective structural factors, we see them as subject to attribution. No opportunity, however objectively open, will invite mobilization unless it is (a) visible to potential challengers and (b) perceived as an opportunity. The same holds for threats, an underemphasized corollary of the model." In short, opportunities and threats cannot be automatically construed from changes in the political environment. Elsewhere, McAdam (1999: xi) asserts that "to trigger an episode of contention, it must be first interpreted as threatening by a sufficiently large number of people to make collective action viable. In this sense, it is not the structural changes that set people in motion, but the shared understanding and conceptions of 'we-ness' they develop to make sense of the trends. The importance of the trends derives, then, from the stimulus they provide to this interpretive process." McAdam's effort to highlight the neglected the role of threat as a factor in prompting collective action has particular relevance for the present study.

McAdam argues that in Tilly's (1978) original formulation of political process theory, he "assigned equal weight to threat and opportunity as stimulants to collective action. But over the years, threat has given way to opportunity as the analytic *sine qua non* of many social movement scholars" (2004: 205). He finds this appropriation of the theory excessively constricted, especially among movements in democratic settings: "That is, in polities where there is some expectation of state responsiveness and few formal barriers to mobilization, we should expect perceived threats to group interests to serve along with expanding opportunities, as two distinct precipitants of collective action" (McAdam, 2004: 205). Yet, the attention given to threat as a stimulus to collective action has remained largely "an underemphasized corollary of the model" (McAdam, Tarrow, and Tilly, 2001: 43). I contend that this failing is linked in part to the dearth of research on right-wing movements, precisely because such movement cultures tend to feature threat more prominently in their political discourse, but I will return to this point later. In any case, McAdam offers an example of how threat may be built into a model of movement origins.

In the second edition of his seminal work, *Political Process and Black Insurgency, 1930–1970*, McAdam revises his earlier analysis to give greater emphasis to the role of threat in the formation of the civil rights movement. This revised examination is careful to articulate the confluence of multiple sets of actors or "combatants" (federal officials, civil rights activists, Southern segregationists) interacting out of complex culturally embedded aims and motives. In addition to the black community activists who were at the forefront of the civil rights movement, various state and nonstate elites were part of the mix of change processes. As McAdam points out, these elites saw their own interests imperiled by changes in the broader political environment. Southern segregationists were alarmed by the "Negro question" and saw the "Southern way of life" threatened by civil rights reforms. The mid-century Dixiecrat rebellion was a product of this perceived threat, organized and driven by the region's political and economic elites. At the same time, policymakers within the State Department and foreign policy community viewed domestic racism as fodder for communist propaganda during the Cold War. They saw racial discrimination in the United States as a threat to the world struggle to spread democracy and defeat communism. Thus, while movement-specific forces were kindled largely by a collective perception of emerging political opportunity, threat played a more significant role for state elites and Southern segregationists. "In my reassessment of the case," McAdam states (1999: xxxi), "threat has as much, if not more, to do with the origin of the conflict as does opportunity. Only movement forces were animated by a shared perception of developing opportunities. The critical early actions of federal officials and southern elites were clearly motivated by varying conceptions of threat." Because there are few social movement studies in which threat is built into a model of movement origins, this case invites careful consideration.

According to McAdam, key state actors during the early years of the Cold War came to view American-style racism as a serious threat to the realization of U.S. foreign policy aims. Policymakers in the State Department and many in the foreign policy community were engaged in a critical debate about the shape of the postwar world and its implications for the execution of U.S. policy both here and abroad. McAdam observes that those in the diplomatic corps were concerned about the Cold War image of American racism giving currency to aggressive Soviet propaganda efforts in other parts of the world. Many U.S. government officials lobbied for policy innovations and civil rights reforms. President Truman's civil rights initiatives – appointment of a Committee on Civil Rights to remedy discrimination, establishment of a Fair Employment Board within the Civil Service Commission, and the gradual desegregation of the armed services – were a response to such calls for reform. Another response was the series of legal briefs filed by the U.S. Attorney General's office in connection with various civil rights cases heard before the U.S. Supreme Court. Among these briefs was one filed in the *Brown v. Topeka Board of Education* case, the ground-breaking school desegregation case decided in 1954. McAdam culls a quote from the brief that clearly invokes a Cold War interpretive frame linking civil rights reform to threatened interests: "It is in the context of the present world struggle between freedom and tyranny that the problem of racial discrimination must be viewed.... Racial discrimination furnishes grist for the Communist propaganda mills, and it raises doubt even among friendly nations as to the intensity of our devotion to the democratic faith" (1999: xxiii).

Growing support and advocacy for civil rights reform among segments of the federal government precipitated reactions by Southern segregationists designed to preserve traditional power structures and race relations. Threatened by changes to Southern heritage and native privilege, the region's political and economic elites mobilized to resist federal attempts to desegregate schools and other public institutions. Mobilization of Dixiecrats, then, arose as a response to threatened interests set into motion by changes in the political environment brought on by the Cold War.

Goldstone and Tilly (2001) have also called for a reassessment of the role of threat in movement formation. They make the following assertion:

> While the literature on contentious politics is not silent on threat, . . . we believe that "threat" has not been explored as extensively as "opportunity." Indeed, "threat" is often treated as merely the flip side of opportunity, a negative measure of the same concept so that "increased threat" simply equates with "reduced opportunities." We believe this is mistaken, that "threat" is an independent variable whose dynamics greatly influence how popular groups and the state act in a variety of conflict situations. (2001: 181)

Goldstone and Tilly further argue that the way "threat" and "opportunity" combine or interact, rather than shifts in the chances of success or the costs of action alone, will influence decisions regarding action (2001: 813). They develop a model of opportunity-threat interaction to explore five possible "pathways" of contention. The researchers suggest that the state's manipulation of concessions and repressive threats converge with perceived opportunities and prospects for success by challengers to shape varied outcomes, including spirals of conflict. For Goldstone and Tilly, opportunity is always in interaction with threats, both current (concessions to alleviate harm) and repressive, which may explain why "an increase in repression or concessions is often followed by more protest, rather than less" (2001: 193).

The challenge to examine perceived threat as an independent variable in social movements while appreciating complex interactions with opportunities, state actions, political environment, countermovements, and third parties is formidable. Luders's (2003) study of the civil rights movement, for example, has shown how state actions against threats brought by countermovement organizations such as the Klan and the Citizens Councils helped to amplify movement mobilization. Luders found that active state suppression of white supremacist mobilization in places like North Carolina and South Carolina severely limited the incidence of violence against blacks,

31

fostering a more favorable climate for civil rights activism. "By opting to suppress, tolerate or encourage countermovement mobilization," Luders concluded, "states can decisively affect the intensity of countermovement activity directed against the initial movement" (2003: 28).

Cunningham (2003) has shown how state organization and allocation of repression can impact protest movements. His study of the FBI's counterintelligence program (COINTELPRO) aimed at left- and right-wing movements demonstrates how intensive mobilization of state resources undermined these efforts. It highlights the innovation of FBI agents and offices developing new tactics over time, described by Cunningham as an "organizational learning process" in response to shifts in the protest field. Local FBI offices were encouraged to devise and test deterrence strategies or countertactics and report successes back to Washington. However, the highly centralized control exercised by J. Edgar Hoover over the agency also created impediments to the effectiveness of COINTELPRO. Cunningham identifies a number of bureaucratic constraints to innovation that adversely affected the program. He concludes by suggesting that more attention be paid to the "repressive apparatus" of the state in order to better understand movement success or trajectories of contention.

Other studies suggest that threats brought by state actions against social movements can lead to increased protest activity (DeNardo, 1985; Gamson, Fireman, and Rytina, 1982; Opp and Roehl, 1990). But little consensus on this point has been achieved, and analysts offer a wide range of possible outcomes in response to state repression (see Koopmans, 1997).

The entreaties by McAdam, Goldstone, Tilly, and others to build threat back into our models of movement origins inform the ensuing work. The attribution of "threat" appears to play a more significant role than "opportunity" in the development of the Patriot movement, as I hope to show. The perception of threat is central to the very identity of Patriots whose *raison d'être* is based almost exclusively on its relation to a defined enemy. The degree to which perceived threat was so palpably evident among Patriot groups suggests the possibility that previous omissions of threat in models of movement mobilization might be linked to the dearth of studies of right-wing movements. Threat has long been recognized as a prominent feature of right-wing organizations and politics. Four decades ago, corresponding to the rise of the civil rights movement, Hofstadter (1965) characterized the politics of right-wing groups as a "paranoid style." Indeed, the notion of "conspiracy" has been a pivotal theme in right-wing literature and ideology since the early days of the Cold War (Bell, 1963; Broyles, 1964; Forster and Epstein, 1964; Janson and Eismann, 1963). Turning the State Department/diplomatic corps' perception of threat (race discrimination feeds communist propaganda) on its head, many segregationist actors and organizations on the right made counterclaims that the civil rights movement was a communist plot designed to divide the nation. Robert Welch, founder of the John Birch Society in 1958, directly attacked Dr. Martin Luther King, Jr., in a pamphlet titled "Two Revolutions at Once" (Welch, 1966) for promoting communist programs and attributed American race disturbances and riots to communist agitation (Forster and Epstein, 1964; Janson and Eismann, 1963). The John Birch Society printed approximately a half-million copies of the pamphlet claiming that King was a dupe of communist forces conspiring to divide and conquer the races for the purpose of instigating a civil war. The conflation of communism and civil rights provided fuel for Southern segregationists and early on helped to swell the membership rolls of the Birch Society. Ideologically, this heralded threat provided a coherent justification for racist organizations like the all-white Citizens Councils to resist court-ordered integration of schools and other public facilities. Welch and the Birch organization maintained strong ties to powerful segregationist politicians, including Mississippi Senator James Eastland and North Carolina Senator Strom Thurmond, both of whom defended the Birch Society as a "patriotic organization" before the Senate Internal Security Subcommittee in 1961 (Diamond, 1995: 56). It was the late Strom Thurmond who led the Southern Democrats to break away from the national party and form the National States Rights Democratic Party (NSRDP; Dixiecrats). The Dixiecrats constructed a party platform that denounced civil rights proposals as "communist-inspired maneuvers to excite race and class hatred" (Berlet and Lyons, 2000: 170–1). Thurmond was the highest-profile luminary in the revolt and represented the new anti-integrationist party as its first presidential candidate in 1948. The Dixiecrats, the Citizens Councils, the John Birch Society, Willis Carto's Liberty Lobby, and numerous other right-wing organizations and elites formed a network of segregationist forces impelled by an unequivocal attribution of threat posed by racial integration and civil rights reform.

Hofstadter's characterization has held over the years as threatened groups on the right have consistently and effectively manufactured enemies, adopting this strategy as a virtual *modus operandi* in campaigns of symbolic politics. Through a "discourse of patriotism," rhetorically revised and periodically reconstructed over time, right-wing movements have invariably postulated a threat by liberal-left state and nonstate actors while invoking notions of cultural and racial superiority through "safe" nationalistic coding (Gallaher, 2003). The Americanist movement and various elements of racial nationalism, including Christian Patriots, eventually came to see state sponsorship of civil rights as a problem rooted fundamentally in the power of the federal government, paving the way for increasing antigovernment sentiments. In the process, the putative source of threat shifted from minority groups to state actors and their allies, increasingly expressed as a conspiracy of the New World Order (Aho, 1990; Crothers, 2003; Dees and Corcoran, 1996; Lamy, 1996; Levitas, 2002; Stern, 1996).

I am not suggesting here that right-wing movements have a monopoly on fear-mongering and conspiracy theories. Certainly, such rhetoric and actions may emanate from the left as well (see Fenster, 1999). I only want to point out that (1) threat appears to be more salient as a stimulus to right-wing mobilization, and (2) the relative failure to recognize threat as an important factor in movement formation among scholars may be due to the imbalanced scale on which the research literature now rests. Only by broadening our research program to include more right-wing movements, however, will we be able to put these ideas to an empirical test.

Threat/Opportunity Spiral

In the continually evolving program of contentious politics, scholars of social movements have recently called for more investigation into intermediate, or "meso-level," causal mechanisms and processes that connect features of contention to more general models. One process requiring greater clarification concerns the problem of "trajectories" of contention. McAdam, Tarrow, and Tilly (2001: 34) write, "When it comes to *trajectories*, we face the problem of explaining the course and transformation of contention, including its impact on life outside of the immediate interactions of contentious politics." Elsewhere, they assert that we must be able to identify sets of factors that help us to explain the "mutation of paths taken by ongoing struggles" (2001: 32). Episodes of contention involve multiple sets of actors – elites, challengers, third parties, the media – in which a dynamic of actions and reactions, or even simultaneous responses of actors to exogenous forces (but ultimately to each other), form a trajectory. Interactive and reciprocal actions take place in a continual process wherein lines of engagement are fashioned based on shifting interpretations of reality. McAdam (1999: xxvi) addresses this dynamic in the following terms:

From this perspective, what comes to be defined as "political opportunities" by challenging groups are themselves byproducts of innovative collective action by state (or other elite) actors designed to counter perceived threats to or opportunities for the realization of their interests. If these state actions are defined as new opportunities (or threats) by challenging groups, responsive episodes of insurgent collective action are likely to follow, setting the stage for yet another round of state action. Once this iterative dance of stimulus-response begins in earnest, we can say that we have left the realm of *prescribed politics* and entered into an episode of *contentious politics*.

McAdam, Tarrow, and Tilly suggest in a later work that the trajectory of episodic contention, depicted so colorfully as the "iterative dance of stimulus-response," may take the form of a "spiral." They introduce the concept of the "opportunity/threat spiral" to describe the configuration and trajectory of contention, defined as a mechanism that "operates through sequences of environmental change, interpretation of that change, action and counteraction, repeated as one action alters another actor's environment" (2001: 243).

The opportunity/threat spiral is an integral concept in the present study that I intend to develop as a centerpiece of the analysis. I contend that the highly charged confluence of a "warfare" frame constructed by Patriot movement actors (challengers) and the state engendered a kind of symbiosis, leading to an escalation of mutual threat. Herein, both parties to the conflict increasingly defined the other as "enemy," seized upon shifting and expanding opportunities, fueling action and counteraction that created an upward spiral of violence. In this dynamic, racist and far-right movement actors, engaged in a struggle with the state, constructed and responded to perceptions of increasing repression by striking back at a designated enemy, exhibiting the dual processes of mobilization and polarization occurring together in a stream of confrontations. Law enforcement agencies, alarmed by the explicit targeting of state actors and organizations by far-right groups, responded in kind to perceptions of heightened threat and seized upon the opportunity to call for expanded enforcement and more resources in the so-called War on Crime. Escalation of the threat of force by the state, in turn, spurred even more intense fear of coercion and violence among far-right groups, particularly as the tactics, weaponry, organization, and culture of police became more military-like (Kraska, 1994, 2001b; Kraska and Cubellis, 1997; Kraska and Kappeler, 1996).

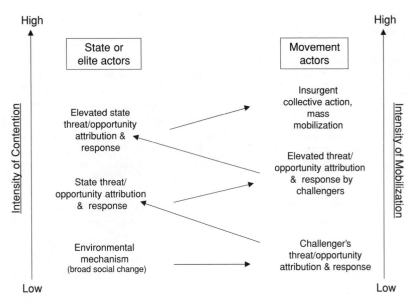

Figure 2.1   Threat/Opportunity Spiral

McAdam, Tarrow, and Tilly (2001: 29) observe that episodes of contention are not linear sequences "in which the same actors go through the repeated motions of expressing preestablished claims in lock-step, but as iterative sites of interaction in which different streams of mobilization and demobilization intersect, identities form and evolve, and new forms of action are invented, honed, and rejected as actors interact with one another and with opponents and third parties." The evolving identity shift of movement actors as "Patriots" was forged in dynamic and interactive waves of contention with the state that transpired over time and in graduated historical moments. Out of this stream of confrontations between the state and poorly organized far-right groups, we discover the eventual crystallization of Patriot identity, culture, and organization, reaching its peak in the mid-1990s, following the federal assaults at Ruby Ridge and Waco accompanied by the passage of tighter gun laws.

Figure 2.1 provides a rough template for the threat/opportunity spiral. I have intentionally placed "threat" before "opportunity" to convey the more significant role of threat attribution in the formation and mobilization of the Patriot movement. I argue that threat attribution among far-right actors is a more prominent catalyst to collective action than perceived opportunity and is a better fit with the data. While building threat back into our models of movement origins may prove to be challenging as a whole, researchers studying right-wing movements should find this task to be considerably less formidable. Depending on the case and context then, the threat-opportunity sequence may vary by political ideology or by some other yet-to-be-specified variable. The model also emphasizes the interactive nature of movement and state and posits that both sets of actors appropriate social and organizational bases primarily in response to perceived threats. Implicit in the "response" of challengers and state actors is the development of innovative collective action and mobilization of resources. I contend that perceived threats are exaggerated or embellished by social actors and strategically framed as a "war" in order to gain political traction and mobilize resources more readily. In the conceptual imagery of a "spiral," which is defined here as a series of ascending planes, the intensity of contention between state and challengers coincides with the mutual and recursive intensity of mobilization. As the mutual intensity of state and movement actors increases, the conflict is pushed upward and across a threshold of violence.

As I will demonstrate, the culmination of domestic policy initiatives (the War on Crime and Drugs, gun control), combined with exogenous forces of change brought on by the end of the Cold War, created expanded political opportunities for state actors. This development in turn provoked elevated fears of state militarism and a new round of threat attribution by Patriots centering on a "disarmament" narrative driven by the warfare motif. Following the unprecedented mass deaths resulting from the federal raid on the Branch Davidians near Waco, Patriot leaders effectively constructed and revised claims of state warfare that now reached new levels of resonance among nascent challengers and networks of gun rights groups. Social appropriation of these networks and sites produced rapid mobilization of more than eight hundred citizen militias and Patriot groups in just a two-year period between 1993 and 1995 (Southern Poverty Law Center, 1996). This insurgent episode of contention, however, was itself a product of a threat spiral that had developed for more than a decade as Patriot movement leaders labored to construct and refine a perception or collective action frame that the state was "at war" with its citizens. In a recursive and interactive engagement with the challengers, the state defined these groups as "terrorists" and sought to expand its law-enforcement/crime-fighting capabilities through development and expansion of counterterrorism or paramilitary training and organization, sometimes referred to as SWAT teams. In conjunction with the War on Crime and Drugs, paramilitary policing became institutionalized in police agencies across the country and at all levels – local, state, and federal. Though the Patriot movement was in disarray and demobilized at the end of the 1980s, the trend of police militarization continued unabated and was in fact boosted by a post–Cold War military shift in mission of enhanced cooperation and joint-tasking with civilian police. As "casualties" of the crime war mounted, particularly with regard to "gun raids," movement leaders were able to frame these aggressive state actions as a campaign to disarm citizens in preparation for creating a New World Order. The lethal casualties at Ruby Ridge and Waco were both products of gun raids, initially involving the investigative actions of the Bureau of Alcohol, Tobacco and Firearms (ATF). It is in this context that Timothy McVeigh, an avid gun rights proponent, was drawn into the Patriot movement through the mobilizing structure of the gun show circuit.

Social Appropriation/Mobilizing Structures

Most social movements develop within established social settings that in turn provide insurgents with valuable resources (leaders, communication channels, networks of trust) critical to launching and sustaining collective action (see McCarthy, 1996). As indicated earlier, political process theorists were among the first to demonstrate that mobilization developed through extant organizations or networks, not disorganized or isolated segments of society. The promise of mobilization is realized largely by a challenger's capacity to appropriate a social organizational base or site from which to recruit, train, and engage in creative cultural/organizational work. Movement entrepreneurs must either create an organizational vehicle or utilize an existing one and transform it into an instrument of contention. These social organizational bases may be referred to as "mobilizing structures," defined as "those collective vehicles, informal and formal, through which people mobilize and engage in collective action" (McAdam, McCarthy, and Zald, 1996b: 3). Mobilizing structures consist of a wide range of informal networks and enabling institutional configurations, including family units, friendship networks, voluntary or civic associations, workplace networks, labor unions, campus networks, and student organizations (Diani and McAdam, 2003; Kreisi, 1996; McAdam, 1988; McCarthy, 1996; Morris, 1984; Zhou, 1989), as well as "cells, branches and militias" (Tarrow, 1994: 135–6).

Some scholars have criticized the use of the term "mobilizing structures" because it is said to convey the same structural bias found in the debate over political opportunity structures (POS). While established organizations and networks are important to movement recruitment and mobilization, most don't ever produce such results. It is not the structures or even prior social ties alone that explain recruitment and mobilization. Rather, established organizations or associational networks must engage in effective and creative cultural work for social appropriation to occur.

McAdam has argued that identifying the structure or networks through which recruitment and mobilization spread is a necessary but not sufficient cause. "Without specifying the mechanisms that account for the affect, movement researchers are guilty of assaying a structurally determinist explanation of movement recruitment. We are left with the unfortunate impression that individuals who are embedded in movement networks are virtually compelled to get involved by virtue of knowing others who are already active" (McAdam, 2003: 286). What is missing is the intermediate mechanisms and processes that account for motivation. Motivation by potential recruits to become activists is better explained by the *creative cultural work* that successfully links salient identity with movement struggle and goals. McAdam (1999, 2003) points out that established organizations or networks are as likely to impede protest or contention as facilitate it. For example, while the black church was indispensable to the emergence of the civil rights movement (Morris, 1984), there was nothing inherent in its organizational structure or culture that guaranteed the translation of black congregations into vehicles of collective protest. For many observers, the black church was essentially a conservative institution with less emphasis on social action than the spiritual rewards accrued in the afterlife (Lincoln, 1974; Myrdal, 1944). Gunnar Myrdal (1944: 851–3) has observed that the black church in the South tended to sublimate frustration into a kind of religious emotionalism, turning deprivation of opportunity into a fixation on the afterlife. C. Eric Lincoln (1974: 108) has argued that because the black church was the one institution under black control, black religious leaders did not want to jeopardize the autonomy of the black church by challenging segregation. It was the task of movement leaders such as Dr. King, then, to *redefine* the collective identity of the black church in terms of the emerging struggle for civil rights, evoking rich religious imagery and symbolism to forge the identity/movement linkage. Given the cultural and political obstacles to mobilization in the black church, it was not a foregone conclusion that the mere existence of a structure or network within the black community would facilitate civil rights activism. It is against this more precarious and imposing set

39

of conditions that scholars can appreciate the extraordinary and creative cultural work by movement leaders that was required to achieve social appropriation.

Focusing on previous social ties through organizations and networks also overlooks the contribution to mobilization made by activists who labor to link previously unconnected organizations or groups. Here I refer to the concept of "brokerage," defined as "the linking of two or more previously unconnected social sites by a unit that mediates their relations with one another and/or other sites" (McAdam, Tarrow, and Tilly, 2001: 26). Brokerage may be distinguished from "diffusion" – the spread of recruitment, relations, and information along established lines of interaction. Brokerage is likely to occur in tandem with the framing mechanism of "frame bridging," which involves the linkage of two or more ideologically congruent but structurally unconnected frames (Snow et al., 1986).

Another important contribution by political process theorists to understanding movement mobilization, alluded to earlier, is the recognition that social appropriation applies to all parties in an emerging contentious episode. Episodes of contention often involve multiples sets of actors, or "combatants." In developing a less movement-centric account of contentious politics, a fuller rendering is required of how complex interactions among different groups influence and shape movement dynamics. Members, challengers, and third parties all confront the problem of mobilizing resources. All parties to the conflict have to contend with established organizational leaders who do not share their interpretation of events as posing threats to, or opportunities for, the realization of group interests. However, members and challengers do enjoy one distinct advantage over subjects or third parties: "[M]ost of the ongoing interpretation of environmental conditions takes place within formal organizations geared to the defense or advocacy of well established interests and organized around stable collective identities explicitly tied to these aims" (McAdam, Tarrow, and Tilly, 2001: 48).

Framing and Social Construction

Social movements are more than carriers of extant meanings and ideas; they involve the amplification or transformation of old meanings and the generation of new ones. Movements function as "signifying agents" that often are deeply embroiled in a contest over meanings with challenges and antagonists – the state, countermovements, the media – in what has been called the "politics of signification" (Hall, 1982). These productive efforts comprise an essential part of the core activities of social movements. Even when opportunities for, or threats against, realization of group interests are perceived and mobilizing structures afford groups the potential for collective action, in the absence of effective framing processes, they are insufficient to account for movement emergence and mobilization. According to McAdam, McCarthy, and Zald (1996b: 5), "Mediating between opportunity, organization, and action are the shared meanings and definitions that people bring to their situation." People must feel aggrieved about some aspect of their lives and hopeful that their grievances can be solved through collective action.

"Framing" refers to the process by which movement organizations and actors actively engage in "meaning-work" or "signification": the struggle over the production and maintenance of ideas imbued with meaning for constituents, antagonists, and bystanders (Snow and Benford, 1992: 136). The verb "framing" denotes an active, process-driven exercise that infers agency and contention at the level of reality construction (Snow and Benford, 1992: 136). It is derived from the conceptual referent "frame," which is defined as "an interpretive schemata that simplifies and condenses the 'world out there' by selectively punctuating and encoding objects, situations, events, experiences, and sequences of actions within one's present or past environment" (Snow and Benford, 1992: 137). Collective action frames are emergent action-oriented sets of beliefs and meanings that inspire and legitimate social movement activities and campaigns. They empower movement actors to articulate and align a wide array of events and experiences so that they are integrated and blended in a meaningful way. Collective action frames function as filtering and collating mechanisms to encode, decode, and "package" portions of observed and experienced reality. The framing process sorts and assimilates the punctuated and encoded bits of information in a way that is innovative and indelible, even though they may appear to be variant and discordant to outsiders. Substantively, collective action frames may accentuate or amplify the gravity and injustice of a particular social condition that was once defined as merely unfortunate. Or they may redefine a circumstance, an event, or policy as unjust and intolerable, making salient something that was previously ignored by society or political authorities. The "striking amount of convergence" regarding content or substance of collective action frames highlights the central theme of injustice, indicating to some that "collective action frames are *injustice* frames" (Gamson, 1992: 68).

The effective linkage of individual and social movement organization interpretive frames is a process referred to as "frame alignment" (Snow et al., 1986). Frame alignment entails a subset of strategic mechanisms that includes bridging, amplification, extension, and transformation. Frame bridging refers to the linkage of two or more ideologically congruent but structurally unconnected frames regarding a particular issue or problem. Frame amplification refers to the clarification and invigoration of an interpretive frame that bears on an issue, problem, or set of events. Frame extension denotes the expansion of a primary framework to encompass interests or ideas incidental to its primary objectives but of considerable salience to potential adherents. Frame transformation involves alteration, reconstitution, or reframing of the attributional orientation (cause of the problem/injustice) constructed by elites or members of the status quo (Snow et al., 1986).

An implicit function of framing is assigning causality or blame for an unjust action, condition, or event. In this regard, Snow and colleagues contend that collective action frames serve as modes of attribution, which specify "diagnostic," "prognostic," and "motivational" tasks (Hunt, Benford, and Snow, 1994; Snow and Benford, 1992). "Diagnostic framing" assigns blame for some problematic event or condition by designating "culpable agents." It entails imputing characteristics and motives for those who are seen as having "caused" or compounded the problem. Culpable agents are then cast as villains, culprits, or "enemies." "Prognostic framing" identifies or outlines a plan of amelioration of the problem, including an elaboration of specific targets and strategies, and the assignment of responsibility for carrying out the action. Finally, "motivational framing" provides the appropriate rationales for action or "vocabularies of motive," which "entails the social construction and avowal of motives and identities of protagonists" (Hunt, Benford, and Snow, 1994: 191). Taken together, these framing tasks assign blame, impute motive, identify targets, and propose strategies for change.

A Broader Research Program for Social Movements

Herein are some of the vital conceptual tools wielded by social movement analysts that must be assessed for their utility in a broader context. With the far-right Patriot movement as the focal point, we have an occasion to evaluate the applicability of an inventory of constructs and theoretical categories. But the case for expanding the research to more right-wing movements does not rest solely on assessing conceptual tools and analytic frameworks. It is imperative that social movement scholars focus more on right-wing movements because the political center of gravity in the United States (and elsewhere) has moved to the right. Movement activism on the right has transformed the political climate in recent decades. Christian evangelical and fundamentalist groups have mobilized at the grassroots level, and they exercise increasing influence over the Republican Party. When George W. Bush finishes his second term in office, it will mark a period in which Republicans have occupied the White House for twenty of the last twenty-eight years. The courts, arguably the last bastion of progressive ideals and minority rights, are under relentless attack by right-wing political and religious groups. Like it or not, right-wing groups have made significant gains in the political arena and successfully redrawn the battle lines in the culture wars as assaults on "liberal media" are used to blunt or discredit criticism of conservative agendas. There are critically important developments in the theater of contentious politics emanating from the right, and they deserve greater attention from social movement scholars.

3

The Historical Context of Patriot Insurgency

The political process model rejects the idea that the immediate premovement period is the proximate cause of insurgency. Classical and resource mobilization models adhere to a tacit view of insurgency in which social movements are depicted as a direct product of recent or relatively new conditions altering the political environment (McAdam, 1999: 65). For classical theorists, severe structural strain produces impaired functioning in the social system and is portrayed as a proximate cause preceding movement formation (Smelser, 1962; Turner and Killian, 1962). Resource mobilization theorists follow a similar logic in postulating increased resource support for challengers by elites that reduces costs and increases the likelihood of success for contentious action (McCarthy and Zald, 1973, 1977; Oberschall, 1973). Historical forces do not play a prominent role in either of these approaches. In contrast to classical and resource mobilization models, political process theorists look to long-range processes that develop over a protracted period of years prior to movement formation. McAdam's (1982, 1988, 1999) study of black insurgency serves as a template for the political process approach. "Instead of focusing exclusive attention on the period immediately preceding the generation of insurgency," he states, "the time frame is broadened to include the entire span of years during which conditions facilitative of insurgency are developing. In the case of the black movement, it is the quarter century preceding the 1954 Supreme Court decision in *Brown v. Topeka Board of Education* that is viewed as especially significant" (McAdam, 1999: 65). McAdam contends that expanding political opportunities for blacks arose following rising northward migration rates to industrial centers where, through labor unions and their growing electoral power in the Democratic Party, they became an indomitable force. These conditions combined with increased American exposure to international political pressure regarding race discrimination after World War II and growing government support of desegregation in response to Cold War threats outlined earlier. By providing this broader historical context, McAdam effectively demonstrates how antecedent factors and conditions facilitated the emergence of the civil rights movement.

In a similar vein, I contend that the explosive growth of citizen militias and insurgent antigovernment Patriots in the early 1990s did not emerge as a full-blown movement overnight but must be understood in a larger historical context. The Patriot movement has its roots in the early Cold War years, when historic international developments in Eastern Europe and Asia accompanied shifting political alignments at home to pose new threats and opportunities. On the domestic front, the "anticommunism hysteria of the 1950s" (Bennett, 1995: 305), the "specter" of racial integration backed by federal policy initiatives, and a series of bold court decisions converged to mobilize collective action by threatened movement actors who sought to link the dual threats in a single conspiratorial narrative. The development of this Patriot narrative among far-right activists was made possible by the exogenous forces stirring widespread fears among Americans regarding international events: communist expansion in Eastern Europe and China, the successful detonation of the atomic bomb by the Soviets, and U.S. engagement in the Korean War. Faced with the triumphs of communism abroad, right-wing anticommunists seized the opportunity to fault liberal foreign policy and make claims of communist infiltration within the State Department. The 1950s' Red Scare involved political witch hunts of alleged communist subversives inside the federal government and was fueled by conservatives who sought to impugn the liberal policies and supporters of the New Deal (Forster and Epstein, 1964: 5; Hamby, 1973) while exploiting Cold War anxieties for political gain (Griffith and Theoharis, 1974; O'Brien, 1974; Rogin, 1967; Tanner and Griffith, 1974). From a political process perspective, we can locate the origins of the Patriot movement in and among third parties on the far right who were mobilized from the same "iterative dance" that enveloped civil rights actors and state actors. The Patriot movement evolved as one "mutation of paths" that developed out of the trajectory of contention in the civil rights struggle.

Cold War Threat, Political Opportunity, and Race Politics

The emergence of the Patriot movement cannot be extricated from the antecedent conditions of the Cold War and the civil rights era that posed the dual threats of communist subversion and race equality to Southern elites and right-wing groups. Though each threat represented a distinct danger to anticommunists and segregationists/white supremacists, respectively, an emergent response by some threatened actors involved the attribution of a conspiracy that wed the two threats in a single narrative. For these groups, the dual threats of communism and racial desegregation were insidiously linked. They saw the force behind the campaign for civil rights as a communist plot by well-placed agents and their liberal allies ("Comsymps") within the U.S. government. Federal officials in the State Department became the primary targets of allegations by far-right movement actors and organizations. From the epicenter of putative communist infiltration in the State Department, the attacks reverberated to the Department of Justice (DOJ), federal district courts, the U.S. Supreme Court, and the White House – Presidents Truman, Eisenhower, Kennedy, and Johnson all supported civil rights reform in some manner. Capitalizing on the political climate that fostered McCarthyism (Fried, 1997), the Patriot narrative combined anticipatory fears of elite government sedition with the emergent threat of state-imposed race equality to form a coherent rationale for resistance that played to the themes of virtuoso patriotism and national loyalty.

After the Second World War, a concatenation of events served to heighten the Cold War threat. Between September 1949 and June 1950, the Soviet Union detonated an atomic bomb, exposing people worldwide to the danger of nuclear war; China fell to the revolutionary forces of Mao Zedong, despite $3 billion in American aid to Chiang Kai-shek's Chinese Nationalists; and the United States became engaged in the Korean War, supporting South Korea against the invasion of North Korean communist armies. The "loss" of China was especially galling to angry Republicans in Congress, who took full advantage of the opportunity to blame Truman and the Democratic administration for the failure to protect the world's most populous nation from communist aggression. Since before the war, conservatives had railed against the "socialist" policies of the New Deal under Roosevelt and Truman. The emergent danger of communist forces abroad gave them fresh ammunition to assail Democrats and liberals, not just on foreign policy, but on domestic issues as well. According to Bennett (1995: 314), "The 'defeats' overseas by communists made it imperative that America be defended at home from such ideologies."

Even as right-wing ideologues portrayed the threat of communism at our back door, a sensational espionage case broke in the United States, the timing of which seemed to confirm partisan claims. In January 1950, Alger Hiss, a former high-ranking official in the State Department under Roosevelt and later director of the Carnegie Foundation for Peace, was sent to prison for perjury. The charge stemmed from the statements of a confessed communist spy, Whittaker Chambers. Chambers claimed that Hiss had secretly been a member of the Communist Party in the 1930s while working for the State Department and had once delivered to him classified government documents. Chambers was a former editor at *Time* magazine and was working closely with a young Richard Nixon, then a Republican congressman from California. Nixon was a staunchly anticommunist voice in the Republican Party and hoped to capitalize on the political opportunity afforded him by the Hiss spy case. Widely recognized as an opportunist by critics in his later years, by 1950 the ambitious Nixon was already seen as "seeking a national reputation as the scourge of communists and their sympathizers" (Bennett, 1995: 290; see also O'Brien, 1974). Nixon worked assiduously with the House Committee on Un-American Activities (HCUA, often referred to as HUAC) and joined forces with other congressional conservatives to pillory Democrats for their laxness toward communism (Tanner and Griffith, 1974: 176). One of the earliest Red-hunting efforts by Nixon surfaced in the form of the Mundt-Nixon bill, first introduced in 1947, which required all communist organizations to register with the Attorney General. Dereliction to register was made a crime punishable by a maximum penalty of $10,000 and ten years in prison. Though the bill failed to pass, significant provisions would later be incorporated into the controversial 1950 Internal Security Act (McCarran Act).

Hiss was never convicted of espionage but rather of perjury for lying to a grand jury. Nevertheless, Hiss was branded a spy by the growing march of anticommunists, and the case became a national scandal. The public face of this well-respected statesman provided the kind of duplicitous image that right-wing politicians had hoped for: a communist spy firmly entrenched in the federal establishment. Hiss's most ardent and outspoken defender – a former associate and later Secretary of State under Truman – Dean Acheson, was soon accused of complicity. Other defenders of Hiss were also assailed as communist sympathizers, perpetuating the guilt-by-association tactic that fostered the culture of the new Red Scare. The defense of accused communists would become a dangerous gesture in this atmosphere, having a chilling affect on would-be guardians of liberty. The Hiss case marked a shift in the strategy of right-wing politics by transforming the *external* threat of communism into the *internal* threat of a subversive enemy (Bennett, 1995: 290).

By 1950, the anticommunist crusade had reached new heights. In September, Congress passed the Internal Security Act, also known as the McCarran Act. The bill was sponsored by a conservative democrat, Nevada Senator Patrick McCarran, and it was crafted to tighten espionage and sabotage laws while extending the statute of limitations. The bill contained a number of disturbing provisions. It authorized the Department of Justice to deny immigration to or deport "subversive aliens" and to detain indefinitely deportable aliens who could not secure permission to enter another country. The law also required all communist organizations and their individual members to register with the Attorney General's office (a provision contained in the Mundt-Nixon bill). In a time of national emergency, it also allowed for the preventive detention of suspected subversives, a provision recalling Japanese internment during World War II (Tanner and Griffith, 1974: 174). President Truman vetoed the bill, citing momentous concerns for civil liberties. But the inhospitable climate of Red hunting had intensified, and the veto was overridden in September 1950 in both houses of Congress, only a few months after the start of the Korean War.

It was in this political environment that Wisconsin Senator Joseph McCarthy delivered his infamous speech to a Republican women's organization in Wheeling, West Virginia, on February 9, 1950, accusing the State Department of harboring 205 communist infiltrators. McCarthy accused Secretary of State Dean Acheson and President Truman of shielding communists in the State Department and demanded that they "lift the veil of secrecy" and allow HUAC to "know about the communistic activities in that Department" (Fried, 1996: 78–9). On February 20, McCarthy delivered a revised version of the original speech on the floor of the U.S. Senate. A portion of the speech transcript conveys the focus of McCarthy's attack on the State Department:

In my opinion, the State Department, which is one of the most important government departments, is thoroughly infested with Communists. I have in my hand fifty-seven cases of individuals who would appear to be either card-carrying members or certainly loyal to the Communist Party, but who nevertheless are still helping to shape our foreign policy. One thing to remember in discussing the Communists in our government is that we are not dealing with spies who get thirty pieces of silver to steal the blueprints of a new weapon. We are dealing with a far more sinister type of activity because it permits the enemy to guide and shape our policy. (*Congressional Record*, 1950: 1954–5)

McCarthy's targeting of the State Department following the Hiss conviction is historic because, as McAdam (1999) observes in his study of black insurgency, the initiative for civil rights reform came in large part from the State Department. By impugning the State Department as a cauldron of communist subversives, McCarthy enabled right-wing opponents of segregation and far-right Patriots to effectively challenge and discredit the foreign policy community's Cold War template of civil rights. The very frame used by federal officials in the State Department and the diplomatic corps to press for civil rights reform was held to be part of the conspiracy. The Hiss case, and McCarthy's framing of it, gave segregationists and far-right activists an opportunity to aver a conspiratorial connection that called into question the basis of civil rights reform. For the record, scholars do not impute explicit racist intent to McCarthy's anticommunism campaign. Some critics surmise that the populist Senator was chiefly concerned with going after Northeastern Ivy League elites, impelled by the politics of "status resentment" (Bell, 1963; Hofstadter,1963; Lipset and Raab, 1970). But by making the State Department the object of McCarthy's most visceral assaults, the vulnerability of a political elite was created that third parties were able to exploit in this episode of contention. As such, McCarthyism provided an effective means for other opponents and challengers to attack civil rights through a discourse of patriotism that used safe nationalistic coding while cloaking racist motives.

By 1954, the year of the *Brown* decision, the Cold War threat was thoroughly diffused in American society, but the civil rights movement had not yet begun to mobilize. Most Southerners did not yet perceive desegregation as a viable threat in the face of deeply entrenched Jim Crow laws and *de facto* institutional support for segregation. To the degree that the "Negro problem" was seen as a threat, it appears that it was treated as a distinctly separate issue from Cold War anticommunism fears. Evidence to support this lack of connection at the time can be found in national-level survey data. Stouffer (1954) provides a gauge of the shared perceptions of internal communist threat in 1954 based on studies commissioned by the Fund for the Republic. Two scientific surveys were commissioned by the fund and conducted by the National Opinion Research Center (NORC) and Gallup. A number of matching questions appeared in both surveys that allowed comparisons of data and furnished a larger combined database. Table 3.1 shows elite and mass-based responses of the combined surveys to the following question: "How great a danger do you feel American Communists

Table 3.1. *Perceptions of Internal Communist Threat in 1954 (%)*

Degree of Danger	Leaders	General Population
Very great danger	15	19
Great danger	22	24
Some danger	45	38
Hardly any danger	15	9
No danger	2	2
Don't know	1	8
Total	100	100
N =	(1,500)	(4,933)

Adapted from Stouffer (1954: 75–6).

are to this country at the present time – a very great danger, a great danger, some danger, hardly any danger, or no danger?"

The data show a relatively high level of perceived threat among both leaders and the larger population in the United States at this time. Thirty-seven percent of leaders and 43 percent of the population thought the internal threat of communism presented a "great" or "very great" danger. Another 45 percent of leaders and 38 percent of the general population said the threat of internal communism presented "some danger." Fewer than 20 percent of the respondents in each category dismissed altogether the danger of communism in the United States. A battery of other items in the surveys revealed the extent of perceived threat to be a dilemma for civil libertarians. Approximately two-thirds (66 percent) of leaders and three-fourths (77 percent) of the larger population favored revoking the citizenship of anyone affiliated with a communist organization. More than one-fourth (27 percent) of leaders and more than half (51 percent) of the rest of the population perceived communists to be such an elevated threat that they should be incarcerated for simply being affiliated with a communist organization. Eighty-six percent of leaders and 89 percent of the general population favored firing a college professor who had a communist affiliation.

The Cold War threat frame in 1954, however, did not make any appreciable link between anticommunism and race or religion. The surveys inquired about the racial or religious shape that the communist threat might take. Respondents were asked the question: "What kinds of people in the United States are most likely to be Communists? What racial or religious groups are they most likely to be in?" Stouffer found that only small percentages of respondents identified "Negroes" or Jews as likely communists (the most likely targets of allegations). Table 3.2 shows that only 5 percent of

Table 3.2. *Respondents Linking Religion/Race and Communist Threat in 1954 (%)*

Race/Religion	Leaders	General Population	White Southerners
Negroes	5	9	15
Jews	11	5	–

Adapted from Stouffer (1954: 172–4).

community leaders nationally identified Negroes, while 9 percent of the general population did so. In reporting regional data that were not provided in the tables but mentioned in the text of the analysis, Stouffer noted that 15 percent of "Southern white respondents" thought Negroes especially likely to become communists. While this is not a large percentage of Southerners by any means, the figure for white Southerners was still three times that of community leaders across the nation and 67 percent higher than the general population. No comparable figure was reported with regard to Jews.

Stouffer's reporting of data on Jews was prefaced by the following statement: "In spite of anti-Semitic propaganda which has made it a point to identify Jews with Communist infiltration, and in spite of the numerous Jewish names which actually have appeared in the news about suspected Communists brought before investigating committees, it is of interest to note that only 5 percent of the national cross-section said that Communists were especially likely to be Jewish" (p. 174). The caveat highlighting anti-Semitism linked to communism is notable because there is no similar reference to blacks (Negroes). Stouffer concludes by saying, "[T]here was no marked tendency to single out a particular racial or religious or other ethnic group as especially likely to harbor Communists" (p. 172).

By comparison, 35 percent of the national sample said communists were more likely to be found among the less educated and working classes. Apparently, structural factors were seen as more significant than such cultural factors as race and religion in determining the nature of the communist threat.

Black Insurgency and White Supremacist Construction of Threat, 1955–1960

The events of the next few years would heighten the perceived threat of the "Negro Revolution," triggering an emergent framing and discourse that tied black insurgency to communist subversion. McAdam (1999: 117–45)

51

describes the period of 1955–60 as the years of movement ferment for the civil rights struggle. A stream of contentious episodes by movement actors and organizations propelled the cause of civil rights forward, giving blacks greater hope that race equality could be realized. At the same time, Southern segregationists saw these episodes as a mounting threat to white heritage and privilege. Organized efforts to resist change and discredit the movement and its leaders followed to counter the threat.

In December 1955, Rosa Parks refused to give up her seat on a public bus to a white man and was arrested in Montgomery, Alabama. The arrest of Parks followed the arrests of two college students in Tallahassee and the outlawing of the NAACP in Alabama, "creat(ing) favorable conditions for the organizational unification of these black communities" (Morris, 1984: 43). The all-black Montgomery Improvement Association (MIA) called for a one-day bus boycott and received overwhelming support within the black community. Sensing that widespread grievances among blacks with Jim Crow policies had been unleashed, and with the additional momentum of the *Brown* decision, the MIA invited a young Baptist minister from Atlanta, Dr. Martin Luther King, Jr., to lead a sustained protest in Montgomery in order to force the city to abandon segregation in public transportation. For eleven months, King and key members of the Baptist Ministerial Alliance coordinated nightly meetings at the Holt Street Baptist Church where the strategic framing of black insurgency was transposed as a deeply religious narrative. The narrative invoked Old Testament themes of "exodus" and "deliverance" and analogies of American Negroes were drawn with the captivity of the children of Israel in Egypt. Social or organizational appropriation of black churches was achieved in large part through the creative cultural work and signification by King and other black ministers, demonstrated so effectively in Montgomery. In concert with the direct-action strategy of the boycott, the NAACP sought legal relief from the federal courts to end segregation in public transportation, which it finally received in October 1956. The Montgomery bus boycott and desegregation campaign was a national story as both black and white audiences saw the resolve and the success of organized black protest.

The *Brown* decision and the Montgomery bus boycott gave blacks new hope. Impelled by these successes, civil rights activists recognized and seized upon expanding opportunities to widen their challenges to Jim Crow. The next year, in1957, black leaders in Little Rock, Arkansas, secured from local public school authorities permission to begin integration of the all-white Central High School. Southern resistance forces, from the governor's office down to white parents and students in the school district, quickly mobilized to block the integration effort. Arkansas Governor Orville Faubus cited the potential racial unrest as a pretext for state intervention, deploying National Guard troops to prevent the black students from attending Central High. The governor's use of state troops to defy federal authority was a futile strategy that was eventually abandoned. With only local police stationed to protect the black students, white supremacists stormed the school and created a riot. President Eisenhower responded to the violence by calling in federal troops to quell the mob and patrol the school grounds. The violent resistance in Little Rock became yet another headline news story as the National Guard remained on the campus for the entire school year to enforce the desegregation mandate. With the aid of the federal government, school desegregation and the call for civil rights reform was now gaining momentum.

According to McAdam (1999: 142), Southern resistance forces reacting to the perceived threat of black insurgency grew increasingly on two fronts during the latter half of the 1950s. At the grassroots level, white supremacist groups mobilized in direct response to the spread of organized black challenges to the system. Analysis of data drawn from the *New York Times Index* of reported race incidents showed a sharp increase in local white resistance/supremacist events or actions taken against blacks in the period after 1954. White resistance/supremacist incidents jumped from 57 between 1948 and 1954 to 352 in the 1955–60 period, a more than six-fold increase. Southern white backlash exploded in the critical six-year period following *Brown*, corresponding to heightened civil rights activism. McAdam found additional support for the "defensive mobilization" thesis by comparing the rate of activities for both black protests and white supremacist activity. Plotting the incident rates on a line chart revealed patterns of collinearity. Incremental increases in black protest were followed by almost identical increases in white resistance/supremacist activity.

McAdam also found evidence for local activity of white resistance linked to black protest in speeches and declarations by officials in the White Citizen Councils. White supremacists boasted of huge gains in membership in the councils following black protest activity. Indeed, the surge of White Citizen Councils and their membership across the South corresponds to the critical period of 1955–60. The estimated membership of the councils prior to the Montgomery bus boycott in November 1954 was 60,000. In the three months following the launch of the boycott, nearly a quarter of a million new members joined (McAdam, 1999: 144).

53

On a second front, anti-integration activity by Southern state officials increased with the goal of minimizing or delaying court decisions and civil rights initiatives by federal officials. Locked in a political struggle with the federal government, state officials used institutional politics to resist integration. Drawing again on data from the *New York Times Index*, McAdam (1999: 144) found the number of government-initiated resistance events or actions attributed to Southern state officials rose from 48 between 1948 and 1954 to 472 between 1955 and 1960, nearly a ten-fold increase. This increased rate of resistance activity also followed a collinear pattern of prointegration activity by federal agencies, evidencing "a sharp increase in supportive federal involvement during the last three years of the Eisenhower administration" (McAdam, 1999: 145).

The John Birch Society: A Patriotic Organization

As the perceived threat of black insurgency spread, third-party anticommunist groups such as the John Birch Society capitalized on prosegregation sentiments marking the genesis of a Patriot narrative. The Birch Society was founded in 1958 by Robert Welch, a retired candy manufacturer and former director of the National Association of Manufacturers. The Birch Society was successful in attracting a significant number of supporters from the upper ranks of business and industry (Broyles, 1964; Westin, 1963: 210). His strong ties to industry and passionate anticommunist sentiments placed him in the midst of a corporate trend of sponsoring "educational programs" to counter labor organizing. In the wake of the 1947 Taft-Hartley Act, businesses and corporations assumed a major role in rallying the public to the anticommunist cause. The Birch Society produced print and audiovisual materials to boost industry's leverage against labor organizations and collectivism (Diamond, 1995: 52). Birchers also formed alliances with political elites as the fallout from McCarthyism created cleavages within the Eisenhower administration between hard-line anticommunists and those loyal to the president. Welch's strident anticommunism placed him in the camp of McCarthyites, railing against the "enemies in Washington" and singling out the State Department, which Welch branded the "Communist headquarters" (Epstein and Forster, 1966: 17). His repudiation of the State Department and attacks on civil rights earned him strong allies among prominent segregationists, including Strom Thurmond and James Eastland, who declared the Birch Society a "patriotic organization" before the Senate Internal Security Committee (Diamond, 1995: 56). According to

Berlet and Lyons (2000: 181), "The degree of political racism expressed by JBS [John Birch Society] leaders was similar to that of many mainstream Republican and Democratic elected officials of the time."

Though Welch and the Birch Society often avoided charges of racism, this was somewhat misleading. The Birch organization discouraged open displays of racism at the same time that it promoted policies of racial oppression by its strident opposition to the civil rights movement. Welch's occasional disavowal of race discrimination ignores his vitriolic attacks on the civil rights movement and Dr. Martin Luther King, Jr. Welch was convinced that the external threat of communism through military conquest was unlikely. But he was thoroughly convinced that communism could prevail through infiltration and instigation of a revolution within American society. In this vein, Welch claimed that the civil rights movement was that revolutionary force fomented by communists with an intent to divide and conquer the nation. In the Birch Society booklet *Two Revolutions at Once*, Welch assailed Martin Luther King for promoting communist programs and openly attributed American race disturbances and riots to communist agitation. Welch suggested that Dr. King and other civil rights leaders were dupes of communist subversion, not fully aware of the consequences of their actions. By engaging in protest – even nonviolent protest – for civil rights and stirring up unrest, they were unknowingly acting as surrogate agents for the one-world socialist government. The Birch organization printed a half-million copies of this sixteen-page document and distributed it throughout the country in an effort to disparage civil rights leaders and bolster prosegregation forces. Every Birch chapter received one hundred copies. Welch likened the Negro rights movement to "national liberation fronts" in the Third World and claimed that Algeria's "murderous guerilla band" was merely a preview of what the NRM – the Negro Revolutionary Movement – [would] do to the people of the South" (Epstein and Forster, 1966: 7).

The Birch organization also used the "states' rights" objection to the federally supported civil rights reforms, echoing the same argument made by the White Citizens Councils. Birchers launched a two-dimensional campaign under the banners of "Support Your Local Police" and "Expose the Civil Rights Fraud" in an attempt to coalesce the issues in a resistance campaign. In one publication, the Birch organization condemned shunting aside local police by a "national federalized police force" and warned citizens of the "communist hands behind it" (Berlet and Lyons, 2000: 181). "Fully expose the 'civil rights' fraud," Welch declared, "and you will break the back of the Communist conspiracy" (Epstein and Forster, 1966: 7). Perhaps the most complete statement of the Birch prosegregation position was made in Alan Stang's book published by the Birch Society: *It's Very Simple: The True Story of Civil Rights*. Stang toed the Birch line, depicting civil rights leaders as pawns in the collectivist plot to sow dissent and foment a revolution. Stang accused the "Negro Revolutionary Movement" of trying to "destroy capitalism" and claimed that the 1964 Civil Rights Act was "a major step toward a Washington dictatorship" (Epstein and Forster, 1966: 9). More than 300,000 copies of the book were printed and sold.

As the civil rights movement reached its apex in the early to mid-1960s, so did prosegregation forces and the Birch Society. The Birch organization was clearly seen as an ally in the segregationist campaign, as the remarks cited earlier by the Dixiecrat leaders in the Senate, Strom Thurmond and James Eastland, attest. The conflation of communism and civil rights provided fuel for segregationists and helped to swell the membership rolls of the Birch Society. By 1965, there were more than two hundred Birch staffers, with a budget of $6 million, a network of 340 bookstores, and an estimated membership of eighty thousand to one hundred thousand in four thousand chapters across the country (Bennett, 1995: 319; Janson and Eismann, 1963: 28–32; Levitas, 2002: 66–73).

Concurrently, by 1965 the Birch Society framing of civil rights reform as a communist conspiracy had apparently reached a large portion of the U.S. population. Whereas in 1954 only 9 percent of the population linked race and the communist threat, a 1965 Gallup Poll revealed that a majority of Americans now believed there was some connection. A search of the Gallup organization's public opinion database, known as the *Gallup Brain*, produced several relevant questionnaire items for this period. Between October 29 and November 2, 1965, Gallup Poll No. 719 asked a national sample the following question: "What extent, if any, have the Communists been involved in the demonstrations over Civil Rights?" As Table 3.3 shows, almost half of the American population (48 percent) answered "a lot," and another 27 percent thought there was "some" communist involvement in civil rights demonstrations. In effect, a surprising 75 percent of American society saw some degree of communist influence in civil rights activism. The widespread attribution of communist subversion to civil rights efforts marked a major shift in attitudes from eleven years earlier.

This also explains the results of a Gallup Poll in the previous two years. A May 1964 Gallup Poll (No. 691) found that approximately the same proportion of Americans (74 percent) said that the "mass demonstrations by

Table 3.3. *Perceived Extent of Communist Involvement in Civil Rights Demonstrations in 1965*

Response Categories	Percent	(N)
A lot	48	1,683
Some	27	943
Minor	10	343
Not at all	6	219
Don't know	10	337
Total	101	3,525

Source: Gallup Organization, Gallup Poll 719, 10/29/65–11/2/65.

Table 3.4. *Perceived Effect on Racial Equality by Civil Rights Demonstrations, 1963–1964*

Question: "*Do you think mass demonstrations by Negroes are more likely to HELP or more likely to HURT the Negro's cause for racial equality?*"

Response	1963 % (Number)	1964 % (Number)
Help	27 (946)	16 (556)
Hurt	60 (2,077)	74 (2,567)
No difference	4 (147)	4 (141)
No opinion	9 (300)	6 (224)
No code	.4 (17)	–
Total	100 (3,487)	100 (3,488)

Source: Gallup Organization, Gallup Poll 674, 6/21/63; Gallup Poll 691, 5/20/64.

Negroes" were more likely to "hurt" the cause of racial equality than help. In 1963, 60 percent of those polled said that mass demonstrations were more likely to hurt the cause of racial equality. The 1964 figure of 74 percent represents an increase of 14 percentage points over the prior year (see Table 3.4). Given that another Gallup Poll in 1964 (No. 699) found that 62 percent of Americans favored a "gradual, persuasive approach" to achieving civil rights, it may be inferred that many people were suspicious of the unconventional tactics of direct action that prosegregation leaders interpreted as "riots." Taken together, these indicators suggest that black insurgency was seen as a diffuse and increasing threat in the early to mid-1960s, fueled by the Birch Society and segregationist/white supremacist claims of communist involvement and subterfuge.

An equally significant impact of the Birch Society's conflated message was that it attracted far-right militants, some of whom thought the JBS was too restrained by its complex organizational structure and misguided in efforts to solicit approval from political elites. Two such insurgent Patriots were Robert DePugh and William Potter Gale, who broke from the Birch Society because they believed the organization was too accommodating and Welch refused to endorse violence. Both DePugh and Gale embraced paramilitarism and the inevitability of a violent conflict with the putative enemy. DePugh founded the Minutemen in 1960 and advocated a strategy of armed "civil defense" units and outdoor survivalism, which Welch called "a foolish idea" (Janson and Eismann, 1963: 125). Gale founded the California Rangers in 1959 and the Posse Comitatus in 1970, combining racist Christian Identity beliefs with his anticommunism, antipathy toward federal government, and vigilantism. Both promoted gun rights, feared a one-world government, and called for radical collective action.

Robert DePugh and the Minutemen: Patriots and Paramilitarism

In 1960, Robert DePugh founded an underground group "organized to become familiar with guerrilla tactics, paramilitary maneuvers in the countryside, and the caching of guns and ammunition (George and Wilcox, 1996: 222). According to numerous sources, DePugh and a small coterie of dissidents conceived the idea of the Minutemen during a hunting expedition. Fearful of an imminent communist attack on the United States, the men despaired over how poorly prepared citizens would be if forced into a violent struggle or confronted with the challenges of self-defense and survivalism. In the face of this perceived threat, DePugh proposed forming self-sufficient guerrilla bands. He devised a plan to launch an underground network of voluntary soldiers operating in small cells. "For two years they read and trained and expanded almost unnoticed, sharing their ideas with other groups that felt the call to self-preservation" (Janson and Eismann, 1963: 117). The Minutemen were organized on the basis of small cells, or "bands," composed of five to twenty-five persons. The units were loosely associated with each other, operating independently so as to avoid detection. "If the Communists were to come," DePugh inveighed, "it might be every band for itself" (Janson and Eismann, 1963: 118). The advantage of the decentralized structure was that it could withstand penetration or infiltration of a single cell by the enemy. The capture or elimination of cell leaders would be less damaging because leadership would be diffuse rather than hierarchical, making ties to other groups difficult to ascertain.

Unlike the Birch Society, which portrayed the gravest threat to the United States as a conspiracy from within, DePugh envisioned a military assault and invasion by communist forces from without, albeit with the cooperation of American subversives. DePugh dismissed Welch's confidence in American military strength. The U.S. military was unprepared to repel an invasion, he claimed, choosing to organize in advance of what was perceived to be an inevitable struggle. Deploying guerrilla cells throughout the country, the Minutemen planned to mount a resistance force to repulse the aggressors and eventually recapture and restore the Constitutional Republic after a "Communist takeover." DePugh condemned the Birch Society and other similar organizations for acquiescing to the political system: "These people think they can talk their way to victory," he said. "I don't think we can. My group is more or less resigned to a Communist takeover of the United States" (Janson and Eismann, 1963: 124).

Membership in the Minutemen was protected through secrecy, and often even the names of leaders and members were not known to each other. DePugh encouraged his cold warriors to gather intelligence and keep files on suspected communists. Like the JBS, DePugh saw the spread of communist influence within the highest levels of government. He issued a call to investigate "by means of our secret members" every suspected "infiltration of Communist sympathizers into any American organization" and to "expose disloyalty in the American defense effort" (Bennett, 1995: 325). Organizational literature probed further, asking, "What do you really know about the Congressman, State Senator or State Representative from your district?" (Bennett, 1995: 325). The Minutemen also adopted pseudonyms to conceal their identities and guard against the seizure of the important files they kept on suspected communists. Weekly cell meetings in members' homes were held furtively, and "security officers" were posted in front of the residences to screen attendees (Janson and Eismann, 1963: 118).

A critical disruption of the Minutemen's stealth operations occurred in 1961, when authorities in Shiloh, Illinois, received complaints of weapons fire near the local community center. Police responding to calls from alarmed residents discovered a guerrilla unit of the Minutemen conducting tactical exercises. Authorities also found a wide array of weapons, including Browning automatics, a.30-caliber light machine gun, rifles, a burp gun, smoke grenades, and other ordnance. DePugh was commanding a small band of soldiers dressed in camouflage and military gear who were engaged in dash-and-cover drills and performing various combat maneuvers. Discovery of the incident created national news coverage, and the Minutemen were thrust, however unwillingly, into the public spotlight. Apparently, the event only made DePugh more determined to shield the activities of the group from the public. A year later, he declared, "We still hold maneuvers all the time, but we make it a studied habit to leave no trace" (Janson and Eismann, 1963: 119).

The Minutemen achieved notoriety because of the furtive paramilitary organization and the stockpiling of weapons, but the group remained quite small. While DePugh claimed in several issues of his newsletter, *On Target*, to have tens of thousands of members, estimates by the FBI and other watchdog groups placed the entire membership of the Minutemen at somewhere between two hundred and one thousand (George and Wilcox, 1996: 224–5). The element of secrecy in the Minutemen served to cloak the actual membership figures and enabled DePugh to exaggerate the success of the organization, a technique he may have learned from the JBS. Though DePugh frequently criticized the Birch Society, many observers saw them as commingled. The Minutemen were occasionally called the "armed division of the John Birch Society" (Janson and Eismann, 1963: 125). Part of the speculation about this association was fueled when on July 4, 1966, DePugh launched the Patriotic Party to serve as the political arm of the Minutemen (George and Wilcox, 1996: 227). The inconsistency in DePugh's philosophy led some to conclude that the differences between Birchers and the Minutemen were insubstantial. But DePugh's brief experiment with conventional politics quickly disintegrated because the organization failed to attract the type of adherents accustomed to political compromise and institutional cooperation required for such an enterprise.

In November 1966, DePugh and fellow Minutemen Wally Peyson and Troy Houghton were convicted in federal court on firearms charges. The defendants were charged with one count of conspiracy to violate the National Firearms Act: making, possessing, and transferring automatic weapons and silencers (George and Wilcox, 1996: 227). DePugh and Peyson were also charged with illegally possessing machine guns and failure to pay the required tax. While awaiting appeal, the two Patriots fled to New Mexico and became federal fugitives. They were captured in 1969 outside the town of Truth or Consequences when the FBI raided a safe house they were occupying and found a large cache of weapons, including rifles, handguns, silencers, homemade bombs, and grenades. In February 1970, DePugh was sentenced to four years in federal prison for jumping bond. Seven months later, he was convicted on nine counts of violating federal firearms laws and sentenced to additional years. With DePugh in federal prison, the Minutemen dissolved. But out of this vacuum, one of the most important figures in the Patriot movement, Christian Identity leader William Potter Gale, was poised to launch the United States Christian Posse Association (USCPA).

According to George and Wilcox (1996: 222), "The head Minuteman was probably inspired by Colonel William Gale (whom he knew well) and Gale's California Rangers. . . . " The California Rangers was a short-lived paramilitary unit organized by Gale in 1959, shortly before the Minutemen formed. The arrest of another member and close associate of Gale's on an illegal weapons charge put an abrupt and unexpected end to the Rangers. Gale would be better known for his formulation of the Posse Comitatus a decade later, but the link between the two men and paramilitary forays is well established (Levitas, 2002: 72). DePugh's organization also cultivated a broader network of right-wing paramilitary groups. Some of these included the Sons of Liberty in New Jersey, the Christian Soldiers in St. Louis, the Paul Revere Associated Yeomen in New Orleans, and the Soldiers of the Cross in Englewood, Colorado (Ridgeway, 1990: 62). There is also evidence that a number of Minutemen had overlapping membership in the Ku Klux Klan and the National States Rights Party (Ridgeway, 1990: 62). According to Carter (1998), "Even the most cursory examination of DePugh's followers reveals a striking range of racists and anti-Semites, including even aging veterans of the Silver Shirts and other fascist groups from the 1930s. . . . [A] number of Klan leaders expressed support for the Minutemen and rallied to the banner of anti-Semitism."

After his release from prison in 1973, DePugh affiliated briefly with Willis Carto's Liberty Lobby, a strongly anti-Semitic organization based in Washington, D.C., that oversees the Institute of Historical Review, a venue for holocaust denial advocates. DePugh later collaborated on a project called "the Committee of Ten Million" with Robert Shelton, the imperial wizard of the United Klans of America based in Alabama (George and Wilcox, 1996: 227–8). In 1974, DePugh attempted to launch a new organization: the Patriots International Organizational Communications Center. The inaugural meeting attracted two hundred participants representing nearly one hundred groups and featured speeches by prominent Klan and white supremacist leaders, tax protestors, and gun rights advocates. Factions and rivalries, however, prevented the new organization from succeeding (Levitas, 2002: 136).

William Potter Gale and Posse Comitatus: Movement Origins

The formulation of Posse Comitatus and its implementation through USCPA suggest an increasingly refined development of Patriot ideas and means of organizing. According to Levitas (2002), Gale is the key figure who bridged old Cold War framing and new threats in an emergent Patriot ideology that fostered a national network of Posse chapters and served as a base to mobilize insurgents in the 1980s and 1990s (see also Berlet and Lyons, 2000: 272–3).

William Potter Gale became a lieutenant colonel in the U.S. Army under General Douglas MacArthur during World War II and helped to organize guerrilla forces in the Philippines. After his military career ended, Gale was drawn to right-wing politics. A strident anticommunist, Gale embraced McCarthyism, condemned Eisenhower's removal of MacArthur from the Korean campaign, and was deeply mistrustful of the federal government. During a meeting of hard-line Republicans at Gale's California home in 1953, he was introduced to the virulently racist and anti-Semitic Christian Identity faith by one of the attendees, S. J. Capt. By his own account, Gale was schooled in the Identity religion by Capt, who later introduced him to Wesley Swift, the man most scholars credit with founding the Christian Identity movement in the United States (Barkun, 1994). Swift ordained Gale as an Identity minister in 1956.

In 1957, Gale and Capt founded the Christian Defense League (CDL), a vehicle designed to promote Christian Identity. The first president and national director of CDL was Richard Girnt Butler, the future leader of the Aryan Nations and pastor of the Identity-based Church of Jesus Christ, Christian. According to Barkun (1994: 67), the organization developed in two stages. In the first stage, roughly 1957–60, the CDL was inactive and existed in name only. The second stage, beginning in 1960, corresponded to the stealth operations of the California Rangers, a "volunteer civil defense organization" that a 1965 California state attorney general's report described as a "secret underground guerrilla force" (Levitas, 2002: 66). The state attorney general's report documented a police raid on the residence of a CDL member that turned up "eight machine guns and an assortment of other weapons" (Barkun, 1994: 66). The Christian Defense League was also linked to other illegal activities, including the theft of dynamite and a plot to assassinate civil rights leader Dr. Martin Luther King, Jr. (Barkun, 1994: 67). In 1963, a member of the California Rangers, George Joseph King, Jr., was arrested for selling a .50-caliber machine gun and a Sten gun to undercover agents with the Bureau of Alcohol, Tobacco and Firearms (Barkun, 1994: 66; Levitas, 2002: 66–7; Seymour, 1991: 89–91). The California Rangers dissolved soon after the arrest of George King, but the CDL remained active and is still in operation today. When Aryan Nations leader Richard Butler left California in 1973 for Hayden Lake, Idaho, James K. Warner became the new national director of CDL and moved the headquarters to Louisiana, eventually forging close ties with white supremacist David Duke.

Gale's Posse Comitatus represents a pivotal component in the development of the Patriot movement. There is some confusion as to how the idea of Posse Comitatus was first formed. Some have credited Gale and Henry L. "Mike" Beach with originating the concept around 1969 (Barkun, 1994: 221; George and Wilcox, 1996: 444). Others have credited Beach because he was the first to issue Posse "charters" (Berlet and Lyons, 2000: 271; Ridgeway, 1990: 111; Stock, 1996: 171). But Levitas (2002: 108) contends that Gale first raised the issue of Posse Comitatus as far back as 1957 in his "indictment" of President Eisenhower. Distractions arising from multiple endeavors such as the Rangers and the CDL prevented him from developing the concept further. Beach appropriated (Levitas says plagiarized) Gale's ideas and began issuing Posse charters from his Portland, Oregon, home in 1969. Gale outlined his formulation of the Posse in 1971 in an article appearing in *IDENTITY* newsletter. Posse Comitatus (in Latin, "power of the county") called on Christian Patriots to reject any authority above the county, declaring all federal and state actions to be unlawful. The county was posited as the true seat of government and the sheriff the only legal law enforcement official. Modern expansion of federal and state government violated the Constitution, Gale claimed, and ignored the English common law tradition and natural law. The vast concentration of power in federal and state hands robbed people of their rights and contradicted the supreme law of the land as it was intended by the framers of the Constitution. Gale repeated Robert Welch's assertion that the United States was a Constitutional Republic, not a democracy. In subsequent *IDENTITY* newsletters, Gale expounded on the idea that "volunteer Christian posses" were citizens summoned by the sheriff to confront lawbreaking and represented the only legitimate police force in the nation. The sheriff alone was authorized to assemble and commission men for a posse, and one of the main duties of the posse was to protect citizens against illegitimate acts by usurpers (that is, federal agents). Gale believed that if a sheriff refused to protect citizens from illegal federal imposition of power, he should be removed from office.

Gale also claimed that "Citizen Grand Juries" could be impaneled to indict government officials who violated the law and called for a system of "Common Law Courts" to adjudicate the violators. The following year (1972), Gale founded the United States Christian Posse Association.

Posse chapters began to spread rapidly around the country after 1972, helped by Beach's aggressive hawking of charter "certificates" and the "Posse *Blue Book*," a sixteen-page booklet containing Gale's writings and named after the Birch Society's *Blue Book*. The first Posse chapter was established in 1973 in Lane County, Oregon, a hundred miles south of Portland. By June 1974, an FBI memo documented chapters in six counties in Oregon and Posse activity in eight other states, including Idaho, Washington, Ohio, Wisconsin, Virginia, Arkansas, and Alaska (Levitas, 2002: 120). By 1976, an FBI report found that the Posse movement had grown to seventy-eight chapters in twenty-three states, involving an estimated membership of between twelve thousand and fifty thousand (Ridgeway, 1990: 115). Posse membership was likely closer to 12,000, with some overlapping involvement of activists in the Identity movement and white supremacist groups.

Posse growth in this initial period can be explained in large part by the frame resonance and bridging to a burgeoning tax protest movement in the 1970s. The Federal Bureau of Investigation's FOIA Web site (http://foia.fbi.gov/foiaindex/posse.htm) has archived 2,147 pages of documents on the Posse Comitatus released under the Freedom of Information Act. Examination of the documents reveals the extent of Posse alignment with the antitax movement. In its operational definition of the group, which appears hundreds of times in letters and memoranda, the FBI describes the Posse chiefly as a "tax rebellion" group. Moreover, the overwhelming majority of Posse activities investigated by the FBI in these documents concern tax violations or advocacy of a tax revolt.

Social appropriation efforts by Gale and others were aimed at the base of growing antitax sentiments among right-wing groups. Exogenous forces in the 1970s produced new threats as the U.S. economy lapsed into a recession with rising interest rates, increased unemployment, soaring inflation, and OPEC manipulation of oil production creating higher gasoline prices and even rationing. The recessionary economy generated deep-seated anxieties about the financial stability and future of Americans, providing new opportunities for reactionary elements to assail taxes and spending. Antitax organizations mushroomed across the country, largely among the working class and the middle class, threatened by downward mobility (Warren, 1976).

64

Gale played a key role in broadening the Patriot message to appeal to anti-tax protestors. He began committing portions of the *IDENTITY* newsletter to promoting the emergent antitax movement and its leaders, including the convicted antitax crusader Arthur Julius Porth. Porth's extended battle with the Internal Revenue Service had transformed him into a right-wing hero and emboldened tax protestors. Gale recognized that this deepening hostility toward government taxation resonated with Posse ideology, giving legitimation to anger directed at the IRS and the increased tax burden on marginal income earners. Gale endeavored to connect populist resentment toward government with Posse claims that the IRS lacked constitutional authority to impose federal taxes. He encouraged all Patriots to resist the taxation powers of government by forming Posse chapters or sovereign townships. Gale organized tax protest meetings, conducted seminars, and mobilized letter-writing campaigns to legislators, judges, and local and county officials. Gale's own letters frequently included threats to government officials with indictments by Citizen Grand Juries and prosecution by Posse-inspired Common Law Courts.

Posse claims designed to discredit powers of taxation also played to right-wing reactions against increased federal spending on social welfare programs thought to be benefiting minorities. With white supremacy messages underlying the antipathies of antitax protests among right-wing groups, Posse overtures effectively packaged racist and antigovernment sentiments in a coded Patriot frame. Berlet and Lyons (2002: 205) make this point cogently in their study of right-wing movements: "This [antitax] movement reflected widespread economic anger, but it was fueled in part by ... White hostility toward government spending on social welfare programs seen – often incorrectly – as primarily aiding Blacks and Latinos, who were stereotyped as lazy parasites in the producerist narrative framework." In the same vein, anti-Semitic attacks were premised on the claim of a Zionist Occupied Government (ZOG) in collusion with Jewish bankers who were driving taxes and welfare spending higher.

According to Levitas (2002: 111), the first tax protestor to embrace Posse Comitatus was George Lee Kindred. A retired Michigan farmer, Kindred was an Identity adherent and a former member of the Minutemen in the 1960s. Kindred published a newsletter, *The Patriot*, which transmitted the letters of Robert DePugh during the time the latter was a fugitive from justice. When DePugh subsequently was convicted of federal firearms charges, Kindred took the opportunity to sound alarms about gun control underscored by far-right racist fears. Kindred trumpeted the threat of black insurgency in his newsletter, warning that black militants would send teams of terrorists into white neighborhoods and communities. To this end, white people should be prepared: "DO NOT REGISTER OR SURRENDER YOUR FIREARMS – REGISTER COMMUNISTS INSTEAD!" he declared (Levitas, 2002: 111). In a manner foreshadowing William Pierce's storyline in *The Turner Diaries*, Kindred advocated "total resistance" to federal gun control laws. Armed resistance to government tyranny was conjoined with the perceived menace of a race war.

In 1972, he and fellow activist James Freed became targets of an investigation by Michigan tax officials. Both men refused to cooperate and were incarcerated for six months for contempt of court. Kindred and Freed responded by founding the Citizen's Posse of Ingham County and, following Gale's rendering of the law, publishing notices of a Citizens Grand Jury impaneling. The two men invoked the 1878 law of Posse Comitatus, charged the state judge who sentenced them with violating his oath of office, and threatened to hang public officials. Only a month after the Kindred incident, *Tax Strike News*, a national newsletter of the tax protest movement, reprinted Gale's "Guide to Volunteer Christian Posses." While the guide, a compilation of Gale's writings on Posse Comitatus, had been circulated among Identity believers up to this time, Levitas (2002: 112) states that "its appearance in *Tax Strike News* brought Gale's message to a much larger and more politically diverse audience." Indeed, the successful appropriation of the right-wing antitax base in the 1970s was critical to movement formation. Beyond the small coterie of Identity believers, antitax protestors were the first recruits to the movement, allowing Gale to expand his base of support and appropriate an existing network of aggrieved groups. The FBI's archive on Posse Comitatus between 1973 and 1977 offers a record of the extensive involvement of Posse movement actors with tax protest organizations and activities.

In August 1974, Thomas Stockheimer, a farmer and founder of the Sheriff's Posse Comitatus (SPC), Marathon County (Wisconsin), orchestrated an assault on an IRS agent near the town of Abbotsford (FOIA/FBI, part 4b, pp. 1–2, 29–30). After the IRS agent arrived at the residence of Alan Grewe, Stockheimer and six other members of the Marathon County Posse forced the agent into a chair, interrogated him, and accused the besieged official of treason. Stockheimer struck the agent in the face and proceeded to lecture him on Christian Common Law while assailing Jewish bankers, the Rockefellers, and the Federal Reserve System. Stockheimer also denounced the federal tax code as illegal. Stockheimer was later indicted and convicted on charges of assaulting a federal agent, but the state court sentenced him to only sixty days in jail. The defiant Posse leader pledged to continue his antitax campaign against the government even in the wake of the criminal conviction. The record suggests that Stockheimer made good on his pledge.

The FOIA/FBI files indicate that Stockheimer helped pilot five other Posse chapters in Wisconsin in 1974. New Posse chapters arose in Grant, Manitowoc, Shawano, Taylor, and Winnebago counties. The six chartered chapters of SPC in Wisconsin centered their energies on tax protest. In October 1974, Stockheimer organized the Midwest National Tax and Posse Comitatus Convention in Milwaukee to promote both Posse and antitax messages, drawing approximately three hundred participants. The *Milwaukee Journal* covered the convention and described the conventioneers as "members of the John Birch Society, American Party and Sheriff's Posse Comitatus." The program featured Henry L. Beach; George Lee Kindred, billed as "Dean of Layman's Educational Guild at Law"; Dr. Martin A. Larson, author of *Tax Revolt:USA!*; Vaughn Ellsworth, an "Authority on Civil Rights Law"; Gerald McFarren, American Party candidate for the U.S. Senate; and Stockheimer, referred to as the "Chairman of Sheriff's Posse Comitatus, Wisconsin." Undercover FBI agents observed and recorded comments from speakers at the convention. Martin Larson told the audience to cut the government off by "using a pit pocket silent revolution." Vaughn Ellsworth advised attendees on ways to "take on the U.S. Courts" and "challenge the criminal government" on its own grounds, pointing out that the "true enemy is unlimited government." But it was Thomas Stockheimer who most attracted the attention of the FBI at the convention. According to an FBI document, during concluding remarks at the convention's end, Stockheimer stated, "You all know what you need to buy." A voice from audience shot back, "Yeah, buy gold and silver." "No," Stockheimer replied, "buy guns and bullets" (FOIA/FBI, part 4c, pp. 10–11).

A few months later, in February 1975, Posse organizers in Washington State and Arkansas sponsored antitax conventions on consecutive weekends. In Seattle, Henry L. Beach organized the Northwest Regional Posse Comitatus and Tax Convention on the weekend of February 8–9. FBI memoranda only document the event, without supplying undercover information. The following weekend, Posse organizers in Arkansas sponsored the Big Tri-State Tax Rally in Eureka Springs. This program featured antitax icon Arthur Julius Porth, who had recently been released from imprisonment on tax evasion charges; Michigan Posse leader George Lee Kindred; and Jerome Daly, billed as the "Man Who Beat the Federal Reserve." FBI undercover agents documented a broad representation of groups, including the People's Reform Movement in Minneapolis; Americans for Constitutional Taxation, based in Pasadena, California; Patriots for Constitutional Taxation, based in Oak Park, Illinois; and Stockheimer's Little People's Tax Advisory Committee, based in Hewitt, Wisconsin. Posse Comitatus materials and information packets were distributed to attendees. Included in the materials was a section in Kindred's Little People's Tax Advisory Newsletter, titled "Who Heads NAACP" contending that "no Negro has ever been the President of the NAACP." The organization, it was alleged, has always been run by Marxists and Jews (FOIA/FBI, part 6a, p. 32).

Antitax rallies, protests, and conventions in collaboration with Posse chapters and organizers expanded across the country in 1975. Activities and events in Ohio, Iowa, Texas, California, Kansas, Missouri, Illinois, Minnesota, Michigan, and Arizona are documented in the FBI archive. By the following year, the FBI reported seventy-eight Posse chapters in twenty-three states, a dramatic surge of growth due largely to the social appropriation and mobilization of right-wing tax resistance groups and networks spearheaded by Gale and Beach.

The Posse network was also making significant inroads into rural areas where another crisis was looming. Resentment of the federal government among farmers and other rural families was building as interest rates charged by banks and other lenders on farmland climbed and the market prices of farm commodities dropped, causing severe financial woes in the Farm Belt. Posse leaders, such as Stockheimer, recognized the growing threat among farmers and pioneered efforts to appeal to rural landowners. According to Levitas (2002: 122), "Of all the Posse leaders, he was the first to recognize the importance of broadening the rural base of the movement and reaching frustrated farmers – the group's most promising recruits. Stockheimer accomplished this by expanding the focus of the Posse beyond its usual litany of conspiracy theories (which he enthusiastically endorsed) to include issues of more immediate concern to farmers and small town residents, like land-use regulations and farm foreclosures." The overtures by Stockheimer and other Identity activists, linking the fortunes of threatened farmers to Posse claims, proved to be pivotal in the formation and mobilization of the Patriot movement.

The deepening crisis in the Farm Belt triggered by broad social and economic changes was generating thousands of angry, destitute farmers. As the farmers sought to organize and express grievances, Posse and Identity leaders recognized a political opportunity. Movement actors attempted to appropriate networks of dissident farmers by taking the message to key sites of unrest, such as farm auctions where rural residents gathered to see long-held family farms sold in the wake of bank foreclosures. Framing the crisis as a conspiracy of state actors and international elites, movement leaders constructed an emergent Patriot script that conferred meaning on and signification to farmers' grievances, using coded nationalistic speech and making appeals to deep-seated patriotism.

4

The Farm Crisis, Threat Attribution, and Patriot Mobilization

If the antitax network of right-wing groups provided an expanded base for the burgeoning Patriot movement, the farm crisis helped solidify its foothold in rural America. Despite pastoral images of rustic agrarian life in America's heartland, where virtues of tradition, family, and hard work are thought to prevail, there is a disturbing history of "rural radicalism" that has fostered populist movements from the Shays' Rebellion to the American Agriculture Movement (Stock, 1996). According to Stock, rural America has always been defined by such traits as antiauthoritarianism, antielitism, deep suspicion of big business and finance, localism, fierce independence, and a certain contempt for federal government that have nurtured a "culture of vigilantism." In the latter half of the 1970s, broad change processes imposed severe economic hardships on farm families that Posse activists effectively exploited to appeal to rural America's culture of vigilantism and latent hostilities toward government. Seizing upon the perceived threat posed by inflation, rising interest rates, heavy loan debts, and declining prices in farm commodities, Posse and Identity leaders framed the problem as a conspiracy of state elites in collusion with an international cabal of Jewish bankers and socialists intent on expropriating farm properties and subjugating patriotic Christians under the New World Order. The farm crisis not only produced a substantial pool of aggrieved farmers, it opened up new political opportunities for movement entrepreneurs to expose the vulnerability of political elites and forge new alliances, fomenting and harvesting rural radicalism.

Joel Dyer's book *Harvest of Rage* (1997) is a compelling account of how economic devastation in rural America belatedly transformed a passive, mostly apolitical population of farmers into antigovernment activists. Drawing on extensive interviews, Dyer's report on farmers in the Midwest

70

vividly documents the psychological toll of a failing economy on count-less individuals and families. Hundreds of thousands of producers whose farms had been in their families for generations found themselves abruptly faced with foreclosure and the loss of their livelihood. Without property or prospects of employment, many became deeply distraught, contemplated suicide, turned to alcohol or drugs, and sometimes became violent. Mar-riages failed, families were disrupted, and entire communities disintegrated. Dyer suggests that angry reactions of dislocated farmers were manifested in two ways. "Inwardly turned anger" resulted in sharp increases in chronic stress, illness, alcoholism, suicide, and depression. By the end of the 1980s, for example, the suicide rate among farmers was three times the rate of the general population (Dyer, 1997: 33). As legendary heirs of rugged individ-ualism, many farmers blamed themselves for their economic misfortunes, provoking guilt and self-denigration. Inability to cope with these inner conflicts gave way to an array of emotional problems and self-destructive behaviors.

There is ample research to support Dyer's observations of the adverse psychological effects of the farm crisis. One study of 503 Ohio farmers in 1987 found that more than 35 percent of respondents indicated significant levels of clinical depression (Belyea and Lobao, 1990). During the peak of the crisis, mental health agencies in Ohio reported record numbers of cases, which overwhelmed the limited resources of rural social services (Hargrove, 1986). The calamity in Ohio was not unique: A number of other studies found direct ties between rising levels of psychological distress and economic hardship among rural households in various states in the Farm Belt, including Iowa (Bultena, Lasley, and Geller, 1986), Nebraska (Johnson and Booth, 1990), Oklahoma (Wallace, 1990), North Carolina (Armstrong and Schulman, 1990), and North Dakota (Rathge, Leistritz, and Goreham, 1988; Kettner, Geller, Ludtke and Kelly, 1988).

A second type of reaction by farmers was expressed through "outwardly turned anger" and translated into antigovernment hostility and episodic violence. This pattern was supported by studies showing sharp increases in spousal and child abuse rates in rural areas. Studies in Oklahoma, Iowa, and Colorado reported exceptionally high rates of domestic violence among rural populations during the 1980s (Farmer, 1986; Hargrove, 1986; Rosen-blatt and Keller, 1983). Still other expressions of violence surfaced in the form of threats and actions against the government by new throngs of rural converts to Posse ideology, affixing blame to external agents of conspir-acy. Dyer posited a connection between the shared meanings of farmers' misfortunes and the virulent antigovernment message of Posse and Identity preachers. "Antigovernment teachings," he observed (1997: 5), "have become the salve for the depression and other mental wounds of rural America. No one knows how many of the millions of rural people who have lost their lands or their jobs since 1980 or how many tens of thousands more who are still holding on under extreme duress have fallen prey to the antigovernment gospel."

During the decade of the eighties, farm foreclosures mounted rapidly, precipitating the largest resettling of rural populations since the Great Depression. Between 1980 and 1990, rural America lost more than 700,000 family farms. Those hardest hit were the families who operated small and mid-sized farms – the younger, better educated who aggressively expanded their operations and were more highly capitalized during the previous decade (Bultena, Lasley, and Geller, 1986; Murdock, Albrecht, Hamm, Leistritz, and Leholm, 1986). The conditions that fostered agricultural expansion and leveraged purchases of land and machinery in the 1970s were reversed by the end of the decade as the value of the dollar rose, demands for U.S. farm products declined, commodity prices dropped, and interest rates and costs of producing farm commodities increased. Returns on land investments diminished as land values declined, falling 27 percent nationally between 1981 and 1986 (Leistritz and Murdock, 1988). Asset values dropped below the total of farm liabilities, eroding any equity. Some found that diminished farm income was no longer sufficient to make interest and principal payments on the debts assumed during the aggressive expansion in the 1970s. As lenders began to refuse further credit to borrowers, farm liquidations increased. Sociologists Larry Leistritz and Steve Murdock found that between 1982 and 1986, "the percentage of farms going out of business nearly tripled, and the percentage going through bankruptcy more than quadrupled" (1988: 17).

Studies reveal that those best insulated from the crisis were older, well-established, debt-free farmers who also had nonfarm income and those with limited resources who resisted leveraging assets to expand (Leistritz and Ekstrom, 1988). Large-scale operations, for example, enjoyed cost advantages due to volume buying or greater production efficiency. On the other hand, small farmers were less likely to have high-debt ratios because they did not borrow to capitalize and extend operations. Tenure status also affected vulnerability to the crisis. Farmers in the early stages of their farming careers in the 1970s generally had less equity, had high debt capital, and tended to rent or lease resources. Overall, farmers under the age of 35 had the highest debt-to-asset ratios. In 1986, about 20 percent of farmers falling into this category had debt-to-asset ratios exceeding 70 percent, an indication of virtual insolvency (Murdock, Hamm, Potter, and Albrecht, 1988).

The findings of rural sociologists yield a reasonably clear portrait of those most vulnerable to the farm crisis. The types of farm operations with the greatest exposure during the 1970s were medium-sized, highly capitalized ventures that were headed by relatively younger, better-educated producers dependent mainly on farm income. The travesty of this demographic portrait is that these more aggressive farmers were responding principally to federal agricultural policies and incentives. The nexus between the exposed cohort of farmers and federal farm policy has not been lost on scholars. One group of researchers summarized the connection succinctly: "Ironically, those most susceptible to displacement seem[ed] to be persons who heeded the call during the 1970s to plant 'fence row to fence row,' treated farming as a business, were quick to adopt new technologies, and sought economies of scale" (Bultena, Lasley, and Geller, 1986: 436). These farmers represented a new generational cohort that embraced the entrepreneurial models and new technologies on the advice of government officials and experts. The younger farmers also held the highest expectations of success, making the consequent failings especially bitter. A closer examination of federal agricultural policy reveals the extent of this link to the farm crisis and its adverse economic impact on farm families and communities.

In 1972, Secretary of Agriculture Earl Butz exhorted farmers to "get big or get out," promoting large-scale farming operations facilitated by readily available credit programs (Davidson, 1996: 15). Secretary Butz told farmers to "adapt or die" and urged them to plant "fencepost to fencepost" to meet the new demands of the global marketplace. According to Levitas (2002: 172), the "get big or get out" ethic "was preached everywhere – from the bully pulpit of the U.S. Department of Agriculture and the lecterns of land-grant universities to the sprawling lots of agricultural implement dealers crammed with the latest four-wheel-drive machinery." Under the direction of Nixon's Secretary of Agriculture, the United States embarked on the most ambitious program ever undertaken to expand the agricultural export trade. In the 1970s, approximately 40 percent of the grain harvested in the United States was destined for the international market (Dyer, 1997: 136). As export demands rose, administration officials assumed they would increase indefinitely. Apparently, little planning or assessment of the economic repercussions was done to anticipate possible problems. President

73

Nixon also had political motives for pushing the new export program. He envisioned the export plan as a means of raising the household income levels of farmers – in hopes of garnering a larger share of the rural vote – while reducing the trade deficit. Though the program was sold as a humanitarian effort to "feed the world," U.S. grains were sold to other countries largely in an attempt to shore up an unfavorable trade balance caused by declining foreign sales in manufactured goods and the rising costs of foreign oil (Davidson, 1996: 15).

The short-term effect of federal farm policy produced a rapidly increasing farm income accompanied by inflated land values. The latter was overshadowed by the success of exports and higher income for farmers, mitigating concerns by some analysts. At the outset of the export boom, banks urged farmers to take out larger loans to modernize equipment and expand farming operations. The export boom was also a banking boom as lenders aggressively shopped loans to farmers. "Some lenders even made house calls to push new loans, or they earned special bonuses based upon loan volume; others simply made next year's operating loan contingent on borrowing more money the year before" (Levitas, 2002: 172–3). The infusion of capital into the rural economy and the aggressive land purchases that followed worked to inflate land values dramatically. The average cost of an acre of farmland increased five-fold in the 1970s. This sudden jump in land values boosted the value of farmers' equity on paper, making them appear to be prime candidates for more loans. The rapid pace of growth and prosperity enjoyed by all parties involved – farmers, banks, and government – evidently mitigated a more cautious approach. The net effect, however, was that farmers became overextended, largely because the loans were based on collateral that was overvalued.

At the center of the lending problem was the massive expansion of government credit programs in the 1970s. "Despite ample private credit available for agriculture, federal farm credit programs exploded during the 1970s and early 1980s – helping to create a huge artificial boom in the farm economy, which contributed to the agricultural recession of the early to mid-1980s" (Bovard, 1991: 130). By introducing large quantities of cheap credit into the rural economy through the Farmers Home Administration (FmHA), the federal government fostered the conditions for boom and bust in the land market. In theory, the FmHA exists as a lender of last resort to farmers unable to secure private credit. But the effect of federal farm credit programs in the 1970s was to make standards of creditworthiness and fiscal accountability irrelevant. When commodity prices fell in the late seventies and farmers were unable to make loan payments, the normal procedures taken to restore borrowers to good standing were ignored. Even as farmers accrued large debts, the FmHA continued to encourage borrowing and provided a means to expedite these transactions. "The Farm Credit system, a system of federally guaranteed farmer-owned banks, continually lobbied Congress to allow it to lend more and more money to farmers based on less and less collateral" (Bovard, 1991: 132). The result was ruinous for the borrowers, leaving many farmers befuddled and feeling betrayed by bankers and the government. "According to FmHA's own records, almost a quarter of the bankruptcies among borrowers from the FmHA [were] due in large part to having received too many FmHA loans" (Bovard, 1991: 138). "As of early 1986, the average FmHA borrower had a net worth of $73,000. Eighty-five percent of FmHA borrowers were losing money farming. Their average annual negative cash flow was $56,000. If the average FmHA borrower had sold out at the beginning of 1986, he could have left farming with a cash sum greater than the net worth of the typical American family (Bovard, 1991: 138).

McVeigh's coconspirator in the Oklahoma City bombing, Terry Nichols, grew up on a farm in the part of eastern Michigan called "the thumb." Nichols's father, Robert, was a struggling farmer who experienced bankruptcy himself when Terry was a young boy. Terry Nichols's early adult years corresponded to the farm crisis in the late 1970s and early 1980s. A number of Terry's friends and neighbors had their farms auctioned off during this time. After Nichols was divorced from his first wife, Lana, he went to live with his brother James, who owned and operated a farm in Decker, Michigan. Both Terry and James held fervid, antigovernment views and blamed the government for their financial plight. In an interview with *ABC News*, James Nichols made the following statement:

Government manipulated the price of corn down to a $1.25 in the early 80s; went from a good high price somewhere around $3 to . . . $1.25. They forced all farmers, everyone, on the welfare rolls. I know farmers that never went into the government program, that signed up for the government program, because the government forced the price of corn so low. (*ABC News*, April 11, 1996)

Misguided government policies were not the only source of affliction for American farmers. According to Davidson (1996), global production of food was also expanding during the 1970s due to technological and political changes. Some of the largest grain-importing countries – such as China, India, and Brazil – saw substantial increases in domestic production. This development produced a flooded market leading to declining grain prices worldwide. Subsequently, the United States was forced to lower its support prices in an effort to sustain access to foreign markets by making domestic grains cheaper. As grain prices dropped in the United States, however, farmers attempting to avoid losses began producing more, resulting in even a greater glut in the market and further declines in commodity prices. By the end of the decade, farmer's frustrations were starting to build as they found themselves in a double bind. The level of rural frustration in the Farm Belt intensified further in 1979, when the Federal Reserve raised the interest rate in order to halt runaway inflation. Interest rates on loans increased sharply even as commodity prices fell, leaving farmers with unworkable debt-to-assets ratios.

Though the seeds of the farm crisis were planted in the 1970s, the failure of government to act on behalf of farmers exacerbated the problem in the 1980s. The Reagan administration brought to Washington a deep ideological commitment to deregulation of markets, free trade, and the dismantling of the Welfare State. In principle, the Reagan Revolution set about to downsize government, although, as we will see, this effort did not apply to crime control and the military. It did, however, slash a number of government programs, with farm subsidies included in this list of casualties. Reagan sought to reverse the New Deal initiative crafted by Franklin Delano Roosevelt to help farmers through the payment of government subsidies, a piece of legislation known as the Agricultural Adjustment Act of 1933. The goal of the New Deal reform was to limit production in order to impact supply, thereby increasing demand and the price of agricultural products. The program was designed foremost to boost farm income through regulation of the market. Over the years, the program was abused and poorly managed, but it was tolerated and periodically revived by succeeding administrations. With the arrival of the Reagan administration, however, farm subsidies were denounced as welfare and as unnecessary impediments to free trade. A distinct shift in the political environment occurred as the Reagan-led New Right coalition engineered a new policy of diminishing support for American farmers, with the intent of realizing its unbounded faith in markets. Tragically, the declining support of government coincided with the worst years of the farm crisis, leaving hundreds of thousands of farmers unprotected and driving up the rate of bankruptcies and foreclosures to Depression-era figures. In this regard, the calculated refusal of the federal government to rescue farmers made it easier for Posse and Identity leaders to frame the deliberate inaction as a conspiracy.

According to Stock (1996: 163), "More and more often, throughout the farm crisis, recruiters for the Posse Comitatus, the Aryan Nations, Lyndon Larouche's many groups, and a host of smaller organizations traveled to farm auctions and solicited funds from, and disseminated literature to, angry farmers." Using assorted networks, groups, and structures, "wherever farmers gathered: grain elevators, feedlots, hardware stores, fields, implement dealers, churches, foreclosure sales and auctions" (Corcoran, 1990: 30), evolving figures in the Patriot movement proselytized, preached far-right conspiracy theories, organized meetings, and gained new converts. Conventional political action was pointless, they declared, because the federal government was under the control of international Zionists and corrupt elites. Berlet and Lyons (2000: 272) reiterate this point: "Posse and Identity organizers capitalized on the farm crisis of the 1980s. . . . While most of society ignored angry and desperate rural families' legitimate grievances, far-right activists urged resistance and offered ready scapegoats, namely, the Jews who supposedly controlled the Internal Revenue Service and the Federal Reserve." The conspiracy narrative was reinforced by the dismissive response of political leaders in Washington, in sharp contrast to the aggressive solicitation by right-wing activists. "Members of the Posse Comitatus and LaRouche representatives could be seen at farm auctions comforting families. While a smiling Ronald Reagan was on TV telling them that it was morning in America, the far right was confirming what rural people knew to be true: that their livelihoods, their families, their communities – their very lives – were falling apart" (Davidson, 1996: 118). Apparently, these efforts were successful, partly out of default; political elites were indifferent to their dilemma. "In a sense," Davidson (1996: 118) observes, "it was less important what theories the far right offered than that its people cared enough to include these marginalized Americans in a broader political framework. In the eyes of many, the fact that Lyndon LaRouche and David Duke spoke to the very real problems that were ignored or even denied by mainstream leaders made them the only legitimate game in town." Davidson concludes by stating, "The new rural poor were ready to follow almost any leader who offered them hope" (p. 118).

Third-Party Challengers and Mobilization

Davidson's observation about the lack of rivals for the allegiance of farmers, however, ignores the critical role played by progressive activists associated with organizations like Rural America, Inc., Prairiefire Rural Action,

FACTS, and the Iowa Farm Unity Coalition (see Corcoran, 1990; Levitas, 2002; Stock, 1996; Wirpsa, 1995; Zeskind, 1985). Rural America, Inc., perhaps the most effective, was formed in 1975 and worked to advance a progressive public policy agenda for rural development. These efforts paid dividends. In the late seventies, a core group of farmers founded the American Agricultural Movement (AAM), a progressive organization modeled after the protest movements of the sixties. In 1977, Alvin Jenkins and more than forty other farmers in eastern Colorado met in a restaurant to voice their grievances in the face of the pending 1977 Farm Bill. They agreed that the federal government was unresponsive to the needs of small producers and perpetuated policies that encouraged indebtedness and dishonesty. Large farm organizations, such as the once-progressive Farmer's Union, were acting largely on behalf of their own interests and neglecting others. What was needed, they claimed, was an organization with broad representation of farmers' interests, and they demanded a return to 100 percent parity – that is, the farmers wanted a return to 100 percent of the buying power of the farm sector during the prosperous years (1910–14) of the so-called base period. The parity demand was calculated as a type of cost-of-living index for farmers. Organized around the demand of 100 percent parity and the vow not to buy, sell, or produce any farm supplies or commodities until the government raised farm prices, the American Agricultural Movement was born (Levitas, 2002; Stock, 1996).

Innovative Collective Action in the American Agricultural Movement

The American Agricultural Movement (AAM) was able to bring national attention to the problems of farmers by mobilizing support for the strike, organizing protests at farm foreclosures and auctions, holding press conferences, and effectively showing the nation the face of the angry farmer. The movement grew rapidly as farmers across the Farm Belt saw the opportunity for collective action; by mid-1978 the AAM boasted eleven hundred local offices in forty states (Stock, 1996: 158). This emergent episode of contention engineered by the AAM also featured a new and particularly innovative form of collective action: the "tractorade," which involved a procession of tractors, as well as campers and pickup trucks, descending on a targeted city for the purpose of gaining public attention through media coverage and the strategy of disruption to leverage demands.

78

The first tractorade was a coordinated protest designed to pressure President Jimmy Carter and U.S. Secretary of Agriculture Bob Bergland in November 1977. Thousands of tractors amassed at the town square in Plains, Georgia, Carter's hometown, on Thanksgiving Day. Concurrently, a similar event was organized in Plains, Kansas, where protestors challenged Secretary Bergland and pushed him for a response to the threatened strike. On December 10, four days before the proposed strike deadline, several thousand more farmers descended on the nation's capital and rallied near the Washington Monument, while concurrent protests were staged across the country in numerous state capitals. The tractorade descending on Atlanta was reportedly ten miles long. News organizations estimated the number of tractors at five thousand, but the AAM claimed that the number was closer to seventeen thousand tractors and fifty thousand farmers (Levitas, 2002: 170–1). On January 18, 1978, the first tractorade on Washington, D.C., descended like an invading army, with more than three thousand farmers participating. The protest succeeded in garnering national media coverage and getting the attention of congressional leaders, who poured out of their offices to meet them. But to the disappointment of AAM leaders, legislators agreed only to some emergency changes in the Farm Bill and balked at the 100 percent parity demand. If they acceded to the parity demand, legislators claimed, they would be effectively raising food prices, which the public would not accept. Lawmakers feared a backlash by voters. Yet AAM leaders refused to back off on their demand for 100 percent parity. Movement organizers continued to turn out thousands of farmers who arrived in Washington in waves, mostly by chartered buses, throughout the winter of 1978, while concurrent tractorades and rallies were organized in local venues around the nation. As the standstill continued, however, the level of frustration within the AAM began to mount. Moreover, the discouragement produced by unresponsive political leaders coupled with worsening economic fortunes for the agricultural sector were pushing some aggrieved farmers toward the overtures made by Posse and Identity organizers.

A second tractorade on Washington, D.C., occurred on February 5, 1979, and, according to Stock (1996: 158), "took an even angrier and less compromising tone as the AAM tried to 'shut down Washington.'" A cavalcade of tractors twenty-five miles long disrupted traffic in the capital as farmers rammed police cars, blocked major intersections, and caused delays for commuters, even forcing the cancellation of a presidential meeting. Demonstrators parked their vehicles on the Washington Mall, and incidents of property destruction and heated exchanges and altercations with police were reported. Some farmers drove their tractors up the steps of the Capitol Building, released chickens and goats, threw tomatoes at Secretary of Agriculture Bergland, and set three tractors on fire in a show of defiance. At least some of the angrier and more aggressive responses of the protesters were due to the chilly reception they received from Washington politicians. Levitas observes that politicians made it clear they had no interest in working with the AAM. Secretary Bergland told a House Agriculture Committee that the president would veto any increases in price supports and later informed reporters that farmers were motivated largely by "old fashioned greed" (Levitas, 2002: 177). Movement leaders were enraged and demanded an apology from Bergland, vowing to remain in Washington until their demands were met. As the tensions and violence mounted, however, the news media, sympathetic allies in the previous tractorade, turned on the farmers, framing the protestors as culpable agents in the conflict.

Frustrated with Bergland and the Carter administration, most AAM supporters backed Ronald Reagan in the 1980 election in hopes of finding a more receptive response. But farmers and other rural families fared even worse under Reagan's agriculture policies (North, 1991). He showed little sympathy for the plight of rural America, calling for a reduction in farm subsidies, deregulation of markets, and slashing of tax revenues and federal aid to state and local governments, affecting their ability to fund rural social service programs. Between 1980 and 1982, for example, the amount of federal support for operating community health centers declined from $314 million to $208 million, a drop of more than one-third (Davidson, 1996: 98). The efforts of distraught farmers to gain allies in Washington and obtain relief for the growing farm crisis did not move Reagan to a sympathetic posture. Reagan's devotion to free markets made him contemptuous of the farmers' demands. In the wake of the second tractorade on Washington, Reagan remarked condescendingly, "Let's keep the grain and export the farmers" (Kohl, 1988: 180).

Social Appropriation of AAM

The repudiation of farmers by Washington "intensified dissension in the ranks of AAM and widened the split that gave far-right militants the opening they needed to ratchet up their propaganda machinery and gain new recruits" (Levitas, 2002: 176). For the growing number of farmers pressed by rising debt, increased production costs, and low market values, "the rhetoric of self-described 'populists' and tax protestors had special appeal.

Like the Posse Comitatus argument that taxes need not be paid because Federal Reserve bank notes weren't backed by gold or silver, farmers were told they should ignore their debts because bank loans were not 'real money' " (Levitas, 180). Daniel Levitas, who worked as an organizer and research director for the Des Moines office of Rural America in the early 1980s, makes a strong case that Posse and Identity leaders were able to socially appropriate the organizational base of AAM around this time. Alvin Jenkins, one of the principal cofounders of the AAM, became increasingly convinced by Posse claims and eventually created a schismatic organization, the Grass Roots AAM (GRAAM), based in Campo, Colorado. Jenkins and others who gravitated to the far-right actively recruited AAM members, using the old organization as a mobilizing structure for the emergent GRAAM. One AAM member who opposed the efforts of Jenkins provided an acute insight: "AAM created this great network of people, but it also gave the right wing a toehold among farmers" (quoted in Levitas, 2002: 179).

Social appropriation efforts appear to have begun as early as the initial AAM call for a strike. Jim Wickstrom, the leader of the Wisconsin Posse Comitatus, published and distributed a pamphlet in 1978 titled, *The American Farmer: Twentieth-Century Slave*. Wickstrom supported the AAM farm strike but framed the conflict in the rhetoric of Posse and Identity doctrine (Diamond, 1995: 260). Bankruptcies and foreclosures were alleged to be part of a conspiracy by Jewish robber barons in order to grab farm lands and enslave white Christians. Wickstrom warned of an impending war on the Christian Republic and admonished farmers to work toward establishing God's laws to fend off the army of the New World Order. The Wickstrom booklet was circulated and adopted by some AAM activists during the siege of the Washington Mall (Levitas, 2002: 179). Willis Carto's *Spotlight* magazine also lauded the campaign by farmers as a protest against the takeover of the U.S. Department of Agriculture by David Rockefeller's Trilateral Commission. Employing largely populist language and images, Carto found some farmers receptive to this approach. According to James Corcoran (1990: 34), "Carto saw in the farm crisis the opportunity to form a new political party that would champion the causes and ideals of the Liberty Lobby, a racist anti-Semitic organization he founded in 1957. In nearly every issue of the *Spotlight*, . . . stories about the plight of the farmers were featured side by side with articles that promoted the formation of a new Populist party that would end U.S. foreign aid to Israel, repeal the income tax, abolish the Federal Reserve System and uncover the Holocaust for what it was: a hoax." The John Birch Society's February 1979 issue of

American Opinion commended the AAM for exposing a government conspiracy. Rick Elliot's antitax National Agricultural Press Association (NAPA) used its publication, *The Primrose and Cattlemen's Gazette*, to weave virulent anti-Semitic ideas into news stories about key farming issues. Elliot supported the AAM farm strike and the demand for 100 percent parity, scapegoating Jewish bankers. By 1981, he claimed to have three thousand NAPA members in thirty states (Diamond, 1995: 260; Levitas, 2002: 179).

Arthur Kirk, a Nebraska farmer, joined Elliot's NAPA in 1984. He became convinced that his financial problems were the result of an international conspiracy by Jewish bankers. On October 23, 1984, sheriffs' deputies arrived at the Kirk farm with foreclosure papers. Kirk owed approximately $300,000 to the bank. The angry farmer met the deputies with a loaded shotgun and ordered them off his property, pointing toward a Posse sign that he had been told by Elliot barred government officials from the land. Later that day, the deputies returned with the SWAT team of the Nebraska State Patrol. Negotiators tried to talk Kirk into surrendering, but Kirk was distraught. "Damn fucking Jews," he yelled into the phone, "destroyed everything I ever worked for. Who's got the power in the world? Who runs this world? The fucking Jews. By God, I ain't putting up with their shit anymore!" (*ABC 20/20*, "Seeds of Hate," August 15, 1985). Kirk later stormed out the back door of his house, outfitted with camouflage and a helmet and carrying an automatic weapon. Gunfire was exchanged and Kirk was killed in a shootout. An interview with Kirk's widow following the incident confirmed that the couple believed that the farm crisis was "no accident" but part of a larger conspiracy by international bankers and Jews to take over the country.

Lyndon LaRouche launched a concerted campaign to win over AAM members. Davidson (1996: 112–14) observes that LaRouche planned to strategically "align himself with farmers' interests and, once inside the organization, steer the AAM in his own direction." LaRouche's courtship of AAM was allegedly designed to build an urban-rural alliance between marginalized inner-city residents and disillusioned rural denizens through his organization, the National Caucus of Labor Committees (NCLC). LaRouche supported the AAM farm strike and linked demands for parity to his attacks on the International Monetary Fund (IMF), the Federal Reserve, and the World Bank. According to Levitas, LaRouche and his operatives "dogged AAM followers at their meetings and national conventions" and in 1980 attempted to persuade AAM president Marvin Meek to run as LaRouche's vice-presidential candidate (2002: 212). Though Meek declined, LaRouche was successful in gaining support among a core of high-ranking AAM activists by early 1983.

Richard Butler, founder of the Aryan Nations and the Christian Identity–based Church of Jesus Christ, Christian, "saw among the desperate farmers recruits for a revolution that would result in the establishment of a national racist state" (Corcoran, 1990: 35). In a 1982 Aryan Nations newsletter, Butler reached out to farmers attempting to link the farm crisis to Identity doctrines and beliefs. "The farmer is being backed into a wall," Butler wrote, "and he's beginning to believe there has to be an answer for all of this. The answer is revolution. . . . He's [sic] been used and abused. . . . He's going to get a lot more angry, and eventually he'll see that the only way to turn things around is to fight to win his country back for white Christians" (quoted in Corcoran, 1990: 35).

Posse and Identity leaders also used radio broadcasts to reach farmers and other rural families. Jim Wickstrom appealed to besieged farmers over Dodge City, Kansas, radio station KTTL-FM beginning in the fall of 1982. Wickstrom's anti-Semitic diatribes warned of the designs of Jewish bankers to steal lands from unsuspecting farmers. He also called for Posse indictments of judges and other "servants of Babylon" who allowed foreclosures on family farms. Wickstrom's broadcasts reached parts of eastern Colorado, southwestern Kansas, and northern Oklahoma. KTTL-FM also broadcast weekly messages by William Potter Gale. In one broadcast, titled "Victory with Jesus," Gale inveighed against Jews and other minorities, calling for a need to "cleanse our land" with a "sword" and with "violence." Identity leader Sheldon Emry, who claimed that all the economic problems of farmers were the fault of the Federal Reserve System, produced a syndicated show, "America's Promise," which was broadcast on more than twenty-five radio stations throughout the Farm Belt (Corcoran, 1990: 30–1).

The effect of these penetration efforts served to fracture the AAM, thus making social appropriation more likely. In 1981, disgruntled AAM supporter Keith Shive founded his own organization, the Farmers Liberation Army (FLA). Shive was rabidly anti-Semitic and racist, condemning international Jewish financiers and advocating the abolition of the Federal Reserve System. The development of spin-off groups like FLA and GRAAM underlined the growing ideological differences among farmers and highlighted the internal fragmentation of AAM. Increasing numbers of rural activists were radicalized by economic deprivation and the unresponsiveness of political elites and embraced the insurgent ideas of the burgeoning Patriot movement.

In March 1982, Jerry Wright and Gene Schroder, cofounders of the AAM, participated in a three-day paramilitary training session, organized by William Potter Gale and Jim Wickstrom, on the farm of Wesley White in western Kansas. The event featured instructions in the making and use of explosives, knife fighting, guerrilla warfare, hand-to-hand combat, first aid, and the use of poisons (Levitas, 2002: 183). This "counterinsurgency seminar" was billed as survivalist training in preparation for the coming "End Time." Participants learned to apply facial camouflage, make explosives, construct booby traps and land mines, set up a perimeter defense, distill poisons, and conduct night maneuvers. The Kansas training session was modeled after the one developed by Wickstrom and Stockheimer in Wisconsin two years earlier at Wickstrom's Posse compound in Tigerton Dells, an illegally constructed township based on Posse Comitatus doctrine. Two months after the counterinsurgency seminar, Wesley White was arrested and charged with transporting illegal explosives to Colorado (Corcoran, 1990: 32).

Gordon Kahl: The First Patriot Martyr

During this same period, a farmer and Posse member from North Dakota named Gordon Kahl was spending the winter with his family in Arkansas, where he attended tax protest meetings and visited the Covenant, Sword and Arm of the Lord (CSA) compound in rural Mountain Home. Kahl befriended fellow Posse member Leonard Ginter, who would later hide him in a safe house after Kahl became a fugitive. Kahl was enthralled with the CSA and even discussed with his wife the idea of moving their family to the compound. According to Corcoran (1990: 64), Kahl was received as a "true patriot and Christian" who was honored by the community. CSA founder and leader James Ellison embraced Kahl and others like him because he "saw the dispossessed and struggling farmers as potential 'Christian survivalists' who would swell the ranks of the Covenant, Sword and Arm of the Lord" (Corcoran, 1990: 34). Ellison anticipated a war between the United States and the Soviet Union that he believed would be the biblical Armageddon. He also believed that Christian Patriots would have to prepare to become soldiers of God. To prepare his two hundred followers for the pending battle, Ellison founded the "Endtime Overcomer Survival Training School" on the CSA's 220-acre property. The school featured "a paramilitary training ground – complete with pop-up targets of blacks, Jews, and police officers wearing Star of David badges – and offered courses in guerrilla warfare, weapons training, bomb-making, and Christian military truths" (Corcoran, 1990: 35). According to former CSA member Kerry Noble (1998: 81), the CSA was modeled in part after the Christian Patriots Defense League (CPDL), founded in 1959 by retired U.S. Army Colonel Jack Mohr, a former member of the John Birch Society (George and Wilcox, 1996: 194). While the CPDL served as a basis for the formulation of the CSA, Noble recounts in great detail how Ellison cultivated ties with Richard Butler's Aryan Nations and Robert Millar's Identity-based Elohim City in southeastern Oklahoma. These two influences became the most important in the evolution of the CSA. A third influence on Ellison and the CSA described by Noble was Dan Gayman's Identity-based Church of Israel in Schell City, Missouri. As we shall see, the CSA would come to play a critical role in linking the farm crisis, Gordon Kahl, Posse and Identity beliefs, paramilitarism, the warfare motif, the Patriot movement, Elohim City, the bombing of the Murrah Building in Oklahoma City, and Tim McVeigh.

In January 1983, Gordon Kahl traveled to Springfield, Colorado, where he joined 250 other farmers to protest the foreclosure of Jerry Wright's farm. As a member of the Posse Comitatus, Kahl made the trek primarily to recruit farmers to the message. Grass Roots AAM members organized a protest featuring speeches by Alvin Jenkins and Gene Schroder. In an effort to block the foreclosure sale by the Baca County Clerk, activists began chanting "No sale! No sale!" while rushing the building. Disregarding the angry protestors, the clerk approved the sale of Wright's farm to the Federal Land Bank, igniting the crowd and precipitating a riot. Sheriffs' deputies dressed in riot gear and armed with nightsticks and rifles managed to turn back the angry farmers using tear gas (Corcoran, 1990: 24–6; Levitas, 2002: 189–90).

Kahl returned home prior to the tumult and learned about the riot the next day. He was heartened by the bold and aggressive confrontation; he would reveal his own willingness to use violence against federal agents the following month. Kahl's antipathy toward government had been growing for years, but it intensified when he was convicted on tax evasion charges in 1977 and served eight months in federal prison. After his release, Kahl hardened his position by refusing to comply with the conditions of his probation and becoming more steeped in Posse activism. Eventually, a warrant was issued. On February 13, 1983, a team of federal marshals and local law enforcement attempted to arrest Kahl in the small town of Medina, North Dakota. A deadly shootout ensued. Two U.S. Marshals were killed and three local law enforcement officers were injured, as was Kahl's son Yorie.

Kahl fled to Arkansas, where he found his CSA compatriot Leonard Ginter. Ginter's home in Smithville was considered too risky because Ginter was well known to law enforcement authorities, so Ginter arranged for Kahl to stay in a safe house owned by another CSA member, Arthur Russell, about four miles north of Smithville. For four months, Kahl managed to hide from authorities using the protection of CSA Patriots. Acting on a tip by Russell's daughter, who sought to collect a $25,000 reward, in June a joint task force of fifteen U.S. Marshals, six FBI agents, three state police officers, and four county law enforcement officers surrounded the hideout. Another shootout erupted, killing both Kahl and County Sheriff Gene Mathews. Not aware that Kahl had been mortally wounded, officers peppered the house with CS gas and weapon fire while one agent placed a container of fuel over a rooftop vent and drained it into the house, igniting some kindling and causing a massive fire (Flynn and Gerhardt, 1989: 114). The house burned to the ground with Kahl inside. Kahl became the first martyr of the Patriot movement, and the fiery inferno that consumed Kahl's body became a disquieting foreshadowing of the conflagration at Waco.

McVeigh provided a stirring confirmation of Kahl's status as a martyr in our first interview in 1995. "He was a hero and a real Patriot," McVeigh said. "He had the guts to stand up to the government and you see what happened. They did to him what they did to David Koresh." McVeigh first learned of the Kahl incident from a documentary film by Jeffrey Jackson titled "Death and Taxes," which circulated widely in the Patriot community and cast Kahl as a martyr. This image of Kahl was inspiring to McVeigh. He saw Kahl's deadly standoff with the state as an act of courage and an empowering signal to other Patriots.

The "War in '84"

If there was a defining moment in the development of a distinct Patriot frame and identity on which the movement was to build, it was the death of Gordon Kahl. Kahl's extensive forays into multiple sectors of the far-right orbit – Posse Comitatus, Christian Identity, farm protests, antitax organizations, the CSA – allowed movement entrepreneurs to expand their reach and begin the process of consolidating grievances within a predominantly antigovernment warfare frame and narrative. The eventual ascendancy of this frame seems to owe much of its impetus to the signification imputed to the Kahl incident. Kahl's death – or rather the interpretation of his death by

Posse and Identity leaders – mobilized the first wave of Patriot insurgency and violence.

Kerry Noble's autobiographical account of his experiences in the CSA provides ample support for this argument. Noble asserts that Kahl "became our catalyst" (1998: 129). He describes how CSA members visited the burned-out house where fellow CSA members Ginter and Russell had hidden Kahl and where he died. Other right-wing leaders demanded to know what Ellison and the CSA were going to do about the "murder" of the *new martyr* of the patriotic movement [who] was killed in our own backyard" (Noble, 1998: 131; emphasis added). Noble states, "[W]e were forced to act or lose credibility" (Noble, 1998: 131). Ellison arranged to attend the Annual Congress of the Aryan Nations in June at Richard Butler's rural Idaho compound near Hayden Lake to address other movement leaders about the Kahl tragedy. Noble makes clear that Kahl's killing became the rallying point and catalyst for the ensuing plan for underground insurgency. The death of Kahl was embellished and framed as a conspiracy by the government to silence a "true patriot." Some Identity members claimed that Kahl acted in self-defense, and one report alleged that the sheriff was actually shot by the FBI, not by Kahl. The hard-core activists at Hayden Lake determined that the killing was "an act of war" that demanded an equal response. Former Klansman Louis Beam introduced his "leaderless resistance" strategy to the attendees, a form of guerrilla warfare designed to oppose "unlawful aggression" by the state against its own citizens.

This strategy involved the deployment of "silent warriors" who would work to overthrow the government through criminal activity in order to "bring back the spoils of war, like money, for the cause" (Noble, 1998: 132). A collateral tactic was the formation of "cells of warriors," utilizing two to five men who were never to combine with other cells but operate independently toward a common goal of insurgency. Beam revised and expanded the leaderless-resistance strategy later, and it was adopted widely in the Patriot movement in the wake of Ruby Ridge and Waco. But at this early stage, only a corps of insurgents was privy to the plan. Noble prepared the infamous four-page document declaring war on the government known as the "War in '84." It asserted "that for every aggression the government did [*sic*] against the patriotic people of the United States, equal and opposite, if not greater reaction would occur against the government. If the government wanted war," Noble proclaimed, "they [*sic*] would get war" (Noble, 1998: 133). The document also declared that "it is inevitable that war is coming to the United States of America.... We envisioned that 1984 would be the year of the Second American Revolution" (Noble, 1988: 133).

It was out of this conclave that Robert Mathews formed the violent underground cell The Order, modeled after the insurgents described in the fictional account of a Patriot revolution in *The Turner Diaries*. All nine of the original Order members, who also called themselves the Brüders Schweigen, or Silent Brotherhood, were present at the 1983 Aryan Nations Congress (Smith, 1994: 68). To Mathews, who studied Odinism (a form of Germanic neopaganism), nine was a magical number in Norse mythology and infused the ideal of "Aryan warriors" with mystical power and meaning (Flynn and Gerhardt, 1989: 123). Order members formed a "blood covenant" marked by an oath that stated in part, "My brothers, let us be his battle ax and weapons of war. Let us go forth by ones and twos, by scores and by legions, and as true Aryan men with pure hearts and strong minds to face the enemies of our faith and our race with courage and determination" (Flynn and Gerhardt, 1989: 126).

Beginning in September 1983, The Order launched a major offensive over the next fifteen months. The radical cell robbed banks, several electronics stores, a truck stop, a video store, and armored trucks. The robbery of a Brinks armored truck in July 1984 alone netted $3.6 million. The stolen money was turned over to Patriot movement leaders and distributed to fund the revolution. The "spoils of war" were reportedly distributed to Richard Butler, Louis Beam, William Pierce's National Alliance, Tom Metzger's White Aryan Resistance (WAR), former Klansman and Identity leader Robert Miles, and Frazier Glenn Miller's Carolina Knights of the KKK (Flynn and Gerhardt, 1989: 296). Some of the stolen money was kept to purchase guns, vehicles, explosives, and hundreds of acres of land to establish "training camps" (Smith, 1994: 71). During the insurgents' campaign, Mathews's group also bombed a Jewish synagogue in Boise, Idaho; executed a patriot, Walter West, for failing to protect the secrecy of the group; and assassinated the Jewish talk-show host Alan Berg.

Berg was a nemesis of Tom Metzger's White Aryan Resistance and frequently berated Identity and Posse figures and beliefs on the air. Berg singled out former Birch member Jack Mohr and Colorado Identity leader Pete Peters, whose organization was based in La Porte and who would later host the pivotal Estes Park meeting in the wake of the Ruby Ridge incident. Order member David Lane called into Berg's radio program on numerous occasions to defend Identity beliefs, leading to intense, visceral exchanges. Rick Elliot, the founder of NAPA and editor of the *Primrose and Cattleman's*

Gazette, also clashed with Berg after Elliot accepted an invitation to be on Berg's radio show. Mathews created a hit list targeting high-profile figures such as Henry Kissinger, Southern Poverty Law Center's Morris Dees, and Alan Berg. Likely as a result of geography and convenience, it was determined that Berg was to be the group's first assassination. On June 18, 1984, Berg was mowed down by automatic gunfire outside his Denver home by Bruce Carroll Pierce, accompanied by Mathews and two other Order members. By November, the group had retreated to three safe houses on Whidbey Island, Washington, located in Puget Sound. The FBI learned of their location and sent its counterterrorism unit, the Hostage Rescue Team (HRT) to conduct surveillance and develop a plan of attack. With the combined effort of SWAT teams from Portland, Seattle, and Butte, police surrounded the three cabins. At dawn on December 7, the HRT-led task force announced its presence and demanded surrender. Randall Duey, armed with a submachine gun, was arrested attempting to flee through the back door of one of the safe houses. Two others, Robert and Carol Merki, were arrested without incident. But Mathews refused to surrender and sent out a letter that stated, "I have been a good soldier, a fearless warrior. I will die with honor and join my brothers in Valhalla" (Coulson and Shannon, 1999: 188). Mathews held off government agents for a day and a half in a shootout. Finally, on the evening of December 8, Mathews was killed "as a result of flares that were fired into the house. Exploding ammunition stored in the house turned the flames into a firestorm" (Smith, 1994: 73).

Danny Coulson, who created the FBI's Hostage Rescue Team in the mid-1970s and later wrote an account of his experiences, described the aftermath of the Whidbey Island standoff in this manner: "Somebody in the command center had the idea of shooting a lighting flare into the cabin to backlight it so that the SWAT teams could see exactly where Mathews was. The flare had set the wooden cabin on fire. Rather than surrender, Mathews had elected to stay inside and burn to death" (Coulson and Shannon, 1999: 191). Following a pattern seen in the Kahl incident, Mathews died in a shootout in which the building he occupied was set on fire by government agents, culminating in a deadly conflagration. Again, it was a disturbing pattern that prefigured Waco. Robert Mathews became the second martyr in Patriot movement lore and The Order became a prototype for future Patriot insurgencies.

The "War in '84" declaration forged in Idaho produced a collateral wave of insurgency from the CSA during this same era. The CSA compound was slated to be "an arms depot and paramilitary training ground for Aryan

Warriors" (Smith, 1994: 64). The key figures in the CSA campaign were James Ellison, Kerry Noble, and Richard Wayne Snell, a self-defined "messenger" between the Covenant, Sword and Arm of the Lord and Elohim City. Elohim City was an Identity compound founded by Robert Millar in southeastern Oklahoma, near the Arkansas border, and Snell was an active member of both Identity communities. According to Noble (1998: 134), on August 9, 1983, Ellison led a cell of CSA members to Springfield, Missouri, where they attempted to burn down the Metropolitan Community Church, home to gay and lesbian congregants. The fire failed to cause major damage and only charred the front doors, where gasoline was placed. On August 15, the CSA cell bombed a Jewish Community Center in Bloomington, Indiana. On November 2, 1983, Snell led a cell of three men who attempted to blow up a gas pipeline with dynamite. The portion of the pipeline targeted was built over the Red River near Fulton, Arkansas, but the blast only dented the structure. The following day, the men drove to Texarkana, Arkansas, where they robbed a pawnbroker. Snell shot the owner, Bill Stumpp, in the back of the head three times with a pistol. Snell justified the murder by saying that Stumpp was Jewish. In December, Ellison, Noble, Snell, and two other CSA members planned the assassination of a federal judge, a prosecutor, and an FBI agent, all of whom were involved in a previous case against the group, but the plan was derailed by a head-on automobile collision en route to the crime. In June 1984, Snell was driving back to Elohim City with a van full of illegal weapons, including hand grenades, when he was stopped by an Arkansas state trooper. Snell rolled out of the van and shot officer Louis Bryant, an African American, twice with a. 45-caliber pistol and left him on the pavement to die. Snell was captured in a roadblock hours later near Broken Bow, Oklahoma, and engaged state police in a gunfight. Snell was shot seven times but survived. He was arrested and later extradited to Arkansas by Governor Bill Clinton and convicted of capital murder. He would remain on death row until all appeals were exhausted and an execution date was set – curiously, April 19, 1995, the day of the Oklahoma City bombing.

Patriot Plan to Bomb the Murrah Federal Building

These assorted actions by the CSA were only a prelude, however, to the "ultimate goal," as Noble put it: "the bombing of the federal building in Oklahoma City" (Noble 1998: 134). In mid-November, Snell and CSA member Steve Scott "went to case out the Murrah Federal Building. They discovered that it housed several federal agencies and had minimal security" (Noble, 1998: 134). The men returned and reported their observations to Ellison. Ellison accompanied the men back to Oklahoma City "to gauge what it would take to damage or destroy the federal building" (Noble, 1998: 134). A discussion ensued about the possibility of launching rockets from a trailer. According to Noble, Ellison declared, "We need something with a large *body count* to make the government sit up and take notice" (p. 134; emphasis added). As noted in Chapter 1, McVeigh made a nearly identical statement to me in November 1995, and it was repeated in the leaked *Dallas Morning News* story in 1996 and cited by Michel and Herbeck in *American Terrorist* (2001: 300) six years later. Noble seems unaware that McVeigh made this statement and makes no attempt to draw a comparison.

At the same meeting in November 1983, Ellison also responded to an inquiry by a CSA disciple about the possible deaths of children and others who were not federal employees. Kent Yates, the inquisitive Patriot, expressed concern about unnecessary carnage the explosion of the Murrah Building might cause. But Ellison dismissed the concern and stated, "There are no innocents in war" (Noble, 1998: 135). Again, McVeigh voiced the identical response to me in 1995 while explaining why he chose not to ignite the bomb at night, when the Murrah Building would be unoccupied. The same attitude was reflected in the "collateral damage" statement attributed to McVeigh in *American Terrorist* (Noble, 1998: 188) that created such a public outcry.

The CSA plan to blow up the Murrah Building was contingent largely on the work of one person, Kent Yates, a former Green Beret trained in weapons and explosives, who had to build and test the rockets. Yates was apparently successful in this endeavor. According to Coulson, the CSA had in its possession a "light anti-tank rocket" in 1984 (Noble, 1998: 219). In one test, however, a rocket exploded in Yates's hand, injuring him and causing the plan to be postponed. Noble suggests that Ellison was less anxious about the plan to destroy the federal building after the Yates accident, wondering if it was a sign from God. The CSA never carried out the plan, presumably because the FBI and Arkansas State Police laid siege to the CSA compound before the bombing plot could be executed. Federal agents were able to link the CSA to Mathews's group through weapons made at the CSA. Moreover, two Order members, Frank Silva and David Tate, who eluded authorities and avoided capture at Whidbey Island, retreated to the CSA encampment. While on the run, however, they were stopped by two Missouri State Police in a routine traffic check in early April 1985. Tate shot one officer and seriously wounded the other. Silva and Tate were apprehended within a few days, and the connection to the CSA was confirmed by police. The CSA link to the weapons supplied by Order members, the arrest of CSA member Richard Snell, and the attempt by Tate and Silva to reach the CSA prompted the FBI to act. The FBI's Hostage Rescue Team, the same unit that led the raid on The Order a few months earlier, organized the assault plan. The FBI-led siege on the CSA took place on April 19, 1985, ten years to the day before the Oklahoma City bombing. It was a massive operation in the wake of the deadly Whidbey Island standoff, with the FBI alone deploying two hundred agents (Coulson and Shannon, 1999: 266). Fortunately, the HRT found Kerry Noble a willing interlocutor in negotiations, and the standoff ended in three days without a shot being fired.

Only five days after Richard Wayne Snell shot and killed a black Arkansas State Trooper and fifteen days before Robert Mathews and The Order robbed a Brinks armored truck outside Ukiah, California, William Potter Gale organized the founding of the Committee of the States (COS) on the July 4 weekend in 1984. The COS was proposed by Gale initially in 1982 as "a remedy to the farm crisis then unfolding in the Midwest" (Levitas, 2002: 287). Gale hosted the 1984 meeting at his Manasseh Ranch in California that was attended by forty-four patriots, including Richard Butler and future members of the Arizona Patriots, all of whom signed a declaration charging government officials with acts of sedition and ordering the dissolution of Congress. The Committee of the States was conceived as a national body or structure to organize Posse chapters across the country. The COS declaration proclaimed its members to be part of the new "self-governing Republic" that was reclaiming the U.S. government for the people, and it announced that it would assume all functions of the Departments of Justice and Defense, among others. Gale specifically addressed the plight of farmers in the COS declaration and called for a repeal of the Federal Deposit Insurance Act and the liquidation of all national and foreign debt. Government officials acting on "unlawfully delegated powers" were warned that interference or noncompliance with the new Republic would result in death. Gale created as an enforcement arm of the new Republic the first "unorganized militia." Gale held paramilitary training operations at the Manasseh Ranch for the militia, featuring lessons in explosives, ambush techniques, knife fighting, and nighttime raids (Levitas, 2002: 287–8). A federal investigation of the Committee of the States resulted in the arrest of Gale and seven other members in 1986 on a ten-count indictment of conspiracy, attempting to interfere with federal tax laws, and mailing death threats to IRS officials.

A Second Wave of Patriot Violence

The War in '84 signaled the first round of Patriot insurgency. An ensuing wave of Patriot violence followed, but it was quickly thwarted by federal law enforcement. The protest cycle model (Tarrow, 1989) posits that through a heightened phase of conflict and intensity across the social system, challengers' actions are communicated to, and produce opportunities for, other groups, which in turn lead states to devise broad strategies of repression and facilitation. Movements may respond to these strategies either by moderation or radicalization. McAdam, Tarrow, and Tilly propose moving beyond the protest cycle model and refocusing efforts on a set of mechanisms often found in "protracted trajectories of contention": *diffusion, competition, repression,* and *radicalization* (2001: 67–70). But they also caution scholars not to expect to find all episodes of contention based on the same mechanisms or describing the same trajectories. "What is important here," they state, "is not to posit deductively linear trajectories and predictable outcomes but to identify the processes and their constituent mechanisms that constitute different dynamics of contention" (p. 70). That the second wave of Patriot violence was by no means "protracted" may explain why these mechanisms, with the exception of diffusion, were not evident to any measurable degree in the groups I examined. Diffusion, as defined in Chapter 2, refers to the spread of recruitment, relations, and information along established lines of communication. The mechanisms of competition and repression are somewhat self-explanatory (see pp. 67–9), while radicalization refers to "the expansion of collective action frames to more extreme agendas and the adoption of more transgressive forms of contention" (McAdam, Tarrow, and Tilly, 2001: 69).

The secondary cycle of violence involved three groups: The Order II, the Arizona Patriots, and the White Patriot Party. The Order II, also called the Bruder Schweigen Strike Force II, was organized in early 1986 by Richard Butler's chief of the security force at the Aryan Nations' property, David Dorr, evincing a process of diffusion. Unlike its predecessor, however, which had drawn members nationally and planned a diverse range of insurgent activities in four states, The Order II recruited from the local area and committed all of its crimes in the same region. The group's activities included several bombings, counterfeiting, and the murder of an informant. Lacking resources and imagination, The Order II's activities spanned only about a year before members were arrested for an unsuccessful robbery (Smith, 1994: 78–9). Order II member Robert Piles pleaded guilty to the murder of the informant, and David Dorr and four other members were convicted on federal racketeering charges under the RICO (Racketeer Influenced and Corrupt Organizations) Act. There is little to suggest that Order II members faced competition for power or repression given their highly localized activity. No compelling case can be made for radicalization either, because The Order II did not expand the collective action frame to more extreme agendas or adopt more transgressive forms of contention. Smith (1994: 79) summarized the negligible impact of the group as follows: "Without the ingenuity and charisma of Mathews, the Order II failed miserably. Born out of frustration over the Order's inability to achieve its stated aims and blinded by rage over the death of Mathews, the Bruder Schweigen Strike Force II struck back wildly and with little forethought."

The Arizona Patriots was founded in 1982 by former actor Ty Hardin, who made several Western movies and starred in the television series *Bronco* in the 1960s. Hardin became embroiled in tax disputes with the IRS in the seventies and left Hollywood claiming that the motion picture industry was controlled by Zionists. Adopting Posse ideology and proclaiming ties with the Christian Patriot's Defense League, the Arizona Patriots began to attract the attention of federal authorities in June 1984 after issuing a Posse-inspired "indictment" of elected officials and making threats. The transfer of claims of contention across these extant lines of communication reveals the effect of diffusion. An FBI informant was placed in the organization and recorded various discussions by Arizona Patriots to engage in acts of insurgency similar to those of The Order, including the plan to rob an armored truck and bomb a Phoenix synagogue and an IRS office in Ogden, Utah. Patriot members also allegedly met to plan bombings of bridges and the assassination of Governor Bruce Babbit. One of the most militant of the Patriots, Jack Maxwell Oliphant, purchased 320 acres of land near Kingman, Arizona, to serve as an Identity training ground and compound. In December 1986, federal agents arrested eight members of the Arizona Patriots on Oliphant's compound and found, among other things, electrical blueprints for the Glen Canyon Dam and the pipe system at Davis Dam, both on the Colorado River, and the power and lighting system at the Ft. Thompson substation on the Missouri River in South Dakota (Flynn and Gerhardt, 1989: 454–5; Levitas, 2001: 289; Smith, 1994: 80). None of the planned actions were ever carried out. Smith (1994: 81) suggests that the Arizona Patriots were compromised by undercover agents and too disorganized to be successful: "Their plans were doomed from the beginning: discord, incompetence, indecision, infiltration by undercover agents, and inexperience characterized the group." Like The Order II, the brief episode of contention displayed by the Arizona Patriots did not expand upon or adopt more extreme agendas and forms than their predecessors. Similarly, any evidence of competition and repression is lacking.

The White Patriot Party (WPP) was founded by Frazier Glenn Miller shortly after the death of Robert Mathews in December 1984. Miller's organization prior to that time was called the Carolina Knights of the KKK. Miller received an estimated $300,000 from Mathews and The Order's various bank and armored-truck robberies (Smith, 1994: 85), thus providing another example of diffusion in the second wave. Miller embraced the insurgent organization and violence of The Order and arranged to steal U.S. military weapons and equipment through Robert Norman Jones, a member of the Carolina Klan who was hired to conduct paramilitary training. Jones also had contacts with military personnel at Ft. Bragg, North Carolina, who were sympathetic to the WPP and assisted him in the paramilitary training. Learning of this connection, the Southern Poverty Law Center's Morris Dees filed a lawsuit asking the Department of Defense to investigate links between the military and the WPP. A federal judge subsequently issued a court order prohibiting any military assistance to the WPP, and three marines were discharged for their involvement (George and Wilcox, 1996: 377). By July, Jones was arrested for trying to purchase C-4 plastic explosives from an undercover agent, and in the spring of 1986 Miller was charged with violating the court order. Enraged, Miller told core WPP members to assassinate Dees, though it is not clear how far this plan actually proceeded. After exhausting his appeals, Miller and two other WPP members fled North Carolina and went underground. While on the run, they drafted a "Declaration of War" modeled after the "War in '84" document. The fugitives were eventually apprehended and arrested in Arkansas in April 1987. Miller, like James Ellison, ultimately agreed to a plea bargain in which he exchanged testimony in the 1988 Ft. Smith sedition trial against other Patriot leaders – Richard Butler, Robert Miles, and Louis Beam – for a lighter sentence. After the arrest of Miller, the WPP dissolved and the remaining members were absorbed into a white supremacy group, the National Democratic Front, based in Maryland (Smith, 1994: 84–7).

95

With the demise of the short-lived second wave of Patriot violence and the highly publicized, though unsuccessful, federal prosecution of Patriot leaders in the 1988 Ft. Smith sedition trial, the movement and its networks lapsed into a period of latency or quiescence. Disorganized and in disarray, the Patriot movement appeared to be depleted of its leadership, organizational stability, and resources, with little evidence of resurgence. However, as Melucci (1989, 1996) has observed, during a phase of latency, movement actors and organizations may continue to meet and interact, effectively sustaining the networks necessary and available for mobilization at a later time. This "continuity in militancy" (della Porta and Diani, 1999: 89), the fact that those who have participated in previous protest movement action are more likely than others to become active again, has been well supported in the research (Diani,1995; Klandermans, 1997; McAdam, 1988; Whittier, 1995, 1997). According to della Porta and Diani (1999: 89), collective identity in such networks can be nurtured by the hidden actions of a limited number of actors, creating "the conditions for the revival of collective action and allow[ing] those concerned to trace the origins of new waves of public action to preceding mobilizations." As we shall see, critical changes in the political environment were brewing that would create new threats and opportunities for the Patriot movement in the post–Cold War era, reinforcing the warfare frame and galvanizing antigovernment sentiments.

5

State Mobilization

BUILDING A TRAJECTORY OF CONTENTION

States and challengers engage in continuous and recursive interaction. As McAdam (1999: xxvi) observes, what comes to be defined as a threat by challengers is itself a by-product of innovative collective action by state actors designed to counter perceived threats to the realization of their interests. If and when state actions are defined as new threats by challenging groups, responsive episodes of insurgent collective action are likely to ensue, setting the stage for yet another round of state actions in an iterative dance of stimulus and response. In this manner, state actors and challengers may create a reciprocal, interlocking helix of escalating conflict that shapes and builds the trajectory of contention. "Each [state and challenging group] defines threats and opportunities, mobilizes existent and newly created resources, undertakes innovative collective action in response to other actors' maneuvers, and in some cases transforms the course of interaction" (McAdam, Tarrow, and Tilly, 2001: 74).

A major challenge facing social movement scholars is explaining *how* and *why* relations among actors and predominant forms of interaction shift significantly in the course of contention. We have already noted McAdam's call for a less movement-centric account of contentious politics. The corollary of this critique is that the dynamic role played by the state has not been fully appreciated in social movement studies: "To the extent that it enters at all, the state generally acts as a *diabolus ex machina*, producing opportunities, awaiting mobilization, landing heavily on some actors and facilitating others, but not participating directly in contention" (McAdam, Tarrow, and Tilly, 2001: 74). States, like challengers and third parties, are not passive bystanders but proactive agents working to affect the course of contention. In this chapter, I want to examine the robust role played by the state in defining threats and opportunities, mobilizing resources, and undertaking innovative collective action, both in response to the maneuvers of challengers and to broader social change processes.

The warfare frame constructed by Patriot insurgents in the 1980s, wherein the deaths of Robert Mathews, Gordon Kahl, and Arthur Kirk in shootouts with state paramilitary forces were posited as acts of state warfare, had resonance with only the most hard-core elements. The failed "War in '84" and its spin-off campaign in 1986 resulted in the demise or criminal prosecution of key movement leaders, followed by pervasive infiltration and surveillance by federal law enforcement. Between 1986 and 1988, more than thirty Patriot leaders and insurgents were arrested, indicted, and/or convicted by the state. In 1986, eight members of the Arizona Patriots were arrested and charged with plotting to rob an armored truck. In 1987, a federal jury in Las Vegas convicted William Potter Gale and four other members of the Committee of the States of conspiracy, violating tax laws, and mailing death threats to the IRS. Gale died the following year (April 1988) of complications from emphysema. In 1987, five Order II members were convicted on federal racketeering charges. Lyndon LaRouche and six aides were convicted in federal court in 1988 of conspiracy and loan fraud. The 1988 Ft. Smith sedition trial cast an even wider net designed to target Posse and Identity leaders not directly involved or charged in the earlier incidents (Dees and Corcoran, 1996; Smith, 1994). These sweeping, aggressive efforts by the state effectively assuaged further insurgency by the end of the 1980s and left the movement in disarray and debilitated. At this juncture, the movement lapsed into a brief nascent phase, persisting largely through informal communications and networks as small cadres of residual activists retreated into "abeyance structures" (Taylor, 1989) or sheltered spaces of contention.

The warfare motif languished as a cloistered claim chiefly among true believers into the next decade, when changes in the political environment provided new threats and opportunities for movement leaders to exploit. What were these changes and how did they alter the relations between challengers and the state? I argue that the culmination of domestic policy initiatives converged with exogenous forces in the demise of the Cold War in the early 1990s to resuscitate claims of a state-sponsored war against far-right groups. The emergent post–Cold War threat attribution of state militarism was grounded in a changing role of the military to assist and support domestic police operations in such areas as interdiction of drugs and contraband and terrorism. The military's new role further advanced police-military integration, which both the Department of Defense and law enforcement officials seized upon as opportunities to expand their resources and solidify their institutional bases. But accompanying this transfer of military weapons, equipment, and resources to civilian police was the inevitable acculturation effect entailing a "militarization of police" (Kraska and Kappeler, 1996). The War on Crime and Drugs had already set into motion the process of police militarization, to be sure, but the developments of the post–Cold War period accelerated and deepened the trend begun more than a decade earlier. Consequently, the recursive interaction between the state and its challengers over time came to be defined and shaped by a mutual attribution of war that can best be understood as part of the iterative dance that produced a violent threat/opportunity spiral.

The widespread perception among Patriot groups in the 1990s that the government was waging war against its own citizens was fostered, paradoxically, in the policies and practices of the state during the Reagan–Bush I era. I say "paradoxically" because the electoral success of Ronald Reagan signaled an astonishing victory for right-wing political groups. Reagan ran on a federalism platform of states' rights and downsizing the federal government that touched on the most politically sensitive issues among far-right groups. But the Reagan administration failed to deliver on these key issues, in large measure because of conflicting agendas within the New Right coalition that helped Reagan win the White House (Diamond, 1995). Indeed, the federal government expanded its domain significantly during this time, belying Reagan campaign overtures and promises to the contrary.

Two distinct policy and funding priorities in the Reagan camp had clear implications for the post–Cold War threat attribution of state warfare made by Patriot movement actors and their allies: (1) rebuilding the military and (2) the War on Crime and Drugs. The notion of devolving federal powers was incompatible with a strong military role abroad and a massive domestic program like the War on Crime and Drugs. These policy priorities mandated extensive government expenditures and major bureaucratic expansion, making unwanted intrusions by the state a growing concern. Concurrent with fiscal and bureaucratic growth, the state aggressively expanded its policies of militarism, on both the foreign and domestic fronts. The central motif running through these policy initiatives, and the cultural text underlying them, was *warfare*.

On the foreign front, the Reagan White House was determined to mount a major offensive against socialist regimes and liberation movements in Central America. Much has been written about the Reagan administration's efforts to revive the Cold War, enlarge the Pentagon budget, obtain military aid for El Salvador and Guatemala, and secure training and support for the Nicaraguan Contras, a rebel fighting force trying to overthrow the Sandinista government (Marshall, Scott, and Hunter, 1987; Nairn, 1981; Robinson, 1992; Sklar, 1988). It is not necessary to reprise this political analysis except to point out that it was through this effort to defeat revolutionary insurgencies in Central America that the military doctrine of "low-intensity warfare" or "low-intensity conflict" (LIC) was developed and institutionalized in the national security bureaucracy. LIC is a strategic framework developed by the U.S. military-security establishment that begins with counterinsurgency and extends to a wide range of other politico-military operations, including foreign internal defense (FID) (that is, any actions taken to assist friendly governments resisting insurgent threats), limited strike force activities, economic destabilization, psychological operations (PSYOPs), propaganda campaigns, terrorism counteraction, and antidrug operations (see Dunn, 1996; Gallagher, 1990; Klare and Kornbluh, 1988a, 1988b). LIC was derived from the Pentagon's index of conflict, divided into three levels: high, medium, and low. Limited conflicts were defined as "low" to describe the avoidance of all-out, sustained deployment of U.S. troops that would result in a high level of casualties. LIC measures were held to be ideal in small wars, indigenous guerrilla campaigns, insurgencies, and terrorism threats that could be carried out against the enemy with relatively inconspicuous special forces, launching clandestine, short-term operations. LIC offered preemptive strategies designed to deter armed conflicts within a host country or as a means to quickly win a limited war. Where the threat was perceived to be a state power, such as in Nicaragua, LIC provided proinsurgency strategies, helping fund and train rebel forces in proxy wars.

LIC ascended to preeminence under the Reagan administration. In 1987, President Reagan signed legislation creating a unified command for special operations and established a Board for Low Intensity Conflict within the National Security Council. The law mandated a new office, the Deputy Assistant to the President for Low Intensity Conflict. Later that year, Reagan signed a highly classified National Security Decision Directive that authorized the board "to develop and implement a unified national strategy for low-intensity warfare" (Klare and Kornbluh, 1988b: 6). A key feature of LIC is the diminution of the line separating external and internal security functions (Barnet, 1988). LIC strategists have promoted a goal of *total integration* of police and military forces in a coordinated or unified command in order to achieve both military and political objectives. Primarily through the War on Drugs, LIC was quietly adopted and deployed back in the United States as the Reagan administration pressured Congress to allow a greater role for the military in drug interdiction. Indeed, a 1983 report by the Pentagon conceded that "low-intensity operations are not confined to overseas but may be necessary within the United States" and proposed that one of the three essential roles for the military in low-intensity warfare is "the federal exercise of police power within the United States" (Dunn, 1996: 27). The Reagan administration's insistence on military intervention in the drug war made "antidrug operations" the domain with the greatest growth potential for domestic LIC operations in the 1980s (see Dunn, 1996: 106–11; Klare, 1988: 71–3).

While Patriot and other far-right groups perceived no viable threat associated with drug enforcement, the Reagan and Bush administrations nonetheless laid the groundwork for an integrated police-military force that would increasingly project a martial image and pave the way for the feared "gun raids" by coordinated teams of paramilitary police units in the coming years. In effect, *the drug war opened the door to police militarization* through government policies that encouraged police-military integration. As the state turned toward aggressive gun control legislation in the early 1990s and police utilized military-like raids to enforce the new gun laws, claims by Patriots and gun rights groups that the state was waging war against its own citizens exploded. Before we turn to the threat attribution of warfare against gun owners, however, it is important to establish the origins of an expanded military role in the state's domestic social control efforts.

The Military and the War on Drugs

From its inception, the Reagan administration wanted deployment of the military in the drug war and lobbied Congress to repeal the century-old Posse Comitatus Act, which prohibited military enforcement of civilian laws. The Posse Comitatus Act was a statute passed after the Civil War in reaction to military occupation of the South during Reconstruction. The act made it a felony for the Army to perform the law enforcement functions of civilian authorities. In practice, a cautious approach by the military had already evolved by the 1970s in which the Pentagon restricted efforts to occasional rendering of "indirect" forms of assistance, such as lending equipment, allowing use of military facilities, and training civilian personnel. In groundbreaking legislation contained in the 1982 Defense Authorization Act, Congress enacted amendments to the Posse Comitatus Act as a part of its "legislative offensive" (Wisotsky, 1990: 92). The new legislation gave formal approval to the military's previous *de facto* support and authorized a greater degree of military collaboration and assistance in drug interdiction. Freed by the statutory amendments, the Department of Defense began responding to political pressures from the White House through the office of the vice president by supplying more military equipment, technology, training, and personnel (see Duke and Gross, 1995; Dunlap, 2001; Dunn, 1995; Kraska, 1993; Miller, 1996).

According to Steven Wisotsky (1990: 5), "Reagan . . . succeeded in literally militarizing what had previously been a rhetorical war by deploying the military forces of the United States in drug enforcement operations." The Department of Defense supplied Cobra and Black Hawk helicopters, pursuit planes, and other equipment to civilian police agencies and programs. Navy Hawkeye EC-2 aircraft equipped with Forward Looking Infrared Radar (FLIR) capable of detecting other aircraft from three hundred miles away patrolled potential water and air routes of drug smugglers. The Coast Guard intensified efforts to interdict drug-trafficking vessels at sea; and for the first time in U.S. history, Navy ships, including a nuclear-powered anti-aircraft carrier, intercepted ships in international waters to search for drugs. Finally, radar systems on the ground at the North American Aerospace Defense Command (NORAD) and NASA satellites were employed to spy on suspected drug operations in and outside the United States.

On the heels of the passage of the amendments to the Posse Comitatus Act, President Reagan delivered a speech at the Department of Justice in October 1982, making official the war on criminals and drug traffickers and pledging an "unshakable commitment" to end the "drug menace." Much to the chagrin of libertarian conservatives, the Reagan administration aggressively expanded the federal government's role in combating illegal drugs. The scale of this enterprise was unprecedented, and the federal drug control budget alone increased from $1.5 billion in fiscal year (FY) 1981 to $6.6 billion in FY 1989, the first year of President Bush's tenure. In 1982, Reagan asked for and received full support for his programs: more than one thousand new federal law enforcement agents; two hundred Assistant U.S. Attorneys (and 340 clerical staff); twelve regional prosecutorial task forces across the nation; 1,260 new prison beds at eleven federal correctional facilities; stricter laws with respect to bail, sentencing, criminal forfeiture, and the exclusionary rule; increased interagency coordination at the federal level, directed by a Cabinet-level committee and chaired by the Attorney General; increased federal-state cooperation, including federal assistance for training state police; $127 million in additional funding above the amount requested, and a reallocation of $700 million that shifted monies from drug rehabilitation and treatment to law enforcement (Wisotsky, 1990: 4).

The central organizing principle of the drug war strategy for the Reagan administration was the development of "multiagency task forces," involving the coordination and integration of civilian law enforcement and the military. The first such task force was organized in 1982 under the direction of Vice President Bush as a prototype and deployed in South Florida. The multiagency task force included 374 federal agents from U.S. Customs and the Drug Enforcement Agency and had access to the resources of other agencies, such as the U.S. Coast Guard, the Central Intelligence Agency, and the Department of Defense. The chief mission of the task force was to lead an intensified air and sea interdiction effort to disrupt the flow of illegal drugs into the South Florida area. The CIA, which had previously exercised only a modest role in drug enforcement, significantly expanded its role as well. In 1982, the president issued an executive order directing the CIA to gather intelligence on criminal narcotics trafficking abroad and authorized agents to render "any other [lawful] assistance and cooperation to law enforcement authorities" (Wisotsky, 1990: 92). The extent of coordination and integration among police, military, and security forces was both innovative and unprecedented during peacetime.

President Reagan later declared the South Florida Task Force an "unqualified success" in the War on Drugs and proposed "nationalizing" the program (Wisotsky, 1990: 95). Though the General Accounting Office conducted an independent evaluation and found only a slight increase in seizures at a cost of $66 million, the Reagan administration pushed forward with its plan, implementing the National Narcotics Border Interdiction System (NNBIS) in March 1983 under the direction of the vice president. Using the South Florida program as a prototype, NNBIS extended federal drug enforcement operations near New Orleans, El Paso, Long Beach, Chicago, and New York. The six new centers functioned as coordinating mechanisms, utilizing intelligence information from the CIA and the material resources of the DOD, Customs, the Coast Guard, and the DEA.

In tandem with the NNBIS, the president also proposed the formation of the Organized Crime Drug Enforcement Task Force (OCDETF) Program. This program consisted of a nationwide structure pooling the resources of enforcement agencies in "concentrated, long-term operations designed to attack and destroy narcotics trafficking organizations" (Wisotsky, 1990: 99). OCDETFs were regional, multitask forces fully staffed with one thousand agents and two hundred prosecutors, supported by clerical and paralegal personnel, and based in twelve cities: Atlanta, Baltimore, Boston, Chicago, Denver, Detroit, Houston, Los Angeles, New York, St. Louis, San Diego, and San Francisco. The centers were coordinated to work with the U.S. Attorney's office in their respective regions. Each region was under the authority of the associate attorney general, who supervised a task force staffed with assistant U.S. attorneys and agents from the FBI, DEA, Customs, ATF, and the U.S. Marshals Service.

According to Timothy Dunn, antidrug operations along the United States–Mexico border in the early 1980s were already beginning to evidence features of low-intensity conflict (LIC) doctrine. "[T]he formation of the NNBIS," Dunn observed, "with its military-civilian law enforcement agency 'interface' mission, exemplified the LIC characteristic of coordinating and integrating police, intelligence, paramilitary, and military actions. The heavy emphasis on surveillance and the participation of forces from a border-area Army intelligence school were also examples of this LIC characteristic" (1996: 111). In addition, Dunn found the preparation and initiation of military training exercises in support of civilian drug interdiction to be consistent with the LIC framework, particularly in very remote areas that required high-tech radar systems, night vision equipment, and other types of sophisticated tracking hardware.

In 1986, the NNBIS launched Operation Alliance to further facilitate interagency cooperation and expand interdiction of drugs, weapons, illegal aliens, currency, and other contraband along the Southwest border. Operation Alliance was designed to coordinate the activities of numerous federal agencies, including the FBI, DEA, ATF, INS, Customs Service, Border Patrol, Coast Guard, U.S. Marshals Service, U.S. Attorney's Office, Secret Service, National Guard, and the Department of Defense (DOD) in this unprecedented program of police-military-security forces. The DOD now assisted the Border Patrol and Customs in various enforcement actions, including ground and aerial reconnaissance, training in patrol techniques, helicopter insertions and extractions, operations and intelligence, Advanced Military Operations on Urbanized Terrain (AMOUT), logistical support (such as barrier erection and road construction and repair), and research to identify technologies combining military and law enforcement applications. Operation Alliance would later play a key role in providing military support and assistance to the ATF (based on a fraudulent claim of a "drug nexus") in its planning and implementation of the disastrous raid on the Branch Davidians near Waco in 1993. The link between ATF and Operation Alliance in the federal siege would serve as a principal theme in the antigovernment narrative of Patriots and gun rights groups igniting the mobilization of citizen militias.

The state's mobilization of military and security resources and the creation of a new infrastructure based on a war paradigm reshaped domestic police organization, roles, and culture. The breadth of this initiative did not stop at the nation's borders, nor did it merely impact policing at the federal level. The Reagan administration's War on Crime and Drugs gave impetus to the development and expansion of paramilitary policing throughout the nation's police departments and organizations in the 1980s.

Militarization of American Police

The "war model" (Kraska, 1993, 1994, 1996, 2001b; Kraska and Kappeler, 1996) or "military model" of crime control (Skolnick and Fyfe, 1993: 113–16) took distinctive shape and became institutionalized under the auspices of the Reagan-Bush administrations in the War on Crime and Drugs. The growing predominance of this model was most evident in the emergent, widely adopted strategy of employing what Kraska and Kappeler (1996) refer to as "police paramilitary units" (PPUs), encompassing such entities as SWAT teams, hostage rescue teams, heavy weapons units, and special operations teams. PPUs are distinguished from traditional policing in the use of militaristic armament (MP5 submachine guns, M16 automatic rifles, sniper rifles, percussion grenades, "street sweepers"), equipment (armored personnel carriers, tactical cruisers, hydraulic door jam spreaders), technology (heat sensors, night vision telescopes, radar detection devices, electronic intrusion devices), training (strike force operations, dynamic entries, reconnaissance, urban warfare, close-quarters combat), and apparel (adoption of camouflage and military issue, flak jackets, Kevlar helmets). In turn, these characteristics resulted in significant transformations of police culture and organizational structure (see Haggerty and Ericson, 2001; Kraska, 1996, 2001c; Kraska and Kappeler, 1996; Skolnick and Fyfe, 1993; Wagner-Pacifici, 1994).

Transformations of police culture have been documented by sociologists and criminologists most frequently in language and attitudinal perspective denoted by the prevalence of "war discourse" or "martial rhetoric" embodied in the "war mentality." The military model transposed the culture and identity of police by socializing officers to think of themselves as "soldiers" and treating citizens suspected of criminal violations as "enemies of the

105

state." Changes in organizational structure produced new role expectations and status sets resulting from the adoption of a military command structure and discipline, with police-training academies giving special attention to close-order drill and military courtesy. Traditional descriptions or terms for police units were replaced with more military-like designations, such as "platoons," "divisions," "squads," and "details" that operate in a "chain-of-command" (Skolnick and Fyfe, 1993: 113).

The dramatic increase of PPUs in police departments in the United States beginning in the mid-1970s provides support for the ascendancy of the war model of crime control. Peter Kraska and Victor Kappeler (1996) conducted a survey of 548 law enforcement agencies serving metropolitan jurisdictions of fifty thousand or more residents in the United States in 1995. The study is based on an impressive 79 percent response rate. The researchers found that in 1980 only 13 percent of the 548 police departments reported having a PPU. By 1985, the percentage of departments with PPUs had climbed past 60 percent, representing an increase of 47 percentage points in just five years. By 1990, 78 percent of police departments in the sample reported having PPUs, and by 1995, the year of the Oklahoma City bombing, the figure reached 89 percent. Because the mere presence of PPUs in these departments is not an indication of how extensively they may be used, Kraska and Kappeler also measured the number of "call-outs" (that is, all emergency or high-risk deployments of PPUs). They found that from 1980 to 1983, the mean number of call-outs remained constant at about thirteen per year. By 1986, the mean number of call-outs almost tripled, to thirty-six per year. By 1990, the figure reached sixty per year, an increase of more than four-fold; and by 1995, the tally rose to eighty-three call-outs a year. The researchers found that the majority of call-outs (75.9 percent) were made to conduct what police termed "high-risk warrant work" involving "drug raids" (p. 7).

They also included items in the survey asking if, and how often, police departments used the tactical operations unit as a "proactive patrol unit" to aid in high-crime areas. Measuring the use of PPUs in patrol work, they argued, was an additional gauge of militarization. The researchers found that approximately 20 percent of departments reported using PPUs for patrol work. Among that 20 percent, the rate of PPUs in patrol work increased steadily from twenty-four in 1982 to ninety-four in 1995, an increase of 292 percent. Finally, Kraska and Kappeler discovered significant joint or cross-training with military special operations personnel among the nation's largest police departments. Forty-three percent of metropolitan police departments had trained with "active-duty military experts in special operations," and 46 percent of departments reported training with police officers who had "special operations experience in the military" (p. 11). "Numerous departments," Kraska (2001c: 7) notes in a later work, "admitted their close involvement with the Navy Seals and Army Rangers."

Kraska and Kappeler offer compelling evidence for both the rise and normalization of police militarization. The diffusion of PPUs at the local level in the first half of the decade, however, did not have a significant effect on the first round of Patriot insurgency. Patriot movement leaders defined the threat almost exclusively in terms of *federal* actors, consistent with Gale's Posse Comitatus ideology, which depicted all government power above the county level as illegitimate. Most Patriot confrontations occurred between insurgents and federal agents (FBI, U.S. Marshals Service, and ATF), with intermittent support from state-level law enforcement. But after more than a decade of federal incentives to involve local police – including the formation of multiagency task forces, the provision of joint or cross-training with special operations personnel, and the transfer of military resources, weaponry, and equipment to form a comprehensive police-military integration program – Patriot threat attribution of state warfare extended to local police departments as well. Thus, while the vertical integration of police militarization still implicated the federal government more harshly in the hierarchy of culpable agents, local police were increasingly seen as an appendage to the federal system.

To the degree that the state pursued a goal of police-military integration, engendering a transformation of police culture that cast officers as "soldiers" and suspected lawbreakers as "enemies" of the state, a martial image was perpetuated that intensified the processes of mobilization and polarization. This profound development within the evolving political environment made the state vulnerable to another round of charges and claims by polarized Patriot and gun rights groups in the 1990s that the state was waging war against its own citizens. Such claims did not arise in a social or political vacuum. The form and contour of a "warfare state" (Tarrow, 1994: 125) did materialize through the state's mobilization of resources and framing of conflict as war, allowing Patriot leaders to exploit a perceived threat made plausible by state policies and paramilitary strategies of social control.

Still, by the end of the 1980s, the Patriot movement was in abeyance and the Cold War was winding down. Many observers on the right thought a retreat from intervention in foreign affairs and a downsizing of the military would follow, diminishing the putative threat of a warfare state. However, in response to broad social-change processes accompanying the post–Cold War era, the Bush administration sought to preserve Pentagon spending at historically high levels by redefining and broadening the military's historical role to include more involvement in domestic social control programs.

Post–Cold War Militarization and Intensification

The George H. W. Bush administration took significant steps to avoid military cutbacks by revising and redirecting the military's role after the Cold War ended. Dunn states that the "end of the Cold War in late 1989 . . . profoundly reshaped international and domestic politics and economics. It created an immense vacuum in U.S. politics that came to be filled in large part by the War on Drugs" (1996: 65). Pursuing a strategy consistent with the LIC framework, military objectives and functions were revised and expanded to facilitate integration with the state's internal social control apparatus. With the passage of the 1989 Defense Authorization Act, the drug war was formally designated as a "high-priority national security mission" for the Department of Defense. This action coincided with the appointment of the first "drug czar," William Bennett, to oversee domestic drug control policy. Bennett openly advocated military support of drug laws and urged military prosecutors and judges to accept the backlog of drug cases (Miller, 1996: 144).

Under the direction of the Bush administration, a post–Cold War military gave the armed forces a much broader role in civilian policing and greatly enhanced the martial image of the state, perpetuating the threat attribution among nascent Patriots that the government was waging war against its own citizens. The concept of "total integration" touted by government and military officials moved inexorably closer to realization through implementation of LIC doctrine in such programs as Military Operations Other Than War (MOOTW) (see *Joint Doctrine for Military Operations Other Than War*, 1995). Kraska (2001c: 8–9) observes that in the wake of the Cold War the "inward turn of the war/military paradigm in U.S. society . . . [toward] crime and drugs had become in some ways *our new Cold War*" (emphasis added). Indeed, the ascendant LIC framework, the war model of crime control and post–Cold War political conditions converged at a historical moment, fueling a powerful matrix of forces. Once these forces were set in motion, subsequent policy and legislative changes turning on increased restrictions of gun ownership transformed defiant gun rights groups into the new targets of police paramilitary raids. But it was in these initial post–Cold War years that the police-military integration trend accelerated, engendering a new round of mutual threat attribution and quickening the threat/opportunity spiral. Thus, I want to examine some of these developments briefly before proceeding to the gun raids.

After taking office, President Bush elevated the war rhetoric against crime and drugs. Criminologists observe that Bush campaigned vigorously for the military model of crime control, surpassing lawmakers in a game of "political one-upsmanship" and battling to be the most bellicose in a war discourse, consistently employing terms and phrases like "battlefields," "drug work camps," "front lines," "drug war bonds," "calling out the troops," and "drug czars" (Kraska, 2001a: 20). Describing the nation as "under siege," Bush was not averse to hyperbole in alleging that there was "no greater threat to the survival of our society than drugs," and he implored Americans to support more involvement of the military. The tactic was apparently effective; soon after Bush unveiled his National Drug Control Strategy in September 1989, a *Washington Post–ABC News* Poll found that 82 percent of Americans said they would favor using the military to control illegal drugs "within the United States" (Sonnett, 1990: 27).

The administration's martial posturing was backed by the passage of new amendments in the 1989 Defense Authorization Act by Congress, outlining a new post–Cold War mission for the military. The 1989 Defense Authorization Act substantially enhanced the role and scope of military support for domestic law enforcement, further relaxing Posse Comitatus restrictions and adding new powers. Operation and maintenance of military equipment, for example, loaned previously only to federal law enforcement, was extended to state and local police agencies, as long as it involved enforcement of prescribed laws (drug trafficking, undocumented immigration, contraband). Various types of support operations were also broadened. Military personnel were now allowed to conduct aerial reconnaissance missions and to intercept vessels and aircraft, rather than simply monitor or supervise. The Department of Defense was also designated as the "lead agency" for the War on Drugs. As a result, military support to civilian law enforcement expanded support activities, such as training civilian police in intelligence analysis and survival skills, providing intelligence support, deploying and monitoring electronic ground sensors, supplying air transportation of law enforcement personnel in interdiction efforts, staffing observation posts, operating remotely piloted reconnaissance aircraft, staging military exercises in suspected drug-trafficking zones, assisting in operation planning, conducting radar and imaging missions, and providing DOD staff to help develop databases, mapping strategies, and reconnaissance folders for Border Patrol sectors. The law also authorized the Secretary of Defense to integrate all U.S. command, control, communications, and intelligence assets assigned to drug enforcement into a single communications network. And finally, the law significantly broadened the National Guard's role in drug enforcement, historically an entity that has enjoyed a dual status as a federal and state force. The 1989 act also provided an increase of $300 million for DOD counter-drug activities, $40 million of which was allocated to the National Guard (Dunn, 1996: 117–19; Palafox, 1996).

Deployment of the National Guard in the drug war from the beginning of the post–Cold War era was important because it symbolized the state's intention to coalesce police and military functions and bypass legal barriers. The National Guard has a unique history, evolving as an agency with a two-tiered mission to serve both the state and federal governments. As such, the Guard was best positioned of any government agency to circumvent the Posse Comitatus restrictions. Guard personnel could work under Title 32 of the United States Code in an Active Duty for Special Work status, essentially meaning that though salary and benefits were paid by the federal government, the soldier was working for a state governor and was not under federal control (Vaughn, 1992). The National Guard under Title 32 could undertake to search vehicles and buildings, enter private property without a search warrant, or sidestep other legal obstacles. Guard personnel need only acquire permission from their immediate commander to engage in these enforcement actions. Under the 1989 Defense Authorization Act, limited active-duty restrictions were lifted, allowing guardsmen to make a permanent assignment out of drug enforcement. Incentives were largely financial. The average pay for full-time active duty in the National Guard in 1992 was approximately $10,000 higher than the average salary of a police officer in the same year. In addition, Guard members under Title 32 received full medical and dental care for themselves and their families, as well as noncontributory 20-year retirement benefits. Congressional funding for the National Guard underscored the intent of policymakers to make drug enforcement a priority. The Guard's budget climbed from $40 million in 1989, to $110 million in 1990, to more than $160 million in 1991 (Dunn, 1996: 124). With the infusion of federal dollars and these economic incentives in place, the number of National Guard on drug patrol exploded.

In the year before the 1989 Defense Authorization Act, the number of active-duty National Guard involved in drug interdiction numbered about three hundred a month. By 1992, the last year of the Bush administration, the number of National Guard on drug interdiction duty jumped to seven thousand a month, more than twenty-three times the figure for 1988. The consequences of the new drug patrol were far-reaching. In 1992 alone, the National Guard assisted in 19,495 arrests. This was accomplished by searching 120,000 cars, entering 1,230 privately owned buildings, and making 6,537 uninvited intrusions into private residences. In a single year, between 1991 and 1992, the number of National Guard vehicular searches increased 267 percent; the number of entries into privately owned buildings jumped 282 percent; and the number of uninvited intrusions onto private property climbed 261 percent (Vaughn, 1992).

The 1991 Defense Authorization Act further eroded Posse Comitatus restrictions by mandating the military conduct training exercises for civilian law enforcement "to the maximum extent practicable" in drug-smuggling zones. It reiterated support for all previously mentioned activities while extending the Pentagon's domestic foothold. The new legislation expanded military antidrug training to law enforcement at all federal, state, and local levels. It also permitted a wide range of additional military support activities, including the establishment of antidrug bases of operations and training facilities both within and outside the United States. The 1991 act called for "improved integration" of law enforcement, military, and National Guard, and integration efforts were not limited to joint training exercises but included active and routine military operations. In effect, the only formal prohibitions remaining pertained to "direct" military participation in search, seizure, and arrest, but even in this regard the distinction was not often clear. Another new provision in the law allowed the military to transfer surplus military products and supplies from the Cold War era, including small arms and ordnance, to state and federal law enforcement agencies for use in antidrug activities. Toward achievement of the goal of improved integration, Congress authorized $1.08 billion in 1991 for the military antidrug budget, a 140 percent increase over the previous year (Dunn, 1996: 119–20; Palafox, 1996).

Finally, though the military's technoscience infrastructure was becoming more difficult to justify at the end of the Cold War, Bush administration officials hoped to shield the military from substantial downsizing and sought to redefine the Pentagon's mission. With widespread support for budget cuts on Capitol Hill pending, legislators from states that had been the beneficiaries of generous federal defense dollars were also anxious to find alternative purposes for military research and development. What emerged

111

out of this clash of interests was the idea of "dual-use technologies" designed to have both military and civilian law enforcement applications. Funding for military research would stipulate that some of the technological benefits be directed to and shared with civilian law enforcement, though the military would maintain control of priorities and agendas for the development of these technologies (Haggerty and Erickson, 2001).

The conception of dual-use technologies developed as police and military roles increasingly overlapped, primarily through antidrug activities. The loaning, sharing, or transference of scanners, night vision scopes, infrared cameras, remote electronic intrusion detection ground sensors, microwave communication systems, low-light television surveillance systems, and other devices prepared the way for the emergent industry of dual-use technologies (Saito, 1994) or "parallel operational strategies" (Rome Laboratory Law Enforcement Technology Team, 1996). The law was first codified in the Federal Technology Transfer Act of 1986, but the Government Technology Transfer Program didn't receive substantial support and funding until after the Cold War ended and a new set of "nontraditional" operations (Military Operations Other Than War) were being promoted. The program was given a significant boost when the Departments of Defense and Justice signed a memorandum of understanding that formalized the agreement to a joint development of "advanced technologies and systems" that could be applied to military operations and civilian law enforcement, creating the DOD's Advanced Research Projects Agency (ARPA). On the domestic side, the Justice Department established the National Law Enforcement Technology Center (NLETC) to help implement the objectives of the memorandum. In the words of David Boyd, the Director of Science and Technology at the National Institute of Justice (NIJ), who led the NLETC effort, the agreement between the DOJ and the DOD "ensures that the high-tech wizardry once employed solely by the military will be used to enhance the capabilities of law enforcement" (Boyd, 1995: 1). Projects identified and approved by ARPA and NLETC were subcontracted to private defense industry partners. With lucrative federal funds as an impetus, industry partners began to produce a dazzling array of high-tech devices and equipment for law enforcement.

Military transfer of weapons, equipment, and supplies to civilian law enforcement also served as stark evidence of post–Cold War militarization. The federal government's 1033 Program established in 1989 was designed to transfer surplus military hardware and weapons to police. By 1995, police forces had already obtained equipment worth $336 million through this

112

program, including sniper rifles, armored personnel carriers, gas masks, helicopters, and assorted aircraft (Haggerty and Erickson, 2001: 57). Dunn (1996) observes that the Pentagon turned over to federal law enforcement agencies Bradley fighting vehicles and the infamous Blackhawk helicopters, the latter a menacing symbol of New World Order armies to numerous Patriot groups. The Department of Defense valued the post–Cold War military transfers to the Border Patrol alone at $260 million (Palafox, 1996: 5).

From Drug Control to Gun Control

The cumulative effect of these developments produced conditions in which a Bush administration policy reversal on gun control laws, leading to new restrictions on gun owners, forced members of the gun lobby and gun rights network to confront the immutable force of a perceived "police state." The decade-long evolution of police militarization and the growth of paramilitary units designed to carry out high-risk raids, chiefly on drug suspects, now turned on a "new class of criminals" (Gibson, 1994: 258): gun enthusiasts who interpreted these actions as state warfare. Recalcitrant, militant gun rights advocates, many of whom were active in the gun lobby, expressed fears of a systematic state campaign to disarm the American public. Drawing on a "disarmament" narrative that painted state actors as agents of a grand conspiracy (for example, the New World Order), Patriot and gun rights groups increasingly trumpeted the threat posed by state-mandated gun control and warned its members of dire consequences. McVeigh was firmly entrenched within this population of gun owners and activists. He saw the War on Drugs as a backdoor ploy by state agents to generate public support for gun control. "The government couldn't just pass a law and tell everyone to give up their guns," he said. "People wouldn't stand for it. The government had to convince people that guns were bad because they were used for selling drugs." The disarmament threat was captured vividly in fictional form by William Pierce's *The Turner Diaries*, which Patriot actors heralded as a prophetic text. When the state stepped up its enforcement of new gun laws through contraband raids by paramilitary police units (PPUs), Patriot and gun rights groups mobilized in reaction to this perceived threat, fueling the threat/opportunity spiral.

6

The Gun Rights Network and Nascent Patriots

RISE OF A THREAT SPIRAL

One of the reasons often cited by state officials for the rapid expansion of paramilitary policing in the War on Crime and Drugs was the pressing need to counter the flow of dangerous weapons into the hands of criminals, gangs, and drug traffickers. Because criminals were obtaining more powerful and deadly weapons, it was claimed, police were forced to respond to this challenge by adopting more military-like tactics and weaponry in crime fighting. The rise of violent crime in the streets of impoverished inner-city neighborhoods during the economically troubled eighties bolstered the tough rhetoric of warfare by officials in fashioning crime control policy. By the early 1990s, the state was intensifying strategies to interdict firearms laws to reduce illegal sales and distribution to criminals and terrorists. Heightened attention to interdicting illegal weapons coincided with the state's efforts to move toward greater integration of police and military forces as the post–Cold War era was providing new opportunities and resources for the domestic war, or what Kraska (2001c: 9) has dubbed "the new Cold War."

In reaction to the state's shift in focus, Patriots and gun rights groups began to decry this new initiative as a threat and increasingly framed gun control efforts as signs of a "police state." The emergent threat attribution impelled and inflamed Patriot actors, leading to the formation of new alliances with gun owners and the gun rights network based on shared fears about state disarmament. Herein, we find the furtherance of a threat/opportunity spiral as state mobilization in response to an increase in crime and violence created the conditions by which a nascent challenger was threatened anew. In effect, the state's efforts to combat perceived threats generated a reciprocal threat and reaction. What came to be defined as a new threat by Patriots was largely a by-product of innovative collective

114

action by state actors setting the stage for yet another round of insurgent episodes and fueling the threat/opportunity spiral. In the escalating trajectory of contention, challengers were able to frame the problem widely and broaden the base of the movement to groups with shared interests and grievances. It is clear that mobilization of the Patriot movement in the early 1990s involved frame alignment, social appropriation, and brokerage, primarily with regard to new and more powerful groups and networks than was the case in the early 1980s. While the first round of Patriot mobilization and insurgency, highlighted by the "War in '84," was tied to appropriation of farm protest organizations and networks, the second relied primarily on the gun rights network.

The Politics of Gun Control

Reagan-era policies of state militarism in the 1980s ironically did not translate into White House support for domestic gun control. Reagan was a card-carrying member of the National Rifle Association (NRA) and often parroted the NRA line that only criminals benefited from gun control. Even after Reagan was shot by John Hinckley in 1981, he affirmed this position in his first press conference after the shooting by noting that the United States already had more than 20,000 gun control laws in place. "Indeed," Reagan stated, "some of the stiffest gun-control laws in the nation are right here in the [District of Columbia,] and they didn't seem to prevent a fellow a few weeks ago from carrying one down by the Hilton Hotel. In other words, they are virtually unenforceable. So I would like to see us directing our attention to what has caused us to have the crime that continues to increase as it has and is one of our major problems in the country today" (quoted in Gibson, 1994: 239). For Reagan, the root problem of crime was criminals, not guns. The Reagan administration and its congressional supporters did not see a direct link between gun control and violent crime in the streets of poor and minority communities. Rather, they maintained unyielding resistance to federal gun control, even overturning some previous regulations of gun manufacturers and sellers.

In 1986, after a long and bitter debate, Congress passed and President Reagan signed into law an NRA-backed piece of legislation called the Firearms Owners' Protection Act, also known as "McClure-Volkmer" for its congressional sponsors, Senator James McClure (R-ID) and Representative Harold Volkmer (D-MO). The new law was designed to roll back broad portions of the Gun Control Act of 1968. Important and wide-ranging legal changes were generated by McClure-Volkmer. These included: (1) allowing federal firearms license holders to sell guns at gun shows located in their home state, (2) allowing individuals not federally licensed as gun dealers to sell firearms as a "hobby," (3) reducing the record keeping of federally licensed gun dealers, (4) restricting the authority of the ATF to conduct inspections of the premises of federally licensed gun dealers, and (5) expanding a federal program that allowed rehabilitated felons to possess firearms. Among the most significant effects of the new law was the rapid growth of gun shows held across the country each year and expanded opportunities for private citizens to buy and sell firearms at gun shows (Rand, 1996). The powerful gun lobby and gun show network flourished under these conditions and provided nascent Patriots and like-minded groups valuable resources, social support, and political opportunity.

A study by the Violence Policy Center (VPC) in 1996 found that the McClure-Volkmer legislation spawned an "uncontrolled proliferation of gun shows," resulting in a "readily available source of weapons and ammunition for a wide variety of criminals – including street gangs, white supremacists, would-be presidential assassins, and domestic terrorists" (Rand, 1996: 2). Although the ATF does not maintain historical records on the number of gun shows, 71 percent of ATF officials surveyed for the Violence Policy Center study observed an increase in gun shows between 1986 and 1995. One regional ATF official estimated an increase of 50 percent over this ten-year period. By 1995, the year of the Oklahoma City bombing, the National Association of Arms Shows (NAAS) estimated that there were more than one hundred gun shows every weekend of the year, a figure that would project annually to 5,200 gun shows. The NAAS also estimated that more than five million people attended gun shows every year, generating more than a billion dollars in sales (Rand, 1996).

The VPC study was one of the first to link the explosive growth of gun shows to increased recruitment and mobilization efforts by Patriot movement actors. "As antigovernment activity by militias and other extremists has grown," the study found, "so has the awareness that gun shows are not only a key source for firearms and other material, but are a town square where extremists can gather information, make contacts, and mingle with the like-minded" (p. 6). One news report from an undercover investigation cited in the study called the gun show circuit a "key dissemination point" for militia and patriot groups (p. 7). The report further noted that "the nation's vast meshwork of gun shows with its thriving commerce in weapons, paramilitary paraphernalia and anti-government invective" served

116

as a "gateway into the militia subculture" (p. 7). No less a luminary than William Pierce, author of *The Turner Diaries*, was quoted as saying that "gun shows provide a natural recruiting environment" for such groups (p. 6). By "natural," Pierce implies that Patriots and gun rights advocates shared mutual interests in and opportunities for forming alliances and expanding a political base to resist state-imposed gun control. These natural allies also perceived a common threat posed by the state to ban firearms, inciting the far-right's quintessential fear of disarmament. With the apparent imprimatur of gun rights groups, "gun shows offered the means for disaffected gun owners to get involved with the militia movement," the study states (p. 6).

The perceived salience of this threat attribution was tied to the Bush administration's unexpected reversal of policy regarding gun control. After a series of violent shootings and killings in the mid to late 1980s (see Gibson, 1994: 231–6), Bush administration officials in March 1989 sounded an alarm about the abundance of military-style weapons available on the streets of the United States. The White House expressed concern that in the first ten weeks of 1989 gun dealers had sought permission from the government to import more than 100,000 combat-style semiautomatic rifles. Despite campaign promises to the contrary, President Bush was compelled to reassess his position on gun control. On March 14, 1989, one day after the California legislature outlawed forty types of semiautomatic rifles, the Bush administration "gave in to rapidly escalating pressure for action on semiautomatic weapons" (Davidson, 1998: 207). At the behest of the White House, Bush's director of national drug control policy, William Bennett, ordered the ATF to impose a temporary suspension of approximately 80 percent of these imports. The suspension covered more than twenty types of foreign-made military-style rifles. Bennett asked the ATF to review the requests to see if the weapons complied with the law that stipulated that imported firearms must be "suitable for, or readily adaptable to, sporting purposes" (Gibson, 1994: 245). On April 5, 1989, Bush officials expanded the suspension of semiautomatic imports to include the remaining 20 percent not covered in the earlier order, raising the number of banned weapons to twenty-nine.

A three-month ATF review found that the military-style imports exceeded the law on many counts. The review determined that some gun features (for example, night vision scopes, flash suppressors) would encourage illegal hunting at night. Others, like grenade launchers, had no applicability to the legal standard of "sporting purposes." The ATF investigators

117

used the marketing and advertising materials produced by the sellers to show that the weapons were designed primarily to appeal to a growing American paramilitary culture, not hunters and sportsmen. Treasury secretary Nicholas Brady, disturbed by the lack of attention paid to semiautomatic weapons manufactured in the United States, informed the White House that seventeen domestic-made assault rifles would be banned if the same standards for imports were applied (Davidson, 1998: 214). The report also highlighted the sheer volume of foreign-made military-style weapons pouring into the country. An audit of import requests by ATF agents revealed that in 1989 importers had already received authorization to bring in more than 640,000 such weapons and was near approval of another 136,000. The ATF review estimated that between two million and three million military-style rifles had been sold in the United States since the end of the Vietnam War. On July 7, only one day after the ATF study was released to the public, Bush administration officials announced that forty-three types of military or combat-style rifles would be "permanently banned" from importation. The list of permanently banned weapons included the popular Russian-made AK-47 and the Israeli-made Uzi, among others (Gibson, 1994: 8, 245–6).

The government's policy reversal on gun control caused shock waves in the gun rights community and ignited a heated political battle. The Bush administration's new restrictions on guns altered the traditional alignment between liberals and conservatives on gun control issues. According to Gibson (1994: 247), officials in the Bush administration sought to take the antigun political position away from the Democrats and expand the Republican Party's appeal to moderates and liberals. Because the ban did not apply to some American-made weapons (for example, the Ruger Mini-14), the White House hoped it would still appease portions of the gun lobby. But Democrats and gun control advocates seized the opportunity to push for more sweeping measures. In late 1989, Senator Howard Metzenbaum (D-OH) and Senator Dennis DeConcini (D-AZ) filed separate legislative proposals designed to ban the sale and ownership of domestic-made semiautomatic weapons. Similar versions of the bills were also introduced in the House. The two Senate proposals varied only in the range of banned guns. Metzenbaum's bill was broader and called for prohibiting the sales of two popular American semiautomatic rifles: the Colt AR-15 and the Ruger Mini-14. It also made illegal the transportation of a rifle by a gun owner outside his home.

118

DeConcini's bill was less ambitious. DeConcini was a tough-on-crime conservative Democrat who had never voted against any NRA-supported legislation – what the NRA called its most favored lawmakers: a "100 per-center" (Davidson, 1998: 211). But after meeting with numerous police organizations, DeConcini was convinced that a reasonable restriction on semiautomatic weapons was essential. His bill sought to prohibit all foreign-made military-style weapons but proposed a limited ban on domestic weapons, excluding the Ruger rifles with ordinary wooden stocks. Instead, DeConcini focused on the more blatantly marketed combat-style weapons, such as the MAC-10, MAC-11, AR-15, TEC-9, and the so-called Street Sweeper. In an effort to gain political advantage, DeConcini framed his legislation in such a way as to assert a link between military weapons and drugs. The bill was named the Anti-Drug Assault Weapon Limitation Act (Gibson, 1994: 247–8). According to Davidson (1998: 213), "the NRA felt betrayed by the Senator" and launched a furious campaign in Arizona to unseat him.

Third-Party Attribution of Threat: Handgun Control, Inc.

Democratic legislators were joined in an alliance with police organizations and the gun control lobby (Vizzard, 2000: 135). Handgun Control, Inc. (HCI), the nation's premier antigun interest group, seized the opportunity to expand its political agenda. HCI was led by James Brady, Reagan's former press secretary – who was shot by John Hinckley and partially paralyzed – and Brady's wife, Sarah. After Reagan left office, Brady became much more outspoken about gun control issues and worked closely with HCI to press for new legislation. Gun control advocates fashioned a new law named after Brady that required a seven-day waiting period before the purchase of a handgun. By putting a face to the Brady Bill, HCI was able to garner significant media attention and political capital for its cause. The media and the public were highly sympathetic to the paralytic Brady, who struggled to articulate his words and spoke from a wheelchair. Brady and HCI put pressure on lawmakers to match their tough rhetoric about the War on Crime and Drugs by supporting the bill. Many conservative legislators who were aligned with the gun lobby were reluctant to give their support, but they also feared a public backlash by voters if they opposed it. With the endorsement of police agencies nationwide, gun control advocates strategically moved to frame opponents as evildoers in league with criminals and drug dealers and specifically targeted the gun lobby for its antagonism to the bill. HCI ads featured James Brady calling on Congress to pass a "common-sense law" so police could run background checks on buyers to determine criminal records. "It seems that the only people against the Brady bill," the ad declared, "are psychopaths, criminals, drug dealers and the gun lobby" (Gibson, 1994: 249). By framing the problem in this way, pro-gun organizations such as the NRA and Gun Owners of America (GOA) were painted as a threat to crime control, police officers, and the larger social order.

In late 1989, HCI sought to exploit the political opportunity to widen support for gun control by organizing a campaign, Operation Spotlight, designed to expose the gun lobby's powerful ties to legislators. HCI used mass mailings and increased its placement of ads in major media outlets in an effort to mobilize public opinion. It also raised the level of aggressive rhetoric in its attack on the gun lobby. In July 1990, HCI placed a series of nearly full-page ads in major newspapers featuring a Klansman wearing white robes and holding an AR-15 with a thirty-round magazine, with the caption "Why Is the NRA Allowing *Him* Easy Access to Assault Weapons?" (Gibson, 1994: 250). In the midst of the HCI campaign, gun owners and gun rights groups already reeling from the torrent of criticism and political attacks received another setback. Former President Reagan reversed his long-standing position on gun control laws and publicly endorsed the Brady Bill. On March 29, 1991, Reagan made it official while speaking at a ceremony at George Washington University marking the tenth anniversary of the assassination attempt on him. Reagan announced his support for the Brady bill, declaring, "I am going to say it in clear, unmistakable language: I support the Brady bill and I urge the Congress to enact it without further delay" (Sugarman, 1992: 237). The endorsement of the Brady Bill by Reagan, the most powerful public figure for gun rights in the prior decade, exploded like a bomb. In less than two years, the gun lobby lost the support of two presidents, saw its congressional support dwindle, and was linked to terrorists and drug dealers by opponents.

Gun rights groups were also losing support among the general public. Numerous public opinion polls showed increased support for gun control during the early post–Cold War years. Table 6.1 shows the findings of a series of Gallup Polls between 1982 and 1993 on the issue of handgun registration, a restriction adamantly opposed by the gun lobby. Support for handgun registration increased from 66 percent in 1982 to 81 percent in 1990 and remained at that level in 1993. The Brady Bill, which proposed a

Table 6.1. *Attitudes Toward Universal Handgun Registration (Gallup Polls)*

Year	% Support
1982	66
1985	70
1990	81
1993	81

Source: Adapted from Robert J. Spitzer, *Politics of Gun Control*, Chatham, NJ: Chatham House, 1995, p. 119.

Table 6.2. *Attitudes Toward Instituting a Waiting Period Before Handgun Purchase (Gallup Polls)*

Year	% Support
1988	91
1990	95
1991	93

Source: Adapted from Spitzer, *Politics of Gun Control*, Chatham, NJ: Chatham House, 1995, p. 119.

"cooling-off period" before the purchase of a handgun, was first introduced in Congress in 1987. Though the bill initially failed to pass, the data showed overwhelming public support for the Brady Bill in three Gallup Polls taken in 1988, 1990, and 1991 (see Table 6.2). With the 1992 election of Bill Clinton, gun control advocates gained a strong ally in the White House. Under the Clinton administration, the Brady Bill was pushed through Congress in 1993 despite fierce opposition by the NRA and other gun rights organizations. Finally, and certainly most disconcerting to the pro-gun movement, Gallup and Harris polls showed increased support for a handgun ban. In 1980, only 31 percent of Americans supported a handgun ban when asked in a Gallup Poll. But by 1993, Harris and Gallup polls showed support climbing to 52 percent and 60 percent, respectively (see Table 6.3). Moreover, a 1992 *New York Times/CBS News* Poll found that 79 percent of Americans favored a ban on military-style assault weapons (Spitzer, 1995: 119). In effect, a majority of Americans supported bans of handguns and semiautomatic weapons, a significant step toward universal disarmament. These opinion poll numbers, in combination with mounting political opposition and new government restrictions on guns, revealed a

Table 6.3. *Attitudes Toward Banning*
All Handguns

Year	% Support
1980	31
1993 (Gallup)	42
1993 (Harris)	52

Source: Adapted from Spitzer, *Politics of Gun Control*,
Chatham, NJ: Chatham House, 1995, p. 120.

changing political climate for gun advocacy groups, giving rise to a heightened perception of threat among the embattled gun rights network.

Polarization and Radicalization of Gun Rights Groups

The NRA, GOA, and other pro-gun groups fought back by conducting their own massive campaigns to stop passage of gun control legislation and reshape their image. The gun lobby first organized an effort to retake control of the framing of issues. The NRA worked feverishly to reframe gun control as an attack on the Second Amendment to the Constitution. This frame was developed out of an earlier political struggle for control of the NRA in which "hobby shooters . . . wary of political activism" lost out to "social movement gunowners" who viewed defense of the Second Amendment as paramount (Sugarman, 1992: 232). The victorious NRA hard-liners, or what one observer called "Second Amendment fundamentalists," crafted their conflict with the state and opposition groups as a "war" (Sugarman, 1992: 232, 239). One special edition of the *NRAction* newsletter distributed at its annual convention in 1991, for example, was titled "War Declared on NRA, Bill of Rights" and warned members that "the primary weapon of freedom's enemies was the Brady bill" (Sugarman, 1992: 239). Indeed, the NRA's true believers imputed religious meaning to the struggle, casting it as a "religious war" to protect the "sacred" right to bear arms (Davidson, 1998: 213). The increasing radicalization of the gun lobby was catalyzed in part by the increasingly aggressive posturing of gun control proponents. Gibson observes that both antigun and pro-gun factions utilized "war" rhetoric in their mutual framing of the conflict. "Both sides fought this holy war in the name of national rejuvenation," he asserts (1994: 259), vying for the higher moral ground in a "mythic replaying of regeneration through violence."

On another front, the NRA employed scholars to make legal arguments and sponsored publications outlining gun ownership as a constitutionally protected right. Specifically, gun rights advocates argued that the Second Amendment ensured the protection of all other amendments in the Bill of Rights and the Constitution. In the face of threats to democracy by enemies foreign or domestic, they claimed, "armed citizens" must be ready to defend their freedoms. Without the Second Amendment, there could be no First Amendment and citizens would be powerless to defeat the forces of tyranny. This theme appeared throughout NRA and GOA ads, pamphlets, and magazines. *American Rifleman*, the NRA's premier magazine, touted gun ownership as the foundational principle on which all other rights stood. According to Gibson,

The NRA could find ample historical evidence for this need in the American Revolution with all its *citizen soldiers*. For the NRA, these heroic stories of armed men rising to defeat the foes of liberty were a key part of an American creation myth. NRA pamphlets and magazine accounts of American history imply that the *militiamen* of the Revolution in effect persuaded God to form a kind of covenant with the American people. America was destined to be a great nation under God's special protection because the Founding Fathers had been willing to fight for their freedom. Moreover, the Founding Fathers bequeathed to their heirs the right to continue the fight for freedom by passing the Second Amendment of the Bill of Rights. (1994: 252; emphasis added)

In a major counteroffensive, the NRA launched an attack to discredit "anti-gunners" and lawmakers as "soft-on-crime" liberals who coddled criminals while targeting law-abiding gun owners (Spitzer, 1995). NRA publications and bumper stickers featured slogans such as "Ban criminals, not guns," "Guns don't kill people, people do," and "When guns are banned, only criminals will have guns." NRA members were cautioned not to let criminals "steal your gun rights." Threatened gun rights leaders likened the gun control group, Handgun Control, Inc., to Nazis and labeled their actions fascist. NRA President Dick Riley called HCI founder Pete Shield's book on gun control a "*Mein Kampf* sequel for the gun control movement" in a column for *American Rifleman* and warned readers that Shields had a "final solution" for guns – disarmament (Gibson, 1994: 257–8). Furthermore, gun owners were told that they would be the logical *first* targets in a state campaign of disarmament because disarmed citizens would lack the hardware to resist. Armed citizens, it was claimed, were freedom's first and last line of defense against tyranny (Stern, 1996: 109).

As the politics of gun control polarized the parties in conflict, embattled gun enthusiasts became increasingly militant. The NRA insisted that more gun control legislation would create a "new class of criminals" because any gun owners who refused to register their guns would be criminalized (Gibson, 1994: 258). Hard-liners encouraged defiance of new gun control laws and adopted a stronger antigovernment framing of the conflict, drawing analogies to freedom fighters during the American Revolutionary War and the underground resistance to Nazi Germany. In this heated political environment, Patriot activists maneuvered to construct a common antigovernment frame, build alliances, and share resources with networks of threatened social movement gun owners and Second Amendment fundamentalists.

Larry Pratt, Gun Owners of America, and the Call for Militias

In 1990, Larry Pratt, Executive Director of Gun Owners of America (GOA), published a manifesto for gun rights activists promoting the formation of "armed militias" or "civil defense units." Pratt has been called the "father of the modern militia movement" (Dees and Corcoran, 1996: 54) and was listed as one of the 117 "Prominent Patriots" by the Southern Poverty Law Center's Militia Task Force (Southern Poverty Law Center, 1996). Pratt's book *Armed People Victorious* (1990) advanced the argument that civil defense patrols or militias in Guatemala and the Philippines helped citizens survive guerrilla insurgency threats from communist and leftist forces and ultimately secured liberty for these populations. In Pratt's highly revisionist account of the situation in Guatemala, he lionized the repressive anticommunist dictator General Efraín Ríos Montt as a model of evangelical Christian faith who rescued the troubled nation from the clutches of communist subversives. The successful struggle for political control of Guatemala by the rabid anticommunist Ríos Montt involved organization of civilian vigilante groups called "Patrullas de Autodefensa Civil" (civilian self-defense patrols), which enabled the citizens to "cooperate with the Army" in resisting guerrilla intrusions. Essentially, Pratt argued that the police and military could not have defeated the insurgents without the aid of armed citizen militias because local populations produced better intelligence and had a greater interest in defending their communities. "Being an armed people," he declared, "made all the difference" (1990: 23). Of course, Pratt's manifesto fatuously ignored or dismissed the findings of

124

international human rights organizations that determined that the patrols were the same death squads that burned and pillaged villages and killed thousands of civilians believed to be aiding leftist forces (Marshall, Scott, and Hunter, 1987; Uekert, 1995).

Pratt's argument for citizen militias was so thoroughly steeped in Cold War anticommunist propaganda that their function was defined largely as supportive of the state. However, in the final chapter of his book, "Bringing the Lessons Home," Pratt outlines a possible solution to deepening social problems in the United States that would utilize the same concept of armed citizen patrols or militias on the home front. Railing against the domestic crisis of crime and drugs, he first claimed that state efforts to disarm citizens robbed people of their ability to control their neighborhoods. "Just as Marcos tried to disarm the people of the Philippines, so many police generals are trying to get the politicians to disarm the people of America. A special effort is being made to disarm the people of the inner city who happen to be the ones living in the conflict areas. . . . These people . . . are forced to tolerate the crime wave that guerrillas and drug dealers bring with them to their neighborhoods" (1990: 70).

According to Pratt, "The War on Drugs can be won the same way the guerrilla insurgents were pushed back in Guatemala and the Philippines," namely through armed citizen patrols. Pratt pressed the case for militias as follows:

America has been losing the War on Drugs, and it is probably safe to predict that the United States will continue to lose this war until the failed theories of professional monopoly in civil defense are replaced with practices that have proven effective. America will either lose the War on Drugs without the people, or win the war with them. The history of the United States for years before and after the founding of the Republic was the history of an armed people with functioning militias involved in civil defense (or police work, if you will). While the United States has forgotten its successes in this area, other countries have rediscovered them. It is time that the United States return to reliance on an armed people. There is no acceptable alternative. (Pratt, 1990: 71)

In Pratt's view, the alliance of government and militias was predicated on a state policy of promoting gun ownership and thus creating "an armed people." Given his harsh denunciation of gun control (which he implies is *de facto* disarmament), a fracture by which the alliance might dissolve was clearly indicated. State programs of gun control were antithetical to democracy, he reasoned. Armed citizens in civil defense patrols or functioning militias were the solution, and according to Pratt, "There is no acceptable alternative."

Pratt's adoption of an antigovernment frame would develop rapidly over the next few years in reaction to the state's heightened program of contraband raids through paramilitary policing to achieve its goal of gun control. By late 1992, in the wake of the deadly federal actions at Ruby Ridge, Pratt was the leading advocate of forming armed citizen militias to fend off perceived state disarmament. Pratt attended a large conclave of Identity and Patriot leaders in Estes Park, Colorado, organized by Pete Peters, pastor of a prominent Identity church in La Porte, Colorado, in October. The gathering drew 160 of the most influential remnants of far-right activists and nascent Patriots. According to Dees and Corcoran (1996: 67), the Estes Park meeting was a "watershed" event that transformed a "disparate" and "fragmented" group of far-right actors into a "serious armed political challenge to the state." Pratt, whose Gun Owners of America organization now claimed 130,000 members, promoted the formation of citizen militias for a new purpose: to "stop future Ruby Ridges from happening" (Dees and Corcoran, 1996: 55). Pratt espoused a new type of antigovernment militancy while condemning the traditional lobbying approach maintained by the NRA. Aggressive state actions taken against law-abiding gun owners required an aggressive response, he declared. "One can only speculate," Pratt later wrote, "that had there been an effective militia in Naples, Idaho, which could have been mobilized after the U.S. Marshal murdered Sammy Weaver by shooting him in the back, ... Vicki Weaver would not have been murdered later on by an FBI-trained assassin" (quoted in Dees and Corcoran, 1995: 55).

Constructing State Disarmament and Gun Raids

Social construction of a disarmament narrative featured in William Pierce's futuristic novel *The Turner Diaries* already outlined both diagnostic and prognostic framing of the conflict in what seemed to many Patriots and gun rights activists to be a prophetic text. First published in 1978, the book chronicled an impending social crisis that prompted passage of the Cohen Act, a fictional law banning all sales and possession of firearms. The ensuing disarmament campaign was undertaken by the state in an effort to subjugate (white) citizens and impose a tyrannical rule, preparing the way for the New World Order. The Cohen Act gave federal and state law enforcement a license to conduct sweeping raids by paramilitary police teams to confiscate all firearms. *The Turner Diaries* was written in the form of a journal recording the organization and day-to-day activities of an armed insurgency by an underground movement called The Order, led by protagonist Earl Turner, in reaction to the "Gun Raids." Pierce, founder of the National Alliance, constructed the disarmament narrative in terms of rabidly racist and anti-Semitic themes, attributing blame to these groups and portraying the insurgency as a desperate fight for survival by embattled whites in a race war. However, it was the disarmament threat, not white supremacy claims, that resonated with the broad population of gun enthusiasts as Patriot movement leaders played to the antigovernment script. Consequently, when the state's program of police militarization expanded to include contraband raids and tougher enforcement of gun laws in the early 1990s, it was this disarmament motif that fueled elevated fears and created opportunities for Patriot appropriation of gun rights networks.

In a study by Kraska and Cubellis (1997: 626) of police militarization in the United States between 1980 and 1995, they voiced concerns about the expanding use of paramilitary police units within smaller localities and jurisdictions, as well as in an ever-growing range of enforcement activities. This study followed previous research by Kraska (1993, 1994; Kraska and Kappeler, 1996) that first documented police militarization in the drug war and then later in a national survey found significant growth and "normalization" of PPUs in the nation's largest metropolitan police departments. In the 1997 study, Kraska and Cubellis shed light on a pattern of PPU expansion aptly described by the researchers as "mission creep." What began as highly specialized units trained to combat drug-related violence, gangs, or terrorism were evolving into routine patrols on a wide range of call-outs, even in small cities and towns. Significantly, they observed broadened use-of-force options such as "contraband raids." The researchers concluded by calling into question the indiscriminate use of paramilitary policing in patrol work and making note of the disturbing propensity to use PPUs as "a new tool to conduct a crude form of investigation into ... gun law violations" (Kraska and Cubellis, 1997: 626). This point was reiterated by Kraska (2001c: 7) in a later work, in which he stated, "In both large and small departments, PPU's routinely carry out dangerous contraband raids on people's private residences, often in the predawn hours, for purposes of conducting a crude form of investigation into drug and gun law violations." Kraska and associates document the use of contraband raids as a part of a broader problem of police militarization, but even more importantly they

127

pinpoint the *mechanism* by which the threat attribution of state warfare and the disarmament narrative materialized.

With some disturbing similitude beginning in the early 1990s (Earl Turner's "Diaries" began in 1991), law enforcement in the United States began to turn its attention to gun law violations. A series of widely circulated accounts of contraband raids by PPUs targeting gun law violations accrued, inflaming Patriots and gun rights groups. Each of these incidents involved alleged elements of property damage, infringement of civil liberties, and excessive force by paramilitary police units. The incidents were significant not merely for their putative frequency, but in the widening net of police violence that ensnared gun owners. The "mission creep" of PPUs to include crude investigations of weapons violations evoked frightening images of state disarmament chronicled in *The Turner Diaries*. The growing perception that the state was stepping up its campaign against suspected gun violators was not purely paranoia. Evidence from federal law enforcement sources suggests that "Gun Raids" intensified in the early post–Cold War years leading up to the Waco debacle in 1993. ATF Director Steven Higgins testified in a 1993 congressional hearing investigating federal actions during the Waco siege and standoff that "in the 18 months prior to the Branch Davidian incident, our ATF Special Response Teams had carried out 341 actual activations to high-risk situations" (*Hearing Before the Committee on the Judiciary*, 1995: 71). According to Director Higgins, in 1993 approximately 60 percent of the agency's time and budget was devoted to the enforcement of gun laws ("Tougher rules urged on explosives, guns," *Houston Chronicle*, March 11, 1993: 18A). The Special Response Teams (SRTs) conducting the 341 raids ("activations") refer to the agency's specialized paramilitary units deployed in high-risk weapons enforcement. Given the concentrated number of SRT gun raids in such a brief period, it was highly likely that abuses would occur, as indeed they did. Moreover, these raids often involved joint or coordinated enforcement actions by multiple federal or state agencies, augmenting the "siege" mentality of state agents and contributing to the warfare image Patriot leaders were attempting to construct. In the face of the intensified gun raids, agitated Patriots disseminated tropes and atrocity tales throughout the gun subculture, inveighing against the "jack-booted thugs" and sounding the alarm of an impending "police state." It is important to understand how these incidents were interpreted by threatened social actors among gun advocates and Patriots and how the state's war/military model of policing helped give credibility to framing the problem as "warfare."

Framing Gun Raids and the McVeigh List

The following cases were culled from literature circulated in the gun show circuit and the Patriot network in the early to mid-1990s. While virtually unknown to the general public, these cases were receiving dramatic attention within the gun show circuit and served to generate an increasing threat of disarmament and talk of state warfare. It is important to remember that these lesser-known cases also coincided with two widely publicized federal gun raids at Ruby Ridge and Waco in 1992 and 1993, respectively, which will be examined in greater detail in the next chapter. Consequently, while the media coverage of Ruby Ridge and Waco brought the attention of these incidents to the public; they were also portrayed largely as aberrational and isolated cases. But to gun owners and Patriots, they were perceived as part of a *much larger and more systematic pattern* of state disarmament. No one was more convinced of this alleged pattern than Timothy McVeigh.

McVeigh was keenly aware of these concurrent gun raids and the stories that accompanied them. It was through my interviews with McVeigh in 1995 and 1996 that he helped me compile this list of "casualties" from the collateral raids. I called it my "McVeigh list." McVeigh could recount an impressive array of detail and minutia in each of these cases with the passion and conviction of a Second Amendment fundamentalist. McVeigh believed that a disarmament campaign similar to the one described in *The Turner Diaries* was being carried by the government and therefore compelled an insurgent action. "This is just like Nazi Germany," he said at one point. "Look at what they did in the Warsaw ghetto. The initial raids were repelled only because people had guns to defend themselves. But the Nazis came back on April 19 and burned the place to the ground." McVeigh perceived that the totality of gun raids in the United States, reaching an apogee in Waco, proved that the state was conducting a domestic war against armed citizens. The passage of the Brady Bill in 1993 and the 1994 Crime Control Act banning assault weapons only confirmed the state's ultimate intent to disarm the people.

The following cases comprising the McVeigh list are not exhaustive, and no claim is made of representativeness. What the cases reveal – through their interpretation by gun rights activists – is a disarmament narrative that facilitated the antigovernment/warfare frame-bridging and brokerage efforts by Patriot movement leaders.

Case of Dave Jermolovich. According to an account appearing in the May 1992 issue of *American Rifleman*, a publication of the National Rifle

129

Association (NRA), the home of tow truck driver Dave Jermolovich was raided by fifteen agents of the Bureau of Alcohol, Tobacco and Firearms (ATF). The raid, or "dynamic entry," was carried out on Flag Day, June 14, 1991, an irony fraught with symbolism and not lost on the NRA faithful. The agents broke through the front door and searched in vain for an illegal automatic .222 identified in the search warrant as a "Mini-14." While the raid was in progress, Mr. Jermolovich was telephoned by a neighbor. The neighbor told Jermolovich that his home was the target of a police raid. The tow truck driver apparently contacted the Montgomery County (MD) police, who confirmed the raid. Eventually, Jermolovich managed to reach an ATF office and have local police attest to his character. The raid was halted, but not before substantial damage was done to the house. ATF agents "battered down the external doors" and took a chisel and hammer from his tool box to pry open a safe. The house was ransacked as agents searched unsuccessfully for a machine gun Jermolovich "never owned." According to *American Rifleman*, the ATF relied on an unidentified informant who gave them faulty information.

Case of Johnnie Lawmaster. The incident involving Mr. Lawmaster received major coverage in the June 1992 issue of *Soldier of Fortune* magazine. The article, written by a former associate editor of the magazine, James L. Pate, was a biting rebuke of federal actions, forcefully conveyed in the unsubtle title, "Gun Gestapo: BATF Brownshirts Terrorize Tulsa." Acting on information that Lawmaster possessed an illegal firearm, thirty agents with the ATF teamed up with state and local police in the Tulsa area on December 16, 1991, to search for what the warrant described as a "Colt AR-15 and .223 caliber machine gun, unknown serial number." The warrant also authorized agents to seize "any tools used in the alteration or modification of firearms, such as files or drills, documents, papers, books, records and other tangible properties that identify occupants or owners of the property to be searched." According to Pate, agents cordoned off the street; took station with weapons drawn in the backyard; used a battering ram to break through the front door; broke into Lawmaster's gun safe; threw personal papers around the house; spilled boxes of ammunition on the floor; broke and pillaged a small, locked box that contained precious coins; and stood on a table to peer through the ceiling tiles, demolishing the table in the process. The multiagency police force failed to find any evidence of illegal weapons. Pate observed that the marauding agents ravaged the residence, then left the house unlocked and unsecured with guns and ammunition lying about. The gas, electric, and water companies were also

130

told to shut off power to the Lawmaster house. When Lawmaster returned home, he found a note left by the agents. It read: "Nothing Found – ATF." Mr. Lawmaster had no previous criminal record.

Pate later wrote in another issue of *Soldier of Fortune* on the Waco Branch Davidian debacle in June 1993 and postulated a "genetic" link between the two events: "The raid that trashed Lawmaster's house and shredded his constitutional rights was a warning beacon along the policy road that led ATF to Waco.... Waco is the culmination of a failed law enforcement policy that first prominently manifested itself on John Lawmaster's doorstep" (Pate, 1993b: 50). The ATF Supervisor of the Lawmaster raid was Ted Royster, who also was a key figure in the development of the ATF raid plan on the Branch Davidians (Kopel and Blackman, 1997: 295–6). The inextricable link between gun raid abuses and Waco would become a tenet of faith among gun advocates and Patriots alike.

American Rifleman also covered the Lawmaster incident and provided some additional provocative details (Gardiner, 1992). Lawmaster had been recently laid off work and his divorce had become final a few weeks earlier, contributing to the image of victimization by "BATF Brownshirts." ATF agents refused to pay for property damage and purportedly told Lawmaster that if "he attempted to retain legal counsel, the agency would not talk to him." When Lawmaster's attorney attempted to obtain a copy of the affidavit supporting the warrant to determine if there was probable cause, he was told by court officials that the U.S. Attorney had asked that it be sealed. A U.S. District Court later denied Lawmaster's request to unseal the affidavit. The NRA subsequently took up the appeal to the Tenth Circuit Court ("NRA Counsel Helps Lawmaster in Court," *American Rifleman*, July 1992: 51–2).

Case of Sina Brush. According to a National Rifle Association press statement (1994), approximately sixty agents in a joint task force of DEA, ATF, National Guard, and U.S. Forest Service, sporting camouflage and painted faces and accompanied by a light armored vehicle, raided the homes of Sina Brush and two of her neighbors on the morning of September 5, 1991, near Mountainair, New Mexico. The 46-year-old Ms. Brush and her 15-year-old daughter were asleep when she heard a car door slam and the sounds of rushing feet approaching the house. Wearing only underpants, Brush arose to peer out her window when the agents kicked in the front door. Yelling and brandishing automatic weapons, the agents grabbed, handcuffed, and forced Brush to lie facedown on the floor. Her daughter was given the same treatment. She later told reporters that she thought she was going to be

131

killed. Agents searched the house for marijuana and weapons. At the same time, the joint task force was conducting raids on several homes and ranches on a seventy-two-acre tract of land. They were acting on drug patrol information garnered during a surveillance overflight that detected "unknown green vegetation." The search warrant indicated that agents believed marijuana was being grown. After two hours, the search was terminated. No drugs were found.

Case of Donald Carlson. The tragic Carlson incident was covered widely by both mainstream and right-wing media. On August 25, 1992, just after midnight, a joint force of U.S. Customs Service and DEA agents launched a raid on the Poway, California, residence of computer executive Donald Carlson. The federal agents first set off an explosion in Carlson's backyard as a diversion while a team of agents battered down his front door. Awakened by the late-night noise and believing the intruders were burglars, Carlson allegedly grabbed a handgun to defend himself while calling the 911 operator. Accounts of what transpired next conflict, but Carlson was shot three times by federal agents. According to Carlson, he was shot once and he threw down his gun in a gesture of surrender. While on the floor wounded, Carlson said, he was shot again in the back. In a joint press release later (1994) issued by the NRA and the ACLU, it was asserted that two of the shots were fired after Carlson was on the floor and disabled. Carlson later testified in congressional hearings and told committee members that even after agents failed to find weapons or drugs, he was not offered any medical assistance. When paramedics eventually arrived, he was taken to the hospital in custody under armed guard and shackled for several days at the hospital. Carlson was so badly wounded that he spent seven weeks in intensive care. Customs officials claimed that they expected to find automatic weapons and a large quantity of cocaine in Carlson's home. No drugs or illegal weapons were found. According to a *Los Angeles Times* report, federal agents apparently had relied on a paid informant, but the informant denied giving agents any specific information about the house to be searched. Moreover, the DEA had previous experiences with the informant and considered him unreliable (Bovard, 1995: 236–7).

Case of Del Knudson. According to the Fall 1992 issue of *Gun Owner*, a publication of Gun Owners of America, approximately thirty ATF agents raided the home of Del Knudson in Colville, Washington, on April 1, 1992. In a brief story titled "Another BATF SWAT Attack on Women and Children," it was asserted that Malisa Knudson was bathing her 21-month-old daughter Kalee when the agents arrived in several vehicles and a Ryder

News from CAMBRIDGE
UNIVERSITY PRESS

Contact: Greg Houle
212-337-5058
ghoule@cambridge.org

Patriots, Politics, and the Oklahoma City Bombing

Stuart A. Wright

On April 19, 1995 Timothy McVeigh parked a truck loaded with explosives in front of the Alfred P. Murrah Building in Oklahoma City. The explosion killed 168 people. He claimed this attack was revenge for what the US government did at Waco and Ruby Ridge. This book explores the escalating spiral of tension between the Patriot movement and the state

leading up to the Oklahoma City bombing. Stuart A. Wright served as a consultant to Timothy McVeigh's defense team and draws on information based on face-to-face interviews with McVeigh. Wright contends that McVeigh was firmly entrenched in the Patriot movement and was part of a network of 'warrior cells' that planned and carried out the bombing. By examining the Patriot movement's history and subsequent reconfiguration of conflicts with the state, McVeigh's role in the bombing can be more fully understood.

Publication Date:

July 31, 2007
Paperback; $22.99

moving van. The agents jumped out of the van, stormed the house, and apprehended and handcuffed Knudson. Mrs. Knudson apparently pleaded with agents to let her retrieve her daughter from the bathtub, but she was ignored. A family friend who was visiting the Knudsons offered to watch the children, but he was also handcuffed. James Pate (1993b: 35), writing in the August 1993 issue of *American Spectator*, added that the family friend was "an elderly neighbor." The Knudsons also had two other daughters, ages 5 and 7, who were in the house. Del Knudson was away at work at the time of the raid. For three hours, the house was searched and Mrs. Knudson "was interrogated about the family's religious and political views." Agents alleged that the Knudsons wanted to overthrow the U.S. government, that they were white supremacists, and that they owned machine guns. The only weapons found in the house were "lawfully owned semi-automatic rifles and other firearms." The weapons were confiscated but later returned. No charges were filed. ATF agents were acting on information provided by an informant, who was described as "deranged." Readers of *Gun Owner* were encouraged to contact their congressperson and demand that the ATF target "real thugs" instead of innocent women and children. Del Knudson later emerged as one of the attendees at the 1992 Estes Park meeting, along with Larry Pratt (Dees and Corcoran, 1996: 62).

The *Gun Owner* account doesn't comment on the "family's religious and political views," but according to a report by Citizens for Hate, one of Del Knudson's neighbors was the Kehoe family. The Kehoes' two sons, Chevie and Cheyne, were brought up as white supremacists, and Chevie was later linked to the bombing of a government building in Spokane, armed robberies, and selling stolen firearms, as well as to Tim McVeigh (Nichols, 2003). As teenagers, the boys spent time with their family at the Arizona Patriots compound of Jack Oliphant (Hamm, 2002: 157). Chevie read *The Turner Diaries* and was enamored with the exploits of Robert Mathews. He also frequented Richard Butler's Aryan Nations compound and attended the 1993 Aryan World Congress. In 1994, Chevie formed a "cell" of "white warriors" called the Aryan People's Republic (APR), modeled after Tom Metzger's White Aryan Resistance (WAR). He became a polygamist around the same time and moved with his two wives to the Identity settlement Elohim City, in Oklahoma, where the planning of the Oklahoma City bombing occurred. The Citizens for Hate report cites an interview with Chevie Kehoe in which he described the 1992 government raid on the Knudsons as a turning point in his life: "For me to see the government come up there with all these police cars and helicopters and all that and tear his house apart, tear books off the selves, confiscate computer disks, confiscate every firearm he had, go through his garage, handcuff his wife, terrorize his children – to see that the government has that type of power, you know something's wrong" (Nichols, 2003).

Case of Louis Katona. The incident involving Louis Katona III was significant for several reasons. First, accounts by the victims and law enforcement officials differed substantially. Second, the target of the raid, Louis Katona, was a part-time police officer, making his claims more convincing in the eyes of aggrieved Patriots and gun rights groups, even though evidence suggests he exaggerated the details of the event. Third, Katona became actively aligned with an NRA campaign challenging ATF "gun grabs" and was party to a civil suit filed against the agency in which he stood to gain financially. According to a variety of news sources, Louis Katona, a real estate salesman and part-time police officer in Bucyrus, Ohio, was the target of an ATF search warrant for illegal weapons sales. The events leading up to the enforcement action were not contested. In the summer of 1988, the Bucyrus Police Department demanded that Katona return an old Bucyrus police chief's badge that his father had bought for him at a gun show. His boss, police chief Joseph Beran, claimed it had been stolen previously from another collector. Katona refused to relinquish the badge and was forced to resign. Katona also collected and sold machine guns; and after the confrontation over the badge, the police chief declined to approve or authorize further sales by Katona. However, Katona continued purchasing machine guns and submitted the required forms to ATF, claiming that Chief Beran had presigned a large stack of forms. Beran denied the claim. After about two years, the ATF was alerted to the possibility of forgery and violations of other federal firearms law. On May 7, 1992, a federal magistrate authorized a search warrant.

From this point forward, the accounts and interpretations of events differ sharply. Katona claimed that ATF agents "rushed" into his residence to seize his firearms collection, worth an estimated $300,000, an investment he hoped would some day fund his children's college educations. During the raid, he asserted in a deposition, agents grabbed his pregnant wife and "shoved" her against a wall, causing her to suffer a miscarriage (NRA, 1994). Katona also charged that agents were shouting, cursing, and sneering as they dropped or threw his guns onto a concrete floor, potentially damaging his investment. When the case came to trial in 1995, handwriting experts could find no conclusive evidence linking the alleged forgeries to Mr. Katona. As a result, a federal judge threw out the government's case and ordered the

134

ATF to return the firearms to Katona. James Pate, writing for *Soldier of Fortune*, later echoed the Katona-NRA version of the account and proclaimed vindication for the victim, assailing the military-style tactics of the ATF (Pate, 1995).

According to a *Time* magazine story covering the Katona incident, the victim's account was embellished. The ATF raid party consisted of only three agents, one in a suit, who went to Katona's real estate office and informed him of the search warrant. When agents entered the residence of Mr. Katona, it was not a paramilitary-style raid and they were even offered coffee while they searched. The firearms were not thrown carelessly on the concrete floor but dropped only a few inches. Mrs. Katona arrived after the search had begun and was furious at the intrusion. The agents claimed that Mrs. Katona was not handled roughly, though she was apparently intercepted by one agent as she approached them in remonstrance. Mrs. Katona began bleeding that night and miscarried a few days later. *Time* obtained the medical records of Mrs. Katona through the litigation and had three specialists analyze them. According to their analysis of a pelvic ultrasound exam, the victim had an "intrauterine gestational sac without echoes, suggesting a blighted ovum." The specialists concluded that Mrs. Katona had lost the baby well before the raid began (Larson, 1995: 24–5).

The framing of the Katona case as another abusive paramilitary raid, however, was made credible to Patriots and gun enthusiasts because it conformed to a pattern seen in other cases. Indeed, the NRA included the Katona incident in a list with other more arguably valid cases of abuse in its mailings and press releases. Activists posted Katona's story on their Web sites and traded information about other ATF abuses within the gun show circuit. Katona was also featured prominently as a guest speaker at the annual NRA convention in Phoenix in 1995, in which gun owners and gun rights advocates from around the country were treated to the victim's narrative firsthand, giving the story a human face and reinforcing antipathy toward ATF (Larsen, 1995: 24). As such, the Katona family became part of the growing list of victims and casualties perpetrated by "jack-booted thugs" and "BATF Brownshirts," arousing the ire of those in the gun subculture.

Case of Janice Hart. According to several right-wing media sources, 36-year-old Janice Hart, returning home from the grocery store, drove up her driveway in Portland, Oregon, on February 5, 1993, with her two daughters, 12 and 4 years old. When they arrived home, they found the front door kicked in and ATF agents ransacking the house. Agents had thrown dishes on the floor, pulled clothes from hangers, and emptied drawers on the floor.

She allegedly screamed out, "What are you doing in my house?" An officer grabbed her arm and said, "You are going to jail." Ms. Hart's daughters were very afraid and began crying. Nina, the 12-year-old, was told to "shut up and get back in the car." Distraught and perplexed, Ms. Hart repeatedly screamed, "What are you doing to my house?" But all they could say was, "You're going to prison," she recalled. ATF agents then took her downstairs and interrogated her in the basement. When she asked to see an attorney, she was refused.

The ATF apparently had a search-and-arrest warrant for Janice Marie Harrell. Ms. Hart insisted they had the wrong woman; her name was Janice Marie Hart, not Harrell. She was told by agents that she was considered "armed and dangerous," that she sold firearms, used crack cocaine, and had escaped from jail. The agents expected to find weapons, but they found nothing. Undeterred by Ms. Hart's pleas, the ATF agents continued their interrogation for two hours, before they finally took her to the Fingerprint Division of the Portland Police Department. "The Portland Police were very, very nice to me," she said. "They treated me like a person." It took less than a minute for the police to determine that the ATF had the wrong person. Ms. Hart and her husband spent two days cleaning up the mess left behind by the federal agents. A lot of things were broken, torn, bent, and beyond repair, she said. The ATF dropped off a form for the Harts so they could record the damages. She and her oldest daughter struggled with stress and had to seek clinical help for sleeping and eating disorders. Her neighbors became aloof (McAlvaney, 1993; Moore, 1995; NRA, 1994). In one account of the Janice Hart incident, an indignant right-wing newsletter editor opined: "How does this differ from Nazi Germany or Communist Russia, China or Romania? . . . In what ways do they [the ATF] differ from the Gestapo?" (McAlvaney, 1993).

Case of Harry Lamplugh. According to an article appearing in the December 1994 issue of *Gun Owner*, a joint force of fifteen to twenty ATF and IRS agents burst into the home of Harry and Theresa Lamplugh in Wellport, Pennsylvania, on May 25, 1994. At about 8 A.M., Mr. Lamplugh answered a knock at the door and the team of agents stormed into the room, brandishing weapons and demanding to know where the "machine gun" was kept. No search warrant was ever shown to the couple, and when Lamplugh asked to see one, he was told to shut up. Lamplugh, who owned the largest gun show promotion business in the Northeast, Borderline Gun Collectors Association, insisted he did not own a machine gun. He did own a semiautomatic Vietnam commemorative Thompson rifle, he said in an interview with the magazine. ATF agents overturned and "smashed" furniture; scattered personal papers everywhere; broke into safes, locks, and cabinets; and "ransacked their home for more than six hours." Agents also seized all the financial and business records of the company, including medical records, birth certificates, school records, and insurance information. Even though the Lamplughs cooperated with the agents during the raid, an MP-5 machine gun was stuck in Harry Lamplugh's face intermittently (see also Kopel, 1995).

The Lamplughs were not permitted to dress and remained in their pajamas. Mr. Lamplugh was recovering from cancer, and agents dumped his prescription drugs out of their bottles, scattering the contents over the floor. Two of the Lamplughs' cats died after ingesting the spilled medication. A third cat was allegedly "stomped to death" and "kicked under a tree" by one of the agents. During the raid, the agents stopped what they were doing and sent out for pizza. The agents "had a little party," according to Lamplugh, and "threw half-emptied soda cans, pizza and pizza boxes everywhere."

According to *Gun Owner* magazine, affidavits in support of the warrant were sealed, and requests by the Lamplughs' attorney to unseal the document were refused by an Assistant U.S. Attorney. No charges were filed, yet the ATF had not returned any property or records at the time of the publication. *Gun Owner* opined that the "persecution" of the Lamplughs should not be ignored or forgotten, citing it as just "one of the many examples of the BATF's abuse of its power." "This government brutality must be stopped," it concluded (cf. Kopel, 1995; Moore, 1995: 8; NRA, 1994).

These low-profile cases of victimization involving contraband raids by PPUs became legendary in the gun show circuit, helping to shape a disarmament narrative infused with Patriot signification and the threat attribution of state warfare. While the tropes were clearly embellished in many instances, the deployment of PPUs to conduct crude investigations of gun law violations in the early 1990s was consistent with the findings of Kraska and colleagues on patterns of police militarization. The shifting *modus operandi* of firearms interdiction in the spirit of the New Cold War allowed Patriot movement actors to weave a narrative that defined the state's heightened campaign of enforcement as analogous to, if not a literal fulfillment of, *The Turner Diaries'* "Gun Raids." McVeigh believed this narrative with great conviction, and this was his principal motive in distributing copies of the *Diaries* to family, friends, fellow soldiers, and gun owners. "The government is trying to eliminate all private gun ownership in this country," McVeigh told me in our first interview. "They want to rob us of our guns; strip us of all firearms. It's not going to happen without a fight. If the government wants to use overwhelming force, then we will meet it with overwhelming force. We have the right to defend ourselves against all enemies, foreign or domestic."

The warfare frame, devised a decade earlier, was reinvigorated by these unfolding events in the early 1990s as movement entrepreneurs took advantage of emergent grievances among new and more powerful groups to issue calls for another round of insurgent episodes. Yet these calls might still have gone unheeded if not for two large, disastrous gun raids by federal law enforcement within a span of six months, between August 1992 and February 1993. What gun owners and Patriots feared on a small scale from the collateral raids was amplified dramatically by the deadly sieges at Ruby Ridge and Waco, helping to transform a poorly organized network of disparate groups into a mobilized mass movement. Placed in the context of a purported disarmament campaign by the state as if scripted directly from the pages of *The Turner Diaries*, the federal sieges at Ruby Ridge and Waco catalyzed antigovernment sentiments that Patriot leaders then exploited vis-à-vis the mobilizing structures of gun rights groups to promote and organize armed citizen militias.

7

Movement-State Attributions of War

RUBY RIDGE AND WACO

Ruby Ridge and Waco have a special symbiotic relationship: They were both targets of weapons violations by state paramilitary units, erupted into deadly standoffs, encompassed many of the same state actors and agents, and were coupled in time. Indeed, Ruby Ridge and Waco were separated by only six months, a time during which the state's heightened campaign of gun control produced a torrent of federal gun raids by PPUs in the early 1990s. The twin tragedies of Ruby Ridge and Waco were the most egregious, lethal manifestations of the military model. War framing by the state produced inflated perceptions of threat posed by the Weavers and the Branch Davidians. In turn, the sieges at Ruby Ridge and Waco, both based on weapons violations, aroused the deepest fears of Patriot and gun rights groups, expressed laconically by NRA president Wayne LaPierre in 1994 as a "full-scale war to... eliminate private firearms ownership completely and forever" (quoted in Stern, 1996: 111). LaPierre's terse characterization was widely shared by those in the Patriot and gun rights networks as this attribution of war galvanized antigovernment sentiment and propelled the threat/opportunity spiral upward. A brief examination of these two federal sieges reveal a host of features that both the state and challenging groups mutually defined as "warfare" in a deadly escalation of conflict.

Ruby Ridge

In August 1983, Randy and Vicki Weaver packed their three children and all their worldly belongings into a moving truck and set out for a secluded mountaintop home, where they planned to live simply and await the arrival of Armageddon. One of Randy Weaver's coworkers in rural Iowa had friends in northern Idaho and suggested that it would be "a good place for people who believed as they did" (Bock, 1996: 38). The Weavers had increasingly come to embrace far-right conspiracy theories about the government, particularly in the face of callous indifference by officials to the deteriorating farm economy. Vicki's brother joined efforts by other farmers to organize and press the Reagan administration for relief from the growing farm crisis, but to no avail (Stock, 1996: 143). Randy and Vicki became convinced that the conventional agrarian way of life was doomed.

The Weavers' sojourn from Iowa ended in Boundary County, Idaho, seven miles outside the town of Naples, in an area called Ruby Ridge. Boundary County bordered Kootenai County, home to Richard Butler's Aryan Nations compound in Hayden Lake. Before long, the Weavers developed ties with members of the Aryan Nations, visiting the compound on a number of occasions, fortifying their Identity beliefs, and mixing with other Identity believers. It was a unique time to be in northern Idaho. As Jess Walter (1995) observes in his definitive account of the Ruby Ridge incident, the Weavers' arrival corresponded with the peak of racist and early Patriot movement mobilization.

In many ways, 1983 and 1984 – when Randy and Vicki Weaver were just getting settled on Ruby Ridge – were the high point for white separatists and supremacists in the Northwest. The Aryan Nations was attracting welcome publicity for its cross burnings and for a rally it staged in Spokane's Riverfront Park. The 1983 and 1984 Aryan World Congresses at Hayden Lake brought big crowds and Butler's church was at its peak of influence in the far right. Sentiment against the government was growing, and scores of people with radical right-wing beliefs were making their way to North Idaho from other parts of the country. (p. 83)

The Weavers found themselves at the epicenter of far-right activism. Robert Mathews founded The Order at the 1983 Aryan Nations World Congress, and the Weavers apparently had some familiarity with the Mathews group, based on later comments. The Weavers' early years in Idaho corresponded to the "War in '84" campaign, followed by the second wave of Patriot violence in 1986. The failed revolution did not seem to discourage the network of nascent Patriots with which the Weavers were associated. Identity leaders and activists in the Patriot movement continued to come to Hayden Lake to meet, exchange ideas, and preserve an embattled identity. The 1986 Aryan World Congress drew William Pierce (National Alliance), Tom Metzger (White Aryan Resistance, or WAR), and Thom Robb and Robert Miles (KKK), as well as many of the widows or spouses of the dead or imprisoned martyrs from the first round of insurgency. A letter from imprisoned Order member Richard Scutari was read to the gathering at

Hayden Lake, exhorting them to carry on the revolution: "Learn from our mistakes and succeed where we failed. The *Bruders Schweigen* has shown you the way" (Walter, 1995: 91).

According to James Aho, "Idaho's pivotal significance in the plans of the revolutionary right [went] far beyond the ambitions of the *Bruders Schweigen*. Speakers at the Aryan World Congress in July 1986 announced that Kootenai County, Idaho, would henceforth serve as provisional capital of a five-state Pacific Northwest Aryan Nation" (1990: 7). Randy Weaver attended the 1986 World Aryan Congress conference at Butler's headquarters and was moved by their resolve and dedication to the cause. He returned to attend the 1987 World Aryan Congress, accompanied by his wife, Vicki, and his children. It was around this time that Weaver came to embrace hardcore elements of Posse Comitatus. In 1988, he ran for sheriff of Boundary County, Idaho, on the platform of promising to enforce only the laws that local people endorsed, while protecting them from the federal government. Weaver inveighed against the federal income tax, calling it a "cunning act of fraud," promised to hand out "get out of jail free" cards, and used his campaign to educate people about the "primacy of the county" (Bock, 1995: 46). Because about 70 percent of Boundary County is owned by the federal government, disputes tended to revolve around land use policies and regulatory statutes. Parroting Posse claims and rhetoric, Weaver told residents that the county had the power to refuse enforcement of federal law and that agents were required to obtain permission from local law enforcement. Weaver garnered only 10 percent of the vote in the Republican primary, which he blamed on negative news coverage. Apparently, Weaver made racist statements to a reporter for the *Spokane Spokesman-Review* that the newspaper printed (Bock, 1996: 46).

At the 1989 World Aryan Congress, Weaver was approached by a man he had met through a mutual friend at the 1987 Aryan gathering. Gus Magisono claimed to be a weapons dealer and security expert and expounded on the mistakes he thought doomed The Order and other Patriot groups. Magisono said he was involved in an underground network that would support a new round of insurgency, but he needed to build a stockpile of weapons to make the plan work. He persuaded the financially strapped Weaver to sell him two sawed-off shotguns for $300. Magisono, whose real name was Kenneth Fadeley, was actually a confidential informant for ATF. Weaver had become entangled in an ongoing federal investigation of white supremacists and Identity activists associated with Butler. The agency was less interested in prosecuting Weaver than in forcing him to gather

141

intelligence on Aryan Nations leaders, particularly Chuck Howarth and John Trochmann. Howarth, a Posse organizer and former Klansman, had been convicted for planning to bomb the offices of two federal judges and the Internal Revenue Service in Denver in 1982 (Levitas, 2002: 185). Trochmann was an Identity adherent and Second Amendment fundamentalist who would later found the Militia of Montana (MOM). Weaver refused to be an undercover informant for the ATF and subsequently was charged with weapons violations. He was ordered to appear in federal court on February 19, 1991, but the notification listed the trial date as March 20. Weaver thought that the government was trying to deliberately confuse him and set him up. When Weaver failed to appear for trial, an arrest warrant was issued.

Construction of an Intrinsic Narrative: Weaver as "Another Bob Mathews"

One approach to examining the construction of situated meanings involves the study of "intrinsic narratives," defined as "the diverse stories that various social actors tell within emergent situations to which they are mutually oriented, but in different ways" (Hall, 1995: 206). This approach can "help show how cultural meanings become nuanced, shaded, interpreted, challenged, and otherwise reworked by participants, and how such meaning shifts affect the course of unfolding events" (Hall, 1995: 206). In situations of conflict, individuals and groups jointly compose narratives that import freighted meanings to legitimize and make sense of projects they are undertaking (see also Hall and Neitz, 1993). Looking at the intrinsic narratives to assess the emergent cultural meanings surrounding Randy Weaver's identity reveals how meanings about Robert Mathews and The Order were adapted and transposed to tropes about Weaver. By utilizing this approach, we can see how state agents reinvoked and reworked narratives about Weaver in ways that shaped the escalating trajectory of contention at Ruby Ridge.

Following Randy Weaver's failure to appear in court and the issuance of the warrant, an incensed Vicki Weaver wrote a threatening letter to the U.S. Attorney's office in Boise addressed to the "Queen of Babylon." The letter cited selected biblical passages and included a quote from Robert Mathews. It stated in part:

A man cannot have two Masters. Yahweh Yahshua Messiah, the anointed One of Saxon Israel is our lawgiver and King. We will obey Him and no others ... a long forgotten wind is starting to blow. Do you hear the thunder? It is that of the awakened

Saxon. War is upon the land. The tyrant's blood will flow. (Department of Justice, 1994: 36)

A second letter from Vicki Weaver was sent to U.S. Attorney Maurice Ellsworth and addressed to the "Servant of the Queen of Babylon." According to an unpublished Justice Department report on Ruby Ridge, the letter stated in part: "The stink of your lawless government has reached Heaven, the abode of Yahweh our Yahshua. Whether we live or whether we die, we will not bow to your evil commandments" (Department of Justice, 1994: 36–7).

Robert Mathews, of course, was well known among federal authorities in the Pacific Northwest. U.S. Attorney Ellsworth was alarmed by the Mathews quote and requested a "threat assessment" from Ron Evans, chief deputy with the U.S. Marshals Service in Boise. Evans had been chief deputy in North Dakota in 1983, when the marshals became engaged in the deadly shootout with Gordon Kahl. Evans also found the language of Vicki Weaver's letters to be disturbing and believed they were intended to send a message. Soon after learning that portions of the letters were quotes from Mathews, Ron Evans reported back to the chief of enforcement operations at Marshals Service Headquarters in Washington "that BATF sources believed Randy Weaver had the potential to be *another Bob Mathews and his homestead another Whidbey Island standoff*" (Department of Justice, 1994: 38; emphasis mine).

Guided by Evans's reading of the letters, the threat assessment constructed by U.S. marshals selectively drew upon ambiguous and speculative statements by ATF agents, local law officials, and Weaver's neighbors and made questionable inferences from legal and military records. When completed, the threat assessment portrayed Weaver in an overly sinister manner. Evidently, the marshals made no effort to corroborate some of the information collected for the threat assessment, for it was replete with erroneous assertions. Among other things, it claimed that Weaver had been involved in a bank robbery, possessed heavy-caliber guns mounted on tripods around the cabin, was likely to shoot officers on sight, had booby-trapped property with explosives that could be detonated from remote locations, had access to a network of underground tunnels, and was barricaded in a fortified house with blackout curtains (Bock, 1996; Department of Justice, 1994: 36–41). It would later be shown that these claims were unfounded, but the extent to which this intrinsic narrative about Weaver took on the profile of Robert Mathews cannot be ignored. Mathews was extremely violent, robbed banks, stockpiled weapons, barricaded himself in a cabin, and was involved in a shootout with federal agents. The threat assessment also speculated that Weaver had been a Green Beret or a member of Special Forces and may have had demolitions training. Weaver was never a member of Special Forces and had no demolitions training during the time he served in the Army. Apparently, Chief Deputy Ron Evans also drew a comparison of the case to Gordon Kahl, augmenting the putative threat. The Justice Department report states that "Evans compared the Weaver situation to the violence surrounding the attempted arrest of Gordon Kahl when Evans was Chief Deputy of the North Dakota District" (p. 52).

The threat assessment also characterized other family members in a highly dangerous manner. The report included a statement by one agent who told investigators that "the entire Weaver family, including the 12 and 14 year old children, were armed at all times" and that "the Weaver children slept with weapons in their beds" (Department of Justice, 1994: 37). The threat assessment further asserted that Randy and Vicki Weaver might use the children as "the first line of defense" in an attack by law enforcement (Department of Justice, 1994: 41). Based on the dangerous and menacing image of the Weavers conveyed in the marshals' report, Evans pressed for a tactical strike. Evans lobbied to bring in the Special Operations Group (SOG) within the U.S. Marshals Service, an elite paramilitary force used for raids and exceptionally difficult fugitives.

Operation Northern Exposure

Federal authorities did not act immediately on the warrant, waiting fifteen months before organizing the Special Operations Group to conduct surveillance on Weaver and his family. The first surveillance cameras were positioned in late April 1992 on the ridge just west of Weaver's cabin. The first SOG arrived on June 17 to make a preliminary assessment. The operation, code-named "Northern Exposure," was designed to gather intelligence for approximately a month before moving forward to the arrest stage. But the operation was interrupted temporarily while the newly nominated director of the U.S. Marshals' office, Henry Hudson, was undergoing Senate confirmation hearings back in Washington during June and July. Northern Exposure became operational again in early August.

The Marshals' SOG sent to Ruby Ridge was divided into two teams of three agents each. The "forward group" consisted of Arthur Roderick, Larry Cooper, and William Degan. All three marshals in the forward group

144

had previous military training and experience. Arthur Roderick served in the Army Military Police (MP) for three years. Larry Cooper was a former Marine and had also served as a Border Patrol agent. William Degan served in the Marines and was a part of the Reserves when he was called up for duty during the Persian Gulf War. In fact, Degan was singled out for the Special Operations Group because of his military training and experience. The back-up team consisted of Dave Hunt, Larry Thomas, and Frank Norris. Of these three, only Hunt had a military background: He was a former Marine, with two tours as "a guerrilla warfare trainer in Vietnam" (Walter, 1995: 156).

During the second week of the surveillance operation, the forward group encountered trouble. The plan, as described later by marshals in court testimony, was to "get the attention of the dog," referring to the Weaver's yellow Labrador retriever, Striker, by throwing rocks at him. Purportedly, this tactic was designed to draw out the fugitive Weaver and give the marshals an opportunity to arrest him. But both the plan and its implementation were badly flawed. Randy Weaver's 14-year-old son, Sammy, and a family friend, 24-year-old Kevin Harris, were walking near the entranceway to the property when the dog started barking. The dog picked up the scent of the marshals and pursued them down a mountain path. Arthur Roderick and Larry Cooper retreated as the yellow Lab chased them through the brush, barking and howling. When the dog finally caught up with the marshals, William Degan, the third member of the forward group, sprang up on one knee and shot the dog. Startled, Sammy Weaver screamed out an invective and returned fire on the unknown intruder, initiating a shootout. As Sammy Weaver turned to run, a bullet nearly severed the boy's left arm. A second round hit the young boy in the back and exited through his chest, killing him instantly. A ballistics test would later show that the bullet that killed Sammy Weaver was fired from Larry Cooper's Colt Commando 9-mm submachine gun. Kevin Harris returned fire with a .30–06 bolt-action rifle and killed Marshal Degan. Harris then sprinted back to the cabin to alert the Weaver family while the forward group of marshals retreated with the body of their slain partner. Randy Weaver and Kevin Harris later retrieved the boy's body from the mountain path and the standoff was inaugurated.

The Standoff

With a federal marshal dead and the Weaver family entrenched in their cabin atop Ruby Ridge, the FBI's elite paramilitary and counterterrorism

145

unit, the Hostage Rescue Team (HRT), was ordered to the scene of the standoff in northern Idaho. The threat assessment compiled previously by the Marshals Service was sent to the FBI to help them prepare for the confrontation with Weaver. Given the apocryphal content of the threat assessment, FBI officials decided to change the "rules of engagement."

While en route to northern Idaho, commander of the Hostage Rescue Team Dick Rogers and Assistant Director of the FBI Larry Potts discussed the threat assessment and related intelligence compiled from other sources. Rogers told a Justice Department task force investigating the incident in the aftermath that the situation at Ruby Ridge necessitated giving agents a broader set of rules to defend themselves. He authorized agents to use deadly force against any adult seen with a weapon in the vicinity of the Weaver cabin. At the trial of Randy Weaver a few months later in Boise, Rogers offered additional justification for this decision by saying he believed Ruby Ridge was "the most dangerous situation the HRT had ever encountered" (Bock, 1995: 171). Potts concurred with Rogers regarding the alteration, though neither discussed the new rules with FBI legal counsel or with headquarters.

FBI Deputy Assistant Director Danny Coulson received the operation plan at the FBI headquarters' Strategic Information and Operations Center (SIOC), but he did not approve the initial draft. Coulson would later describe his response to the draft plan in a biographical account as follows: "What I had in my hands didn't resemble anything that the HRT or any law enforcement agency should do. *It was a military assault plan*" (Coulson and Shannon, 1999: 406; emphasis mine). Coulson ceased reviewing the plan, in part because the negotiations component was missing, a foreshadowing of the conflict between the negotiations unit and the tactical unit that would arise during the Waco standoff (see Wright, 1999, 2003). The FBI's on-scene commander at Ruby Ridge, Special Agent Eugene Glenn, mistakenly believed the operation plan was approved in its entirety. The legal standard governing deadly force, as set forth by the Supreme Court in *Garner v. Tennessee*, permits officers to fire only in life-threatening situations (Fyfe, 1995). But the FBI instituted shoot-on-sight orders, which were, in effect, *military* rules of engagement. The change in the rules of engagement dramatically altered events at Ruby Ridge.

The shootings took place on August 21 and precipitated the eleven-day standoff. The FBI's HRT was ensconced in strategic positions around the perimeter, wedged between rocks and trees, approximately two hundred yards from the cabin. Sammy Weaver's body was placed in a small shed adjacent to the cabin. On Saturday, August 22, Randy, his daughter Sara, and Kevin Harris walked to the shed to check on the body. When Weaver reached for the door handle, a sniper's bullet ripped through a portion of his arm. As Weaver and Harris ran back to the cabin, Vicki Weaver jumped up frantically with infant in arms to hold the door open. As Kevin Harris reached the top of the stairs and lunged toward the cabin door, FBI sniper/observer Lon Horiuchi took aim at Harris and fired. The .308-caliber bullet penetrated the upper left arm of Harris before hitting Vicki Weaver, who was standing behind the door. It pierced her neck, severed her carotid artery, and then exited, ripping away most of the left side of her jaw and half of her face. At this point, Vicki Weaver lay dead and both Kevin Harris and Randy Weaver were wounded.

Over the next several days, Harris's condition worsened. Weaver's wounds were healing, but Harris desperately needed medical attention. The barricaded inhabitants of the cabin were not hopeful about the resolution of the standoff. They feared that they would be killed off one by one by FBI snipers who had shoot-on-sight orders. Efforts by FBI negotiators to send an armed robot with messages to the cabin were unsuccessful. It didn't help that the HRT was beaming high-intensity lights on the cabin at night to induce sleep deprivation, circling the cabin with tanks, and bulldozing the area around the cabin while the phone on the arm of the robot was ringing incessantly. No one inside the cabin was able to sleep more than a few hours for the first four days of the standoff.

A break in the impasse occurred on Wednesday, August 26, when Patriot and GOA activists Bo Gritz and Jack McLamb arrived and announced that they wanted to act as intermediaries in the negotiations. Gritz, a former Special Forces commander and militia advocate, brought a letter from Identity pastor Pete Peters endorsing Gritz as a mediator. Special Agent Eugene Glenn was amenable to the idea but had to obtain approval from FBI officials at SIOC. Approval was given by SIOC, and the FBI negotiators made contact with Weaver to see if he would allow Gritz to approach the cabin. On Saturday, August 29, Gritz spoke with Weaver and Harris from the cabin porch. The two men said they were not ready to leave yet and expressed their reservations and concerns. Gritz conveyed their message to the FBI and then spoke to the media and to the crowd of approximately one hundred protesters gathered at the base of the mountain around the staging area. Most of the protestors were Identity and Patriot adherents who had come to support Weaver. Some held signs exhibiting angry antigovernment epithets such as "FBI Burn in Hell" and "Zionist Murderers." Others were shouting "baby killers" at federal agents entering and leaving the scene. Gritz told the raucous crowd that Weaver and Harris felt that they were the victims of criminal actions by the government and that they did not believe they could receive a fair trial in "the Babylonian courts." The standoff continued, and Gritz subsequently contacted Gerry Spence, the iconoclastic Wyoming defense attorney who tentatively agreed to represent Weaver if he and Harris surrendered. On Sunday, August 30, Gritz and McLamb persuaded Weaver to let them transport Kevin Harris to a hospital for medical treatment. The next day, August 31, the standoff ended as the Weaver family walked out of the cabin together with Gritz and McLamb.

The criminal trial of Randy Weaver and Kevin Harris highlighted the special symbiotic relationship to Waco. Weaver and Harris were charged in state court with murder, aiding and abetting murder, conspiracy, and assault and were told to prepare for a trial in February 1993. Jury selection began just a few days before February 28, 1993, when an ATF Special Response Team (SRT) laid siege to the Branch Davidian settlement outside Waco. Potential jurors in Idaho were engaged in *voir dire* for the greater part of March, thus coinciding with the fifty-one-day standoff in Texas. With jury selection completed by the month's end, the trial began on April 14, just five days before the disastrous FBI CS gas assault on the Branch Davidians. Judge Edward Lodge was clearly unsettled by the similarities between the two incidents, so he instructed the jury not to watch, listen to, or read news coverage about the burning of the Davidian complex. But the incidents involved significant comparisons and overlapping that could not be ignored. Federal agents who were actively engaged in the Branch Davidian standoff, most notably HRT commander Dick Rogers and FBI sniper Lon Horiuchi, had to leave Waco on more than one occasion to testify in the trial in Boise. A parade of FBI, ATF, and Justice Department officials ferried between the two sites during this critical time. Moreover, media coverage of the Branch Davidian standoff cast more intense light on Ruby Ridge and the Weaver trial, drawing comparisons for a wider, unwitting public.

On July 8, 1993, while government investigative committees, journalists, and scholars were still attempting to get answers to the Waco debacle, the jury in Boise acquitted Randy Weaver of all serious charges, determining that he had been entrapped by the ATF. If most Americans had not thought to make comparisons before, they certainly were treated to the notion during the media-saturated coverage of Waco for nearly four months. But it was the Patriot and gun rights networks that ascribed to these federal "gun raids" a fundamental connection and more malicious intent.

148

Estes Park: Patriot Frame Alignment and Innovation

Strategically and historically situated between the twin tragedies of Ruby Ridge and Waco, Identity leader Pete Peters convened the Estes Park conference on the weekend of October 23–25, 1992, calling on a wide cross section of far-right leaders to unify against an emergent police state. The 160 attendees featured prominent right-wing activists such as Louis Beam, Larry Pratt, Richard Butler, John Trochman, Del Knudsen, Kirk Lyons, and Greg Dixon, among others. Pete Peters told the conferees in opening remarks that they were convened to confront the injustice and tyranny evidenced in Idaho by a government out of control. Peters read a brief letter written by Randy Weaver's daughter, Sara. Speaking on behalf of the family, she thanked all Identity believers for their support and stated her hope that the tragedy would "lead people to the truth." Peters announced that the killings in Ruby Ridge had awakened "a host of Christian soldiers" who were prepared to carry out the judgments of God. Playing down the racist and anti-Semitic elements of Identity beliefs, Peters denounced government and media reports that the Weavers were white supremacists. He referred to them as "good Christians" and intoned that the racist labels were merely ploys by agents of the New World Order to defame the Weavers.

It was Louis Beam's presentation to the conclave, however, that epitomized the frame alignment efforts of conference leaders:

The federals have by their murder of Samuel and Vicki Weaver brought us all together under the same roof for the same reason.... The two murders of the Weaver family have shown all of us that our religious, our political, our ideological differences mean nothing to those who wish to make us all slaves. We are all viewed by the government as the same, the enemies of the state. When they come for you, the federals will not ask if you are a Constitutionalist, a Baptist, Church of Christ, Identity Covenant believer, Klansman, Nazi, home schooler, Freeman, New Testament believer, [or] fundamentalist ... Those who wear badges, black boots, and carry automatic weapons, and kick in your doors already know all they need to know about you. You are enemies of the state. (quoted in Dees and Corcoran, 1996: 51)

Beam placed the Ruby Ridge standoff squarely within the warfare frame, invoking the image of the police state and alluding to the threat posed by "those who wear badges, black boots, and carry automatic weapons, and kick in your doors." Because the gathering represented a wide range of disparate and contentious far-right factions, some of whom maintained only the most tenuous contacts, efforts by conference leaders clearly involved some degree of frame bridging and brokerage. Beam, Peters, and others saw the Ruby

Ridge siege as an opportunity to unify a fragmented, nascent network of Patriots against a common enemy. Comments after the conference by Peters support this observation: "Men came together who in the past would not normally be caught together under the same roof, who greatly disagree with each other on many theological and philosophical points, whose teachings contradict each other in many ways. Yet, not only did they come together, they worked together for they all agreed what was done to the Weaver family was wrong and could not, and should not, be ignored by Christian men" (quoted in Dees and Corcoran, 1996: 50).

During the three-day conference, GOA founder Larry Pratt expanded on the need to form armed citizen militias as an innovative strategy of collective action. Pratt repeated the claim made in his book (1990) that only an "armed people" could defend against attacks on liberty. But now he declared the "enemy" was the state rather than communist insurgents, articulating what Snow et al. (1986) called "frame transformation," or reframing of the attributional orientation. In reframing the struggle, Pratt infused the idea with deeper religious meaning and justification, calling it a "spiritual battle" based on biblical precepts. "What I see in Scripture is not that we have a right to keep and bear arms," he said, "but that we have a responsibility to do so. For a man to refuse to provide adequately for his and his family's defense would be to defy God" (quoted in Dees and Corcoran, 1996: 54). Pratt told conference participants that organizing citizen militias in their own counties and states would likely prevent any future Ruby Ridges.

Pratt's battle cry for citizen militias was accompanied by Louis Beam's call for innovative insurgency in the form of "leaderless resistance." Beam first introduced the concept of leaderless resistance in 1983 in a Klan newsletter, promoting it at the 1983 Aryan Nations Congress (see Noble, 1998). Robert Mathews's group, The Order, and the CSA cell led by Richard Snell were both loosely based on this idea. Beam (1992) published a revised version of leaderless resistance in his own newsletter, *The Seditionist*, which he promoted again at the Estes Park gathering. Beam proposed leaderless resistance as an insurgent strategy that employed decentralized, semiautonomous cells to oppose the growing threat of police state actions. Beam echoed Pratt's redefinition of "the enemy," replacing the old enemy of communism with the new enemy of federal government: "Communism now represents a threat to no one in the United States," Beam declared, "while federal tyranny represents a threat to *everyone*" (1992: 1).

Beam stressed the need to formulate innovative collective action as a response to new conditions. He described the strategy as a "child of necessity" to a "changing situation"; those opposing state oppression, he stated, "must be prepared to alter, adapt, and modify their behavior, strategy and tactics as circumstances warrant" (1992: 2, 4–5). The extensive surveillance and undercover capabilities now developed by federal agencies compelled new tactics. The only effective method to combat the "modern police state," he argued, was to form "phantom cells" operating independently of each other with only intermittent communication for direction. Without a centralized command structure, or "pyramid" organization, detection, infiltration, and exposure by federal agents would be less likely. "In the pyramid type of organization," Beam argued, "an infiltrator can destroy anything which is beneath his level of infiltration and often those above him as well. If the traitor has infiltrated at the top, then the entire organization from the top down is compromised and may be traduced at will" (1992: 3). Beam warned fellow Patriots that relying on "old methods" would only aid the state: "Patriots are required . . . to make a conscious decision to either aid the government in its illegal spying, by continuing with old methods of organizations and resistance, or to make the enemie's [sic] job more difficult by implementing effective countermeasures" (1992: 5).

From an operational standpoint, there were clearly features of leaderless resistance that were problematic. For example, Beam seemed to leave the challenge of communication among the independent cells to the insurgents: "It becomes the responsibility of the individual to acquire the necessary skills and information as to what is to be done" (1992: 4). He provided only the vaguest guidelines, suggesting that communication could be accomplished through "organs of information distribution," such as newspapers, leaflets, or computers. But he also averred that intercommunication was not essential because members shared a common ideology and a unity of purpose. Mixing metaphors and calling on individual initiative, Beam appealed to Patriots to fill the coming night "with a thousand points of resistance" and become "the fog which forms when conditions are right and disappears when they are not" (1992: 6).

Beam and Pratt offered to the small conclave innovative forms of collective action even as federal agents were preparing the next "gun raid" on a relatively unknown religious sect outside Waco, Texas. This next gun raid was especially significant because it highlighted the expanding campaign of paramilitary policing beyond traditional targets. The object of the ATF raid in Texas had no connections to Patriot and racist groups on the far-right. The Branch Davidians were not white supremacists or Identity believers. Indeed, many of the Davidians were racial and ethnic minorities – twenty-seven of the eighty-six people who died in the standoff were black (Wright, 1995a: 379–81). Neither did the sect embrace anti-Semitism or engage in the scapegoating of Jews. The sect's leader, David Koresh, traveled to Israel to study the Torah with Orthodox Jews at a rabbinical school in the late 1980s. The Branch Davidians did not subscribe to Posse ideology or make assertions about the structural or constitutional illegitimacy of federal government. However, there is ample evidence to suggest that state agents *perceived* the Davidians as a violent extremist group that was preparing for a war with the government. This attribution of warfare shaped the response of federal law enforcement and helps to explain the martial logic of the ATF raid plan.

Waco

The ATF investigation of the Branch Davidians began in early June 1992, just two months before the shootout and standoff at Ruby Ridge. A UPS driver making a delivery to Mt. Carmel, Texas, the home of the Branch Davidian religious community near Waco, discovered empty pineapple grenade shells in a box that was broken open. The driver reported the incident to the McClennon County Sheriff's Department, and the case was referred to the ATF. The Department of Treasury report (1993) reviewing the Waco debacle documents that the investigation was headed by ATF Special Agent Davy Aguilera. Agent Aguilera soon learned that the sect's leader, David Koresh, and some of the Davidians were buying and selling weapons. Aguilera tracked down the gun dealer, Henry McMahon, who sold weapons to Koresh and interviewed him at his home in Waco on July 30. McMahon confirmed to Aguilera that he was a licensed gun dealer and that he was selling Koresh semiautomatic weapons. Koresh and the Davidians hoped to turn a profit by purchasing the weapons wholesale and selling them retail at gun shows. Evidently, McMahon had persuaded Koresh that it was a good investment because many gun owners believed the government would ban semiautomatic rifles in the near future, driving up the price of the weapons on the market. McMahon was disquieted by the investigator's questions and later testified in congressional hearings that he withdrew to another room and telephoned Koresh to tell him that he was being investigated by the ATF, a fact that didn't appear in the Treasury report. According to McMahon, Koresh invited the agent to come and inspect his weapons. McMahon relayed the message to Aguilera and tried to hand him the telephone. Aguilera refused to talk to Koresh on the phone, and the ATF never made an attempt to contact him or conduct an inspection of the weapons prior to the deadly raid on February 28, 1993, seven months later. The final report from the joint hearings on Waco by the House Committee on Government Reform and Oversight and the Committee on the Judiciary documented this failure by the ATF investigation, stating that "Koresh's offer should have been accepted" and that the agency missed "an invaluable opportunity to gather intelligence" (*Investigation into the Activities of Federal Law Enforcement Toward the Branch Davidians*, 1996: 10). The report's conclusion was even more succinct: "The agent's decline of the Koresh offer was a serious mistake" (p. 10).

That Koresh's attempt to cooperate with federal law enforcement was rebuffed inflamed gun rights advocates and Patriots. Ben Wattenberg, writing for *American Spectator* in a piece titled "Gunning for Koresh" (1993), claimed that the decision by the ATF to use deadly force in a military-like raid had been decided in advance. Wattenberg's assertion was echoed in numerous gun rights and Patriot publications (Pate 1993a, 1993b) and proclaimed boldly in far-right talk radio programs around the country. In part, this claim appeared to be supported by the Department of Treasury's own report, which castigated the ATF for prematurely determining a high-risk course of action, ignoring less lethal options in serving the warrants obtained, and describing the raid plan as "steps taken along what seemed . . . to be a pre-ordained road" (Department of the Treasury, 1993: 27). Even more damning, the final congressional report by House Subcommittees found that the ATF dismissed or refused multiple opportunities to avoid the high-risk, paramilitary raid: "It is unclear why the ATF did not accept the offer to conduct a compliance inspection of Koresh's firearms. What is clear is that the agents' refusal of Koresh's invitation was *the first of a series of instances* in which the ATF rejected opportunities to proceed in a non-confrontational manner" (1996: 13; emphasis mine). Both government reports found that the ATF could have avoided the raid altogether because (1) Koresh could have been arrested outside the Davidian residence (he left the property on numerous occasions despite ATF claims to the contrary), and (2) on the morning of the raid, the ATF had an undercover agent inside Mt. Carmel who told the raid commanders that the element of surprise was lost and the operation compromised. The Davidians knew the ATF was preparing to launch the raid, but inexplicably the officials in charge proceeded anyway. In effect, the frequent contention by Patriot and gun rights groups that "law-abiding gun owners" were being targeted by federal "storm-troopers" or the "Gun Gestapo" in a domestic war campaign was given some merit by the government's own investigations.

The Patriot framing of the federal siege at Waco as an illegal action taken to mask the disarmament motive was also given some credibility by official investigations. The final joint congressional report found that the affidavit filed in support of the warrants by the ATF "contained numerous misstatements of the facts, misstatements of the law, and misapplication of the law to the facts." It went on to say:

The affidavit included misleading and factually inaccurate statements, contained substantial irrelevant and confusing information, and failed to properly qualify witnesses' testimony when obviously called for based on their backgrounds. Consequently, the affidavit gave the appearance that the ATF was not going to let questionable facts or evidence stand in the way of moving forward on their timetable. (1996: 12)

The combined failures and missteps of the ATF furnished opponents and critics with ostensible proof that state agents had extralegal or ulterior motives for the gun raid. If more evidence of a conspiracy was needed, the House Subcommittees' report provided additional fodder, documenting that "The [ATF] decision to pursue a military-style raid was made more than 2 months before surveillance, undercover, and infiltration efforts were begun" (*Investigation into the Activities of Federal Law Enforcement Agencies Toward the Branch Davidians*, 1996: 3). Moreover, investigative subcommittees learned that ATF agents misrepresented to Defense Department officials that the Branch Davidians were involved in illegal drug manufacturing in order to obtain military training and support. The fabricated drug nexus apparently was made to circumvent Posse Comitatus restrictions regarding military involvement in domestic counterdrug enforcement.

The request for military assistance was made to Operation Alliance through Joint Task Force 6, which coordinates counterdrug missions for the U.S. Army's Special Operations Command. The "dynamic entry" by the ATF's Special Response Team was planned with military assistance by the U.S. Army Special Forces Rapid Support Unit at Ft. Hood, Texas, in three days of training in close-quarters combat/close-quarters battle (CQB) exercises. Other military assistance provided to the ATF included surveillance overflights by counterdrug National Guard units, direct support of National Guard units through aerial diversion during the raid, and postraid support.

In the summary of findings by the congressional investigation on the ATF's raid plan and misuse of military assistance, the subcommittees concluded that "the ATF was predisposed to using aggressive military tactics" (1996: 17).

Construction of an Intrinsic Narrative: Davidians a "Dangerous, Extremist Organization"

Elsewhere, I have argued that the most critical question arising from the Waco debacle concerns the state's fixed reliance on martial logic to define the Branch Davidians, casting them as such a perilous threat that a massive paramilitary raid was required (Wright, 2005). As in the Ruby Ridge incident, assessing the construction of an intrinsic narrative can help to show how cultural meanings became interpreted, nuanced, and reworked and how such meaning shifts affected the course of unfolding events. The ATF developed an inflated martial image of the Davidians as a violent extremist group bent on war with the government, but this image did not develop in a vacuum. In the Waco incident, third-party claimants – the cultural opponents of Koresh – played a significant role in fashioning a warfare narrative that served the interests of an opportunistic state agency. The receptiveness of the ATF to the received warfare narrative of Koresh's opponents was due in part to its strong affinity with the military/war model of crime control. "As such, ATF investigators and officials framed the information they received to fit the narrative of warfare, causing them to overlook or ignore contradictory, conflicting, or ambivalent evidence. This explains the puzzling decisions by ATF officials who failed to consider less lethal options or opportunities as they arose in what the Treasury report referred to as 'steps taken along what seemed to be at the time a preordained road'" (Wright, 2005: 91).

The early construction of a warfare narrative about the Branch Davidians was evident in the communication and claims-making activities of disgruntled apostates, particularly one key claimant, Marc Breault. Breault's efforts were recorded in a scandalous paperback titled *Inside the Cult*, coauthored with a reporter for the now defunct TV program *A Current Affair* (Breault and King, 1993). The blurbs on the book cover dramatize the warfare motif, trumpeting sensational claims of violence. Marc Breault was a principal figure in the construction of a warfare narrative and in the mobilization of organized opposition against Koresh that fueled the fears of authorities (see Wright, 1995b, 2005). He organized groups of ex-members in Australia and the United States, hired a private investigator to collect disparaging information about leaders, lobbied authorities to act against Koresh, and eventually became a primary source for the ATF and other federal agencies. Breault, who hailed from Australia, provided a record of these activities prior to the raid and boasted of almost daily phone calls from "senior officials of the United States Government, which included the ATF, the FBI, Congress, the State Department, and the Texas Rangers" (Breault and King, 1993: 295).

Breault claimed that as early as 1988 the sect began to post armed guards or sentries around the perimeter of Mt. Carmel, conducted paramilitary training exercises on the grounds, and gave the guards shoot-to-kill orders regarding any suspicious intruders (Breault and King, 1993: 172, 178). These claims were significant because they became part of the evidence record in support of the federal warrants. Breault was named as the source for both the shoot-to-kill orders and the 24-hour armed sentries cited by ATF Special Agent Aguilera in the federal affidavit (U.S. District Court, 1993: 12). Yet critical details in Breault's recounting of events to authorities have been challenged by other eyewitnesses, raising doubts about its validity. These doubts are further amplified by the unsubtle vilification efforts by Breault that eviscerate even the appearance of impartiality.

Breault's description of one incident in the book involved Davidian Wally Kennett, who was standing guard at the entrance of Mt. Carmel when allegedly a newspaper delivery man was almost shot. Breault claimed Kennett shouted "Halt" and fired two shots into the air with a Ruger .223 rifle, acting on Koresh's shoot-to-kill orders. But what Breault or coauthor King didn't say in the text was that Breault is legally blind and could not have seen "the shadow of the guard leveling his .223 Ruger rifle at a man" from an estimated twenty yards at 5 A.M., while it was "still dark" (p. 172). The Branch Davidians whom I interviewed in 1993 for my book on the Waco tragedy (Wright, 1995a) were quick to point out that Breault could not read without holding printed materials up to his face and that he could not recognize people or objects from a short distance even in broad daylight. Breault's blindness was also omitted from the affidavit filed in support of the federal warrants by ATF agent Aguilera, even though Breault was named as a primary source for the investigation. Moreover, in addition to excluding the information about Breault's blindness, the affidavit erroneously asserted that Breault was one of the armed guards who were posted at Mt. Carmel (U.S. District Court, 1993: 12). I have argued previously that the dereliction of Special Agent Aguilera to disclose Breault's visual impairment was a major failing of the ATF investigation (Wright, 2005: 88–9). Concealment of Breault's condition by the ATF investigator, given his importance to the investigation as an "eyewitness" to the accounts, certainly undermines the evidentiary claims on which the warrants were approved by the federal magistrate.

Breault's story is further plagued by a conflicting account of the incident by the guard in question: Wally Kennett was one of the Davidians I interviewed, and he disputed Breault's account. Kennett was Marc Breault's roommate during part of his stay at Mt. Carmel and came to know him quite well. Kennett said that Breault was prone to exaggeration and "had a tendency to tell tall tales." He offered to give several examples of embellished stories told to him by Breault. In an unsolicited comment, referring to the alleged shooting incident, Kennett stated, "The guy also claimed he had seen me level a Ruger mini-fourteen at the paperboy's head at four o'clock in the morning when it was pitch dark" (Interview with Wally Kennett, 1993a). Kennett dismissed the claim with disgust and said, "This guy is full of crap." Kennett intimated that the other members tolerated Breault's tendency to embellish because he was "a nice guy." Kennett's characterization of Breault was supported by a number of Davidian survivors, including Catherine Matteson, Sheila Martin, David Thibodeau, and Clive Doyle.

One warfare trope proffered in Breault's book involved repeated references to the "Mighty Men," which he asserted was an elite security cadre organized to protect Koresh and carry out his commands. The Mighty Men were portrayed as Koresh's "most intimidating weapon" and as "hand-picked goons" serving as guards and enforcers of the "cult" (p. 10). But the Davidian survivors I interviewed said the term "Mighty Men" was taken from the book of Psalms in the Old Testament and referred to spiritual qualifications, not martial qualities. Apparently, the term originated from a biblical story of the guards who protected King Solomon's bed (Bromley and Silver, 1995: 62). Davidian survivor David Thibodeau, in an autobiographical account, later said the term referred to "anyone who was given strength by faith" (Thibodeau and Whiteson, 1999: 125).

According to Breault, Koresh was obsessed with the idea of war and told his followers, "You've gotta be ready for war" after forcing them to watch a "marathon of violent Vietnam War movies" (1993: 184). Breault opined that the movies served as *de facto* training videos and were part of a broader "psychological conditioning" program where "mind-control reached such a pitch that his subjects were putty in his hands" (p. 184). Other efforts to invoke warfare rhetoric and framing included references to Koresh's

"100-man army" and likening Mt. Carmel to "an army base" (pp. 186, 250). Through these and other tropes, Breault offered a composite picture of Mt. Carmel as a paramilitary compound run by a war-obsessed cult leader who brainwashed members into violence and stockpiled weapons and who was preparing for a war against the government.

The influence of third-party claimants was acknowledged by the government investigations and reports in the aftermath of Waco. The Department of Treasury report documented that agent Aguilera's contacts with Breault "continued until the ATF raid on February 28" (1993: 29). The allegations of armed guards, shoot-to-kill orders, Wally Kennett's alleged shooting at the newspaper delivery man, and claims that "many cult members carried firearms, including AK-47's" (p. 29) were all attributed to Breault. Accounts by other opponents of Koresh were also recorded in the ATF affidavit, including ex-Davidians Robyn Bunds, Debbie Bunds, Janine Bunds, and David Block. In an interview with Debbie Bunds, agent Aguilera cited as evidence the opinion of Ms. Bunds that gunfire she heard at Mt. Carmel was from a machine gun. "She is sure the firearm was a machinegun because of the rapid rate of fire," the agent stated (p. 10). Janine Bunds claimed to have identified an AR-15 from a photograph shown to her. In neither case was information offered to explain why these witnesses were qualified to make technical judgments about firearms. The congressional report later criticized the ATF affidavit for failing to take into account these and other descriptions of possible gun law violations by unqualified claimants (*Investigations into the Activities of Federal Law Enforcement Agencies Toward the Branch Davidians*, 1996: 12). The Treasury report noted that some legal semiautomatic weapons could be equipped with a "hellfire trigger" that would create the "rapid rate of fire" heard by the women (Department of the Treasury, 1993: n. 35). Lt. Robert Sobozienski, a New York City police officer who served as an expert on the Treasury Department's review panel, later criticized the ATF's uncritical acceptance of accounts by ex-members: "Former cult members were interviewed and apparently much, if not all, of their statements are reported to be facts. No thought is given to the idea that these ex–cult members had been away from their residence for some time, or to the individual biases, or if they had an ax to grind with present cult members" (*Investigation into the Activities of Federal Law Enforcement Agencies Toward the Branch Davidians*, 1996: 46).

The received warfare narrative of third-party claimants converged with the warfare mentality of federal agents to produce an exaggerated martial image of the Branch Davidians. Some of the information appearing in the ATF affidavit filed with the federal court clearly reflected an encoding of information in the attribution of warfare. For example, Aguilera recorded that Koresh played a videotape for the ATF undercover agent Robert Rodriguez that was produced by Larry Pratt's Gun Owners of America. The video was titled "Breaking the Law . . . in the Name of the Law: The BATF Story." The affidavit states that the "film portrayed the ATF as an agency that violated the rights of gun owners using threats and lies" (U.S. District Court, 1993: 15). Evidently, Koresh also expressed a fear of state disarmament and echoed Pratt's views about a biblical basis for firearms to the undercover agent. According to the affidavit, "David Koresh told Special Agent Rodriguez that he believed in the right to bear arms but that the U.S. Government was going to take away that right" (p. 15).

The assertion of an impending state disarmament campaign likely aroused deep suspicions about the intentions of Koresh in the context of the warfare tropes offered up by third-party claimants. Koresh's familiarity with Pratt and the GOA also linked the Davidians to the gun rights network and increased the perceived danger of the group in the eyes of ATF officials. The encoding of these statements and actions was further exacerbated by the labeling of the group as a "cult" in the affidavit, implying a host of dangerous attributes associated with the pejorative term (see Hall, 1995; Lewis, 1995; Wright, 1995b). The affidavit also recorded the following observation: "David Koresh stated that the Bible gave him the right to bear arms" (p. 15). This peculiar blending of faith and firearms reflected Pratt's evolving ideology, and it is certain that ATF officials were aware of Pratt's increasing activism and the GOA's absolutist stance on gun rights. ATF also may have had intelligence from the Estes Park gathering a few months earlier in which Pratt espoused organizing armed militias to challenge the state's enforcement of gun laws.

In the emergent play of cultural meanings, we should also consider that the intrinsic warfare narrative served to consolidate the interests of ATF, whose officials saw the state's increased attention to interdicting illegal firearms as providing new opportunities and resources for the bureau. The presidential campaign of Bill Clinton featured the call for stricter gun laws, infuriating gun rights groups while delighting top officials at the ATF. With the election of Clinton, gun control advocates and their allies enjoyed open support from the White House for the first time in twelve years (Vizzard, 2000: 135). The new Clinton administration took office in January 1993 and was determined to push through tougher restrictions on guns, making the ATF the greatest beneficiary of the new policies. Clinton administration officials lobbied for passage of the Brady Bill and subsequently pressured lawmakers to pass the 1994 Federal Crime Bill, which outlawed seventeen types of assault weapons.

Clinton was a particularly polarizing figure in the conflict between Patriots/gun rights groups and state actors. Not only was Clinton a strong proponent of new gun control legislation, he was also the governor of Arkansas during the deadly shootout between Gordon Kahl and federal agents in 1983, and he approved the federal siege of the Covenant, Sword and Arm of the Lord in his state in 1985. It is likely that Clinton was seen by ATF officials as an ally, sympathetic to a similar enforcement action against what the bureau called "a dangerous, extremist organization" eight years later in Waco, as the new president took office (*Investigation into the Activities of Federal Law Enforcement Agencies Toward the Branch Davidians*, 1996: 46 n.). The affinity between the ATF's primary mission and the new administration's preference for reducing violent crime through heightened gun controls was clear.

Clinton's election in November 1992, not coincidentally, stimulated an increased pace in the ATF investigation of David Koresh. Despite the fact that in December 1992 officials at ATF headquarters in Washington "decided they did not yet have probable cause to support a warrant" (*Investigation into the Activities of Federal Law Enforcement Agencies Toward the Branch Davidians*, 1996: 11), the bureau rushed ahead with a raid plan. The decision to pursue a military-like raid was made around the same time in December, approximately two months before surveillance and undercover operations were begun. The determination of ATF to take this "pre-ordained road" while ignoring chances to arrest Koresh or take less lethal options may be explained partly in terms of perceived opportunities and organizational interests (Wright, 2005).

Operation Trojan Horse

The federal raid on the Branch Davidian complex was the "largest enforcement effort ever mounted by ATF and one of the largest in the history of law enforcement" (Department of the Treasury, 1993: 134). The raid plan, given the code name "Operation Trojan Horse," marshaled eighty federal agents outfitted in camouflage and full combat gear, including Kevlar helmets and flak jackets, wielding MP-5 submachine guns, semiautomatic AR-15 rifles, Sig Sauer 9mm semiautomatic pistols, .308-caliber high-power sniper rifles, shotguns, and concussion grenades. The raid plan called for agents to arrive in the rear of two cattle cars covered with tarps on the morning of February 28. The objective of the raid was to execute search-and-arrest warrants for Vernon Wayne Howell (a.k.a. David Koresh) for firearms violations and possession of a destructive device. The Mt. Carmel complex housed approximately 130 people, more than 60 percent of whom were women, children, and elderly persons.

The ATF raid planners hoped to use the element of surprise and catch the Davidians off guard, thereby minimizing resistance to the enforcement action. As investigators later learned, the Davidians were tipped off about the raid by a Waco news cameraman who stopped a postal delivery worker to get directions to Mt. Carmel. The postal worker was David Jones, a Davidian who learned of the raid and returned to Mt. Carmel to alert Koresh. ATF undercover agent Robert Rodriguez was inside Mt. Carmel that morning when David Jones arrived and informed Koresh of the impending raid. Rodriguez promptly departed the building, went immediately across the road to the surveillance house, told his superiors that the element of surprise had been lost, and advised that the raid be called off. ATF raid commanders Phillip Chojnacki and Chuck Sarabyn ignored the agent's warning and proceeded with the raid. Accounts differ about who fired first, but a shootout ensued and six Davidians and four federal agents were mortally wounded.

The ATF enjoyed extensive military assistance and cooperation in the planning of Operation Trojan Horse. Counterdrug National Guard units in January and February 1993 conducted surveillance overflights of Mt. Carmel in UC-26 aircraft equipped with infrared cameras (FLIR). The ATF's paramilitary Special Response Team trained and prepared for the raid with active military personnel for three days at Ft. Hood. Assistance in planning and rehearsal of a proposed "takedown" by U.S. Army Special Forces Rapid Support Unit included close-quarters combat exercises, company-level tactical C2, medical evacuation training (techniques for treating battlefield injuries), and assistance with Range and MOUT (Military Operation on Urban Terrain) sites. On February 28, the day of the raid, Texas National Guard supplied ten counterdrug personnel and three helicopters: two OH-58s and one UH-60 Blackhawk. ATF's stated mission to National Guard officials initially was to use the helicopters as a command-and-control platform during the raid and to transport personnel and evidence after the area was secured. Only after the National Guard team arrived at Ft. Hood, less than twenty-four hours before the raid, did ATF agents inform them that the helicopters would be deployed as an aerial diversion during the raid itself (*Investigation into the Activities of Federal Law Enforcement Against the Branch Davidians*, 1996: 37–8).

The ATF was able to obtain military assistance in the planning and implementation of the raid by fabricating a drug nexus. The ATF alleged to the Department of Defense that it had evidence of an active methamphetamine lab on the premises of Mt. Carmel. According to the McClennan County Sheriff's Department, Koresh found methamphetamine lab equipment upon taking possession of Mt. Carmel in 1988 and reported it to authorities. An associate of the previous occupant, George Roden, was responsible for the drug lab equipment. The Sheriff's Department investigated the incident and supervised the removal of the equipment. But at the behest of ATF officials, Marc Breault sent a fax to agent Aguilera implying that the drug lab might still be operational. Evidence for a drug nexus claimed by ATF was based largely on this fabricated, deceptive tip. The congressional report provided a detailed description of the bureau's elaborate prevarication (pp. 42–53), noting among other things that the building in which the alleged drug lab was housed burned down three years prior to the raid.

The Standoff and FBI/HRT Assault

In the aftermath of the failed ATF raid and shootout, the FBI's Hostage Rescue Team (HRT) was dispatched to Waco, marking the start of the fifty-one-day standoff. Only six months removed from the Ruby Ridge tragedy, the pattern of a failed gun raid followed by the insertion of the FBI's HRT did not escape the attention of Patriot and gun rights groups. Many Patriot activists came to Waco to protest the federal siege. Louis Beam arrived under the auspices of a reporter for *The Jubilee*, a publication of William Pierce's National Alliance. During a press briefing on March 18, Beam challenged FBI spokespersons over the official explanation of the ATF raid and became engaged in a shoving match. Beam was arrested and charged with criminal trespass. Linda Thompson, founder of the Unorganized Militia of the United States of America, based in Indianapolis, summoned Patriots to the police barricades around Mt. Carmel. Thompson sent a fax through the newly organized American Patriot Fax Network (which later became the American Patriot Friends Network) that read: "JOIN US! The Unorganized Militia of the United States of America will assemble, with long arms, vehicles (including tracked and armored), aircraft, and any available gear for inspection for fitness and use in a well-regulated militia, at 9:00 a.m. on

Saturday, April 3, 1995, on Northcrest Drive off I-35" (Stern, 1996: 61). Some heeded the call, and FBI and Justice Department officials worried that militant groups would descend on Waco and compound an already difficult situation (Bragg and Asin, 1993: 5A).

Tim McVeigh was one of the Patriots who journeyed to Waco. McVeigh arrived at the site of the standoff with a carload of antigovernment pamphlets and bumper stickers to distribute. Police roadblocks were set up approximately three miles from Mt. Carmel. McVeigh attempted to get past the checkpoint on Farm Road 39 but was turned away by agents he described as "soldiers dressed in camouflage" and "armed to the teeth." McVeigh told me in an interview that he entertained the idea of "ramming his car through the roadblock" and "taking out" some of the agents but thought better of it. Instead, he found a place to park his Chevrolet Geo Spectrum in an adjacent field, where hundreds of protesters and onlookers were camped out. McVeigh slept in his car and spent the next few days proselytizing, distributing literature, and selling or giving away bumper stickers that featured familiar claims and slogans to Patriots and gun rights activists:

Fear the Government That Fears Your Gun
When Guns Are Outlawed, I Will Become an Outlaw
Politicians Love Gun Control
A Man with a Gun Is a Citizen. A Man without a Gun Is a Subject
Ban Guns. Make the Streets Safe for a Government Takeover

While holding vigil outside the standoff at Mt. Carmel, McVeigh was approached by a young journalism student, Michelle Rauch, from Southern Methodist University requesting an interview. Rauch's interview with McVeigh for the college newspaper, *The Daily Campus*, provided an extraordinary window into the insurgent's evolving ideology and political beliefs. McVeigh echoed the Posse Comitatus position that the ATF lacked authority to carry out the raid: "[O]nly the local sheriff," he said, "had the proper authority to serve the warrants." McVeigh buttressed this claim with what was essentially an article of faith among gun rights activists: "The government is afraid of the guns people have because they have to have control of the people at all times. Once you take away guns, you can do anything to the people" (quoted in trial transcript, *United States of America v. Timothy James McVeigh*, 1997: vol. 143, 8). McVeigh also took pains to say that America's armed forces should not be used against civilians – a theme he would repeat many times in my interviews with him. He warned that the standoff was "only the beginning" and "that people should watch the government's role

163

and heed any warning signs." Rauch's article appeared in the March 30 edition of *The Daily Campus* and included a photograph of McVeigh sitting next to the bumper stickers prominently displayed on the hood of his car. McVeigh left Waco two days after the interview but still weeks before the deadly denouement.

By March 17, the HRT's response plan was referred to as a "stress escalation" program in the Justice log (U.S. Department of Justice, 1993: 138, n.2). FBI negotiators had managed to convince the barricaded Davidians to release twenty-eight persons. But tensions between negotiators – who called for patience and waiting out the Davidians – and the HRT's increasingly aggressive tactics were threatening to undermine the publicly declared goal of a peaceful resolution (see Wright, 1999, 2001, 2003). After March 21, largely in response to the increased show of force by the HRT, no more sect members left Mt. Carmel. Failed negotiations subsequently were cited by FBI officials as a rationale for organizing a CS assault on the group. On April 19, military tanks fitted with special booms breached the buildings and fired canisters of CS into the Mt. Carmel complex for six hours before a fire erupted, killing seventy-six Branch Davidians, including twenty-four children. The fiery inferno was caught live on television feeds and broadcast around the world to horrified viewers. McVeigh, who was visiting Terry and James Nichols at their farm in Decker, Michigan, was enraged by what he saw. The three men agreed that the bloodbath was not an accident and that Waco was a pivotal turning point for the antigovernment insurgency. McVeigh insisted that action had to be taken. "Waco was a declaration of war," he told me.

The war analogy posited by Patriot and gun rights groups was not a strained interpretation of events. In the aftermath of the federal assault, the scene at Mt. Carmel resembled a war zone, with Bradley fighting vehicles, combat engineering vehicles (CEVs), and M1A1 Abrams tanks surrounding the charred ruins and scores of burned corpses mingled together in a mass of black debris and smoke. Federal agents in military garb patrolled the area, maintained a tight perimeter, and assessed the damage. Jack Zimmerman, one of the Branch Davidian attorneys and a former military judge, observed in the Emmy Award–winning documentary film *Waco: The Rules of Engagement*, that even as the complex was burning to the ground the ATF ran its flag up the Davidian flagpole to signify "a military victory."

The image of yet another standoff with the government ending in a fiery inferno evoked memories of Gordon Kahl and Robert Mathews among Patriot groups. Not only did they perceive this to be a deliberate pattern by state agents, but following the siege and standoff in Ruby Ridge, it appeared that the scale of warfare carried out by the state was growing. Waco was a massive operation involving more than eight hundred federal and state agents, supported by military equipment, ordnance, and personnel, including on-scene advisors from U.S. Army Special Forces and the 22nd Regiment of the British Army's Special Air Services. The target of the assault was not merely a few individuals residing in a cabin but an entire religious community. For Patriot and gun rights groups, Waco represented a significant escalation of warfare. There now appeared to be no limitation on the lengths to which the state would go to realize its goal of disarmament and subjugation.

8

Patriot Insurgency and the Oklahoma City Bombing

In the recursive dynamic of state-movement attributions of war, the 1993 Brady Bill and the 1994 Crime Control Bill were perceived by Patriot and gun rights groups as the final broadside. The two controversial gun control bills followed a torrent of paramilitary gun raids, highlighted by the deadly sieges at Ruby Ridge and Waco. The trajectory of contention can be understood as a derivative of this escalating threat attribution of warfare between the state and challenging groups. What doubts many movement sympathizers and marginal free riders may have had about Patriot claims of state disarmament were quickly dispelled by the new gun control legislation. Patriot leaders construed the new legislation as an unabashed push toward a gun ban and drew comparisons to the fictional Cohen Act described in *The Turner Diaries*. Even as the Cohen Act and the "Gun Raids" triggered the insurgency of Earl Turner and the violent underground insurgency in the *Diaries*, the threat attributed to the Brady and Crime Control Bills in the wake of disturbingly similar gun raids by state PPUs, capped by Ruby Ridge and Waco, galvanized the Patriot movement and incited acts of insurgency.

Making effective use of the strategy developed at the Estes Park meeting in 1992, the Patriot movement broadened its base among a wide range of far-right groups as leaders worked to both facilitate diffusion along existing lines of communication and broker new social sites. Berlet and Lyons observe that "the Patriot movement drew from several preexisting movements and networks," including Posse Comitatus, Freemen, sovereign citizens, antitax protestors, Identity and white supremacy networks, the confrontational wing of the antiabortion movement, the dominion theology sector of the Christian evangelical right, especially Christian Reconstructionism, and the most militant wings of the antienvironmentalist "Wise

166

Use" movement, the county supremacy movement, the states rights move-ment, and the Tenth Amendment movement (2002: 289). The researchers found that Patriot movement leaders were able to integrate multiple themes involving alleged "government abuse of power," "fears about globalism and sovereignty," and "apocalyptic fears of conspiracy and tyranny from above," among others (Berlet and Lyons, 2002: 289).

This grand conspiracy script defined an assortment of state actions as elements in a designed takeover by agents of the New World Order. Patri-ots pointed to numerous post–Cold War developments as evidence of the NWO threat. The increased integration of military and police forces and the consequent militarization of police was chief among the developments, but additional "proof" of the conspiracy included the deployment of U.S. troops under UN command, the joint- or cross-training of foreign troops on American soil, and expanding federal government preparations for a national emergency – a program that some Patriot leaders claimed would result in the suspension of the Constitution and the declaration of martial law. Patriot activists believed that a secret plan had been contrived to turn control of the government over to the Federal Emergency Management Agency (FEMA) while transferring authority over local and state govern-ments to military commanders. In one Michigan Militia publication, leaders asserted that the state was preparing to exploit a crisis event as a ploy to institute martial law wherein "a whole array of socialist/totalitarian actions could be foisted on a captive American populace" (Olsen, 1994: 9).

Variations on this conspiracy motif proliferated among groups coalesced under the Patriot tent, but at the core of this perceived threat was gun control. By targeting gun owners in a universal-disarmament campaign, claimants argued, the state hoped to quell any future resistance to the ascen-dant New World Order. Patriot leaders strategically joined with gun rights groups and insisted that armed citizens were the last line of defense against the imposition of tyranny. As I have tried to show, a key mechanism for uniting disorganized, fragmented far-right groups into an allied antigov-ernment movement was the brokering of ties to the gun rights network by Patriot actors. Strategic framing by Patriot leaders produced an emergent warfare frame that bridged the disarmament narrative to Posse Comitatus fears of federal tyranny, historical revisionist constructions of the Second Amendment and militias, and a host of obdurate and wide-ranging conspir-acies among far-right organizations.

The most visible manifestation of the insurgent campaign was the rapid formation and mobilization of armed citizen militias, which operated under the assumption that a war with the government was already under way. Though the militia movement represented only a small faction of the much larger Patriot movement, the latter estimated at about four million (Berlet and Lyons, 2002: 288), the organization of insurgents into "private armies" created much greater public attention and official consternation.

Mobilization of Citizen Militias

With passage of the Brady Bill only months removed from the Waco debacle, Larry Pratt's call for armed citizen militias was seized upon and refined by Patriot activists. In January 1994, Sam Sherwood founded the Idaho-based United States Militia Association (USMA). Sherwood expressed a strong antipathy for federal authority, calling for a repeal of all gun control laws, the abolishment of the ATF, and the establishment of a national militia under the states. In 1992, Sherwood predicted that a "political war" with Satan and the New World Order would have to be fought, destroying the corrupt American system and giving rebirth to a new society led by Christian Patriots.

Sherwood outlined his ideas in two books: *The Guarantee of the Second Amendment* (1992) and *Establishing an Independent Militia in the United States* (1995). The USMA leader believed that militias should be established in every county to counteract the threat of federal deployment of the National Guard at the state level. Sherwood condemned the National Guard as the only office of government that took an oath to the president, making it more likely that "unconstitutional" gun laws would be enforced, leading to the feared NWO takeover. "That we now desert the Constitution," he wrote, "and swear all allegiance to the personality of the president is deplorable and reprehensible in the least, and probably traitorous in execution" (Sherwood, 1995: viii). Sherwood feared that the loyalty of the National Guard might devolve into a blind allegiance to unlawful orders, "as they did at Ruby Ridge." Expanding the threat attribution, he drew comparisons between National Guardsmen and Nazi soldiers, issuing this warning: "Our attitude as citizens must certainly be that any soldier at any level who executes an order of the president which is unconstitutional will be held to the same level of accountability as [were] the German soldiers who blindly followed Adolph Hitler" (Sherwood, 1995: viii).

Sherwood served primarily as an organizer for the movement. He worked feverishly to organize local activists and met with Patriots in counties across Idaho to build a grassroots movement. In April 1994, Sherwood delivered a fierce harangue against the federal government to a mass rally sponsored by Tom Stetson's Idaho Liberty Network in Coeur d'Alene. Though not an Identity adherent, Sherwood collaborated with Identity leader Stetson in the organization of the rally that the Coalition for Human Dignity (CHR) later described as a "Christian Patriot festival" that promoted citizen militias (Crawford, Gardiner, and Mozzochi, 1994). The CHR report also noted that Stetson was a member of Sherwood's USMA. Stetson, who attended the 1992 Estes Park meeting, wrote a piece promoting the rally in the March/April 1994 issue of the *Jubilee* that touted Sherwood as a featured speaker and described him as a "political writer."

On July 3, 1994, Sherwood addressed a crowd of approximately fifteen hundred people in Boise gathered for the Citizens Rally for Constitutional Rights to support the Second Amendment and oppose enforcement of the Brady Bill. After making a provocative speech, Sherwood manned a table under the banner "Idaho Militia Information," soliciting potential recruits, distributing antigovernment tracts and materials, and collecting fees from new members (Levitas, 2002: 308). By November 1994, Sherwood had organized militias in twelve Idaho counties with more than one thousand members. Sherwood also claimed to have USMA groups in ten other states and was working to form militias in another thirty-five states.

Sherwood emulated Larry Pratt's model of citizen militias as self-defense or "civil defense" units. He insisted, like Pratt, that militias were not organized for violence but rather to defend the Constitution and the freedom of citizens. In the Fall 1995 USMA newsletter, *Aide-de-Camp*, staff assistant Gabriel Taylor attributed the "revived interest in the militia concept" to a reawakening of Americans to "the basic concept of self-defense that has been the bedrock of our philosophy for over 350 years" (Hamilton, 1996: 100). The newsletter extolled the virtue of the "citizen soldier" in defending family, nation, and religion, a theme found throughout Pratt's writings. The USMA connection to Larry Pratt and the GOA was more than ephemeral. Pratt was the featured speaker at Sherwood's USMA meeting in Boise in March 1995, when Sherwood was quoted by media sources as stating, "Go up and look legislators in the face, because some day you may be forced to blow it off." Sherwood denied making the statement, and Pratt later told William Jasper, writing for the John Birch Society publication *The New American*, that Sherwood "never suggested or hinted at any violence" (Jasper, 1995: 3). But this disclaimer ignored the fact that both Pratt and Sherwood believed federal gun control laws to be unconstitutional, thus making any "defensive" action or resistance to enforcement potentially violent. Subsequent actions and statements by Sherwood belied his disavowal of violence.

Sherwood was willing to threaten violence when conflict with the federal government was believed to be warranted. In March 1995, after a federal judge in Idaho closed six national forests to protect endangered salmon, inciting angry ranchers, loggers, and miners, Sherwood urged a crowd to "get a semiautomatic assault rifle and a revolver and a uniform" because there might be "blood in the streets" if the ruling was upheld. "We want a bloodless revolution," he declared, "but if the bureaucrats won't listen, we'll give them a civil war to think about" (quoted in Levitas, 2002: 312).

Sherwood's view on defensive violence was entirely consistent with Pratt's. After passage of the Brady Bill, Pratt promoted the idea that local sheriffs and militias could resist federal gun control laws in his book *Safeguarding Liberty* (1995c). "Now that the Brady bill has become the law of the land," Pratt wrote (1995b: ix), "does that mean it has to be obeyed?" Pratt went on to note that numerous sheriffs in several states had refused to conduct background checks mandated by the Brady Law and lauded the efforts of the Lincoln County, Montana, militia "to lawfully support the sheriff in case the federal government might contemplate another Waco or Weaver-type massacre" (Pratt, 1995b: ix).

Northern Idaho, eastern Washington, and western Montana served as the center of early militia mobilization. At about the same time Sherwood's USMA was forming, John Trochman founded the Militia of Montana (MOM) with the help of his brother David and nephew Randy. John Trochman was one of the principal targets of the ATF operation that ensnared Randy Weaver, and the Trochman family held vigil at the police barricades during the Weaver standoff in 1992. Trochman and Weaver met at the Aryan Nations compound in the late 1980s. Following the Ruby Ridge incident, Trochman, who was cochair of Louis Beam's United Citizens for Justice (UCJ), used the mailing list and contacts from UCJ to initially build an organizational base for MOM (Stern, 1996: 41). Unlike Sherwood, Trochman was an Identity adherent, and he utilized the Identity network to promote formation of armed militias. Much like Sherwood, Trochman emphasized gun control as a primary threat around which militias should organize. According to an Anti-Defamation League report, "Initially at least, MOM organized among ardent opponents of the proposed Brady Bill and the 1994 Assault Weapons Ban. The potency of these issues helped the Trochmans attract impressive numbers to some of the group's earliest gatherings" (1996: 2). Similarly, Stern asserts that the Trochmans "used gun control as fuel to launch America's first active militia group" and "used Montana's anti–gun control sentiment to attract huge crowds to its meetings" (1996: 71–2).

MOM availed itself of Beam's UCJ mailing list to effectively create a Patriot communication network and disseminate one of the most widely read newsletters in the militia movement. Randy Trochman edited MOM's newsletter, *Taking Aim*, which increasingly expanded its focus on gun control to a wider conspiracy of the New World Order. The newsletter featured interviews and articles with other Patriot leaders and hawked videos such as Linda Thompson's *Waco: The Big Lie* and *Pestilence* by James Wickstrom. Thompson, who founded the Ohio Unorganized Militia, claimed in her video that the tanks that breached the walls of Mt. Carmel used flame throwers that ignited the firestorm that killed the Branch Davidians. Wickstrom, who assumed the title of National Director of Counter-Insurgency for the Posse Comitatus in the 1980s, asserted in his video that AIDS was a biological weapon released by agents of the New World Order to eliminate two billion people by the year 2000. MOM also developed a catalog offering caps, T-shirts, and fatigue jackets as well as a range of training manuals and books on militia preparedness, weapons breakdown, methods of resistance, and other revolutionary skills needed for the impending war. In one issue of *Taking Aim*, John Trochman declared that Ruby Ridge and Waco "provided ample evidence of the government's willingness to wage war against its own citizens who refuse to relinquish their weapons and constitutional freedoms" (Dees and Corcoran, 1996: 80).

Paul de Armond (1995) monitored MOM meetings for the Northwest Citizen Project (NCP), a progressive watchdog organization, in February 1995. He reported finding vendor tables full of videos; training manuals on guerrilla warfare, booby traps, hand-to-hand combat, sniper training, and small-arms defense against air attacks; several varieties of "pepper spray"; camouflage clothing; a "stun baton"; and a library of books promoting conspiracy theories, including one authored by John Trochman titled *Escape from Controlled Custody*. Trochman's book provided detailed instruction on how to break out of NWO concentration/detention camps that he claimed were being operated by FEMA. Stern (1996: 75) avers: "Of all the militia groups that formed across the United States in 1994 and 1995, Trochman's was not only the first significant organization, it was also the most active disseminator of militia propaganda around the country."

Between February and May 1994, John Trochman traveled across Montana and Washington, speaking to hundreds of potential recruits and issuing warnings about an invasion of UN troops in black helicopters and decrying the federal sieges at Ruby Ridge and Waco. In March, more than eight hundred people gathered in Kalispell, Montana, to hear Trochman speak about the growing militia movement. He told crowds of Patriots that American soldiers were being trained in preparation for an assault on civilians to facilitate the ascendant New World Order. A key part of the conspiracy, Trochman claimed, was the prevention or elimination of militias. "This federal government has rendered the several states defenseless by taking away their organized militia," he announced, "and is now in the process of disarming the unorganized militia – that's you and me – by laws which are unconstitutional. . . . A government which turns its tanks upon its own people for any reason is a government with a taste for blood. . . . We are on the brink of an invasion, surrender, annihilation . . . " (quoted in Levitas, 2002: 305).

MOM literature delineated the role of militias as one that would counterbalance the military power of the federal juggernaut to use force against the people. MOM's own manual provided a structure for the organization of militias based on the phantom cell system promoted by Louis Beam. The manual instructed militia members to restrict each cell size to only seven members, splitting and reproducing as growth occurred. Members were encouraged to keep communication between cells at a minimum to prevent "infiltration and subterfuge" by federal agents (Stern, 1996: 76).

In Texas, Jon Roland founded the Militia Correspondence Committee on the first anniversary of the April 19 federal assault on the Branch Davidians. In August 1994, Roland posted a communiqué on a Patriot Web site, titled "The Modern Citizen Militia Movement." Roland reported that militia units had been formed in ten Texas counties, "with more forming each week." Roland also declared that constitutional militias had been organized in fifteen states: Arizona, California, Colorado, Florida, Idaho, Indiana, Michigan, Montana, Nevada, New Mexico, Ohio, Oregon, Tennessee, Texas, and Utah. Most militias, he claimed, were "keeping a low profile" until they became established, while recruitment was occurring "through word of mouth and announcements on talk radio." "The main motivating factor for this recent upsurge of activity," Roland wrote, "has been the ill-conceived gun control provisions of the current Crime Bill. People everywhere see it not only as a major assault on their constitutional rights to keep and bear arms, but as a more sinister preparation for depriving them of their other constitutional rights after they have been disarmed" (Roland, 1994: 1).

Roland also posted a December 4, 1994, *Sunday Telegraph* news article written by right-wing journalist Ambrose Evans-Pritchard, entitled "Patriot games turn deadly." The newspaper reported the claim by militia leaders that "several thousand Texans" were actively participating. Militia members interviewed for the news story framed their intent as defensive, but in underlying Posse Comitatus terms: "The main purpose of the movement... is deterrence. Every time the government oversteps its authority it will have to consider the possibility of armed opposition. And if it tries another Waco, it will have a minor war on its hands." The news report also noted that numerous police, sheriffs, and reserve guardsmen were surreptitious members of the militias in Texas and Oklahoma, suggesting that any future enforcement actions like Waco would be problematic.

By fall 1994, recruitment and mobilization efforts had spawned militia groups in more than twenty states. In Colorado, militias formed in Boulder, Ft. Collins, Greeley, Lakewood, and Longmont (Hamilton, 1996: 38). In Missouri, militias organized in eleven counties. The 51st Militia named its group after the fifty-one-day standoff in Waco and called on Patriots to defend against a government raid on guns by stockpiling weapons (Hamilton, 1996: 39). Citizen militias in Missouri grew from 4 to 40 of the state's 114 counties during 1994–5 (Levitas, 2002: 306). State officials in California, Florida, and New York reported intensified militia activity and growth in their states, which forced their legislators to consider new laws prohibiting private militias.

In April 1994, the Michigan Militia was founded by gun dealer and Baptist minister Norman Olsen and Patriot activist Ray Southwell. The Michigan Militia quickly became the largest militia in the United States. The Michigan Militia claimed to have ten thousand members in sixty-three of the state's eighty-three counties by year's end (Levitas, 2002: 306). In 1995, Olsen warned that its leadership cadre could "muster more than a million soldiers in 24 hours who will help defend our country" (Olsen, 1997: 17). Though critics questioned these figures, the Southern Poverty Law Center's online *Intelligence Report* noted that the Michigan Militia could probably make a legitimate claim to as many as six thousand members.

Tim McVeigh and Terry Nichols attended one of the meetings of the Michigan Militia in 1994 near Nichols's farm in Decker. McVeigh was intrigued by the concept and even considered forming his own militia with Michael Fortier in Kingman, Arizona, in 1993. But McVeigh also thought some of the militia group meetings he attended were disorganized and unfocused, he told me in one interview. He wanted to find Patriots who were willing to sacrifice everything, to make a total commitment. "In wartime," he said, "you need soldiers who are not afraid to engage the enemy." McVeigh was interested only in recruiting like-minded warriors for the insurgency. He did not expend much time or energy in militia groups, for reasons I hope to make clear. He did however help militia members obtain illegal assault weapons through the gun show circuit after the 1994 ban.

The militia movement grew rapidly after its inception in early 1994. The Southern Poverty Law Center's Militia Task Force identified 441 armed militias in all fifty states by 1996. Berlet and Lyons (2002: 289) estimated a total membership in armed militias of between twenty thousand and sixty thousand. Other estimates, from both boastful militia leaders and intermittent news reports, ranged as high as a million, but these larger figures were clearly inflated. Some of the perplexity was due to definitional problems distinguishing militias and the much broader Patriot movement. While popular media often used the terms "militia" and "Patriot" interchangeably, most Patriots were not members of citizen militias. However, most, if not all, militia members were Patriots and most, if not all, possessed arms and opposed federal gun control.

In the months preceding the Oklahoma City bombing, incidents of insurgent violence among militia and Patriot groups began to mount. In January 1994, Patriot common-law adherents who were angered by the refusal of a California state official to vacate an IRS lien stabbed and sodomized the official with a gun. In August 1994, two members of the Minnesota Patriots Council were arrested for making the deadly toxin ricin, with the intent to poison federal argents (Southern Poverty Law Center, 1996). In September 1994, Timothy Thomas Coombs shot and killed a Missouri Highway Patrol officer in retaliation for the officer's role in the arrest of fellow Patriot and white supremacist Robert N. Joos, Jr. (Levitas, 2002: 306–7). In November 1994, a militia activist threatened a California Audubon Society official with a noose after the official testified in support of an environmental law (Southern Poverty Law Center, 1996). On March 3, 1995, Militia of Montana leader John Trochman and six others were arrested after allegedly carrying concealed weapons and intimidating officials at the Musselshell County, Montana, jail. Armed and carrying radio equipment and plastic handcuffs, the men were suspected of planning to kidnap a local judge whose rulings had enraged Patriots (Levitas, 2002: 305). In late March, Patriot insurgents launched an attack on U.S. Forest Service offices in Nevada. On March 29, a pipe bomb blew up a facility on the Forest Service campground near Elko. The next day, another bomb blew out windows and ripped a hole in the wall of the Forest Service office in Carson City. The following day, the Forest Service headquarters had to be evacuated after a receptionist received a bomb threat from a caller who reportedly said, "You're next" (Christenson, 1995). These incidents and others, however, were only a prelude to Oklahoma City.

Gun Show Subculture and McVeigh's Insurgent Consciousness

As the Violence Policy Center study cited earlier found, the gun rights subculture provided a vast recruiting network for nascent Patriots in the national gun show circuit. By 1995, there were roughly one hundred gun shows each weekend of the year, drawing an estimated five million people into the cultural sphere of Patriot influence and recruitment (Rand, 1996). The VPC study aptly called the gun show circuit a "gateway" into Patriot and militia groups. Indeed, evidence suggests that gun shows provided at least three important functions for Patriot movement mobilization and insurgency: (1) they furnished virtually unlimited supplies of high-powered weapons and ordnance that could be stockpiled for the burgeoning war with the state, (2) they afforded the movement a "natural recruiting environment" to build a membership base, and (3) they served as a safe conduit for phantom cells of insurgents to communicate with other cells.

In the wake of the 1986 McClure-Volkmer Act, the sales of weapons increased, along with growth in the number and size of gun shows. According to a Department of the Treasury report, *Commerce in Firearms in the United States*, annual firearms manufacturers' sales surged from about four million in 1987 to a peak of nearly eight million in 1993 (2000: 6). Secondhand or retail sales accounted for about two million additional firearm sales (Cook and Ludwig, 1996). Finally, a large but unknown volume of illegal firearm sales comprised a thriving commerce of contraband sold at gun shows. A 1993 General Accounting Office report conducted between November 1991 and January 1993 found that "large-scale theft and . . . stolen material was widely available at gun shows across the country. GAO personnel were able to purchase stolen military parts at gun shows in each of the six states visited, and at 13 of the 15 gun shows they visited. At almost every gun show, GAO staff also found 30-round M-16 magazine clips in government packaging. In five states, GAO personnel were able to purchase all of the parts necessary to convert a semiautomatic AR-15 assault rifle into a fully automatic M-16 machine gun" (U.S. Government Accounting Office, 1993: 18–19). The GAO report noted that the value

175

of these stolen parts (for example, automatic sear, hammer, trigger, bolt carrier) more than doubled at gun shows, making such transactions very lucrative for the sellers. As news spread of the assault weapons ban contained in the 1994 Crime Control Bill, the market value of military-style rifles and parts soared even higher within the gun show circuit, and Patriots and gun rights activists rushed to purchase and stockpile the weapons, an opportunity David Koresh and the Branch Davidians also attempted to exploit. Taken together, the sales and transfer of weapons, stolen gun parts, and military hardware at gun shows turned the circuit into a major supplier to the Patriot insurgency.

The extent to which Timothy McVeigh's insurgent consciousness flourished in this gun show circuit has not been fully appreciated. Following the April 19 disaster in Waco, McVeigh immersed himself in the gun rights network and culture. McVeigh attended more than eighty gun shows in forty states over a two-year period, between the federal assault on the Branch Davidians and the April 19 bombing in Oklahoma City. McVeigh journeyed from gun show to gun show, buying and selling books, distributing antigovernment literature and bumper stickers, and sharing fears of disarmament and the New World Order. He also fronted for militia and Patriot groups as an independent buyer/collector.

As the 1994 Crime Control law loomed, McVeigh began acting as a "straw buyer," purchasing military-type assault weapons for militia members and Patriots who wanted to circumvent federal tracking and record-keeping. According to the Violence Policy Center study, "Straw purchases occur when a person who is not in a restricted category (the 'straw man') purchases a weapon for someone who is prohibited by federal, state, or local law from purchasing or possessing a firearm. Straw men are used by criminals, minors or others in proscribed categories to transact sales with both Federal Firearms License holders and unlicensed hobbyists. In some cases the seller does not know that the weapon is being passed on to an illegal buyer, but in others the seller is aware of the straw sale" (1996: 4). McVeigh was nonplussed by the government forms and paperwork required of buyers, making straw purchases and selling weapons to other Patriots. "Most people didn't want their names on government forms," he said. "They were paranoid. So I bought the guns in my name and sold them for a fee of like twenty dollars in a private sale." He also took satisfaction in defying federal gun laws after the 1994 Crime Control bill took effect, making purchases and sales of guns that were banned. The kind of defiance exhibited by McVeigh was not uncommon in the political environment of gun shows.

176

The gun show circuit cultivated an atmosphere in which federal restrictions on weapon sales were challenged or ignored.

By the time of McVeigh's sojourn through the gun show circuit, the Patriot movement had thoroughly penetrated the gun rights network. Exhibitor's tables at the gun shows were lined with pamphlets, fliers, videos, audiotapes, books, and other materials featuring the Patriot framing of warfare with the state. A sampling of titles commonly found at gun shows reveals the promotion of warfare in the gun show circuit:

The Art of War
A Call to Arms, Battle Preparations Now
Citizen Soldier
Equipping for the New World Order
Field Manual of the Free Militia
Guerrilla Warfare
Improvised Weapons of the American Underground
Militiaman's Handbook
Operation Vampire Killer 2000
Sniper Training and Employment
To Break a Tyrant's Chains: Neo-Guerrilla Techniques for Combat
Toward a Police State?
The Ultimate Sniper
Unconventional Warfare Devices and Techniques
Vigilante Handbook

The gun show network was seeded with revolutionary ideas, reaching its climax as a cultural refuge and incubator for Patriot warrior identity and socialization coinciding with McVeigh's pilgrimage. McVeigh embraced the Patriot warrior identity with uncommon conviction. Though he hailed from a conventional social background, was something of an idealist, and achieved the status of a decorated Gulf War veteran, McVeigh's growing disillusionment with the military, federal government, and new gun control laws contributed to a self-perception of outsiderness.

The Patriot identity construction appealed to McVeigh as both a veteran and an outsider in ways that Gibson's (1994) analysis of "New War heroes" in American paramilitary culture has captured well. Gibson argued that many traditional American males were culturally dislodged by social change in the post–Vietnam War era, making them uncertain of their identity. This threat to traditional male identity helped foster an emergent paramilitary culture that saw men developing fundamental narratives about an empowered

177

warrior role, one that involved "reinterpretations or reworkings of archaic warrior myths" where heroic warriors rescued the sacred order (1994: 11). These narratives, Gibson asserted, were essentially "ways of arguing about what is wrong with the modern world and what needs to be done to make society well again" (1994: 12). In the modern world, Gibson argued, the enemy is perceived as the "New Order," defined as a "world without law or individuals rights" (1994: 70). "There are neither rules nor rituals to give the world rhythm and meaning. Instead there is only the will and desire of the leader(s).... The New Order that the evil ones so fervently desire is both a form of social organization and a continuation of chaos" (Gibson, 1994: 70).

For years, the abstract evil embodied in the "New Order" enabled far-right leaders to locate the enemy in many different individuals, groups, events, and actions, accounting for the far-ranging attributions of conspiratorial threat. But Patriot movement entrepreneurs attempted to effectively rework and recode the various attributional orientations and culpable agents, in order to construct a unified frame that designated the state as the principal enemy. In the Patriot construction of reality, those who resisted the state's disarmament campaign fought a sacred war to preserve a mythical culture and heritage; they were the true heroic warriors. This framing of the conflict resonated powerfully with McVeigh.

By September 13, 1994, when the assault weapons ban became law, McVeigh believed the state disarmament campaign was in high gear. It was at this juncture that McVeigh said he was catalyzed and, as he later told his sister Jennifer, he decided to move from the "propaganda stage" to the "action stage." McVeigh later confirmed this transformative moment of insurgent consciousness with Michel and Herbeck (2001: 159–61). McVeigh wrote Michael Fortier around this time to enlist his help in an unspecified plan to commit a major act of violence against the government. A few weeks later, McVeigh revealed to Fortier his intention to bomb a federal building. Fortier initially expressed reluctance, though he later capitulated, going so far as agreeing to sell stolen guns to help fund the bombing plan. By the end of September, McVeigh and Nichols were purchasing large quantities of fertilizer for the purpose of constructing a bomb.

McVeigh's insurgent activities related to the Oklahoma City bombing originated around mid-September. Court records from the federal trial reveal that on September 12, 1994, McVeigh checked into a hotel in Vian, Oklahoma, roughly twenty minutes west of the Christian Identity compound Elohim City in Muldrow. Kerry Noble, the former Identity and

CSA leader who authored the four-page "War in '84" declaration, suggests that McVeigh went to Elohim City the following day, September 13, to "take part in military maneuvers that [security director] Andi Strassmeir organized for some seventy participants. It was at this time the initial conspiracy to bomb the federal building was hatched" (Noble, 1998: 212). Noble doesn't cite his source for this information, but the source was, in fact, J. D. Cash, a consultant and investigator hired by McVeigh's defense team who had covered Elohim City for years as a reporter for the *McCurtain Gazette*, a small newspaper in Idabel, Oklahoma.

Noble was part of the CSA–Elohim City contingent, along with James Ellison and Richard Wayne Snell, that devised the original plan to bomb the Murrah Federal Building in 1983. Ellison and Snell first cased the Murrah Building in November 1983 (Noble 1998: 134). The plan was derailed by the federal siege of the CSA compound in 1985, but the legacy of the planned bombing and the insurgent acts of these "silent warriors" from the CSA and Elohim City remained a powerful symbol of resistance among nascent Patriots. Noble disclosed the continuing residual ties between CSA and Elohim City in the wake of the 1985 federal siege. CSA members who were not indicted or convicted migrated to Elohim City. Convicted CSA leaders Ellison and Snell remained strongly connected to Elohim City and its leader, Robert Millar, who served as Snell's personal minister throughout the time he was awaiting execution in Arkansas. Following the execution – which occurred on April 19, 1995, the day of the Oklahoma City bombing – Snell's body was claimed by Millar and taken to Elohim City, where it was buried and memorialized. James Ellison cooperated with federal authorities in the 1988 Ft. Smith, Arkansas, sedition trial in exchange for a reduced sentence. Upon release from federal prison in April 1995, Ellison promptly moved to Elohim City and married one of Robert Millar's granddaughters. Noble stressed the ritual meaning of the marriage: "The fusion of Ellison's blood and seed into Millar's" signified a "covenant" between them (Noble, 1998: 219).

Noble argues that the targeting of the Murrah Building for bombing derived from McVeigh's association with a CSA remnant at Elohim City. McVeigh's introduction to Elohim City came through a Tulsa gun show where he met its security chief Andreas Strassmeir in early April 1993, coinciding with the government standoff with the Branch Davidians. The two Patriots discussed Waco and federal gun control. Strassmeir invited McVeigh to visit him at Elohim City and gave him a business card (see Hamm, 2002: 117). That McVeigh traveled to Elohim City to see Strassmeir on at least two occasions is not surprising. As prosecutors pointed out in the federal trial, McVeigh was ticketed for failing to signal during a lane change less than four miles from the property line at Elohim City on October 12, 1993, on County Road 220, roughly six months after the Tulsa gun show meeting. Noble provides an important footnote to the incident; County Road 220 is "the only access road to the compound" (1998: 211). Eight days later, on October 20, McVeigh wrote in a letter to his sister Jennifer that he had found "a network of friends" he could rely on in case of trouble. The second known visit by McVeigh to Elohim City occurred approximately eleven months later, on September 13, 1994, the day the assault weapons ban took effect and the day, McVeigh told me and others, that he was catalyzed into insurgency. The confluence of events on September 13 readily explains McVeigh's activities after this date.

McVeigh's connection to Elohim City has been described by others (Cash, 2004a, 2004b; Hamm, 1997, 2002; Jones and Israel, 1998; Noble, 1998; Solomon, 2003a, 2003b) and confirmed by an ATF undercover operation a little more than a year after the Waco debacle. McVeigh was identified by ATF undercover informant Carol Howe, who said she saw McVeigh with Strassmeir in the months before the Oklahoma City bombing. Howe began working as a paid ATF informant in August 1994. She gained access to Elohim City through a relationship with Dennis Mahon, the Tulsa-based White Aryan Resistance (WAR) leader. As early as November 1994, Howe warned her superiors in the Tulsa ATF office that three residents of Elohim City were surveying federal buildings for the purpose of a bombing. She identified one of the visitors to Elohim City during this time as "Tim Tuttle," an alias that McVeigh was known to have used. Howe filed more than seventy reports with her supervising agent, Angela Finley, detailing efforts by Strassmeir to obtain black market explosives, grenades, and other contraband. Howe's reports also included a warning about Strassmeir's cell, "the Aryan Republican Army underground," which she said was planning to blow up a federal building. The target date was set at April 19, 1995, and Howe told ATF agent Finley that the Aryan Republican Army had narrowed the list to federal buildings in Tulsa and Oklahoma City (Hamm 2002: 238; Jones and Israel, 1998: 191–2).

The upshot of this evidence is that McVeigh became part of a larger effort by Patriot actors to carry out the bombing, and the base of operations was Elohim City. To be sure, McVeigh vehemently denied this connection. But McVeigh had ample motive to protect fellow Patriots involved in the insurgency while solemnizing his own status in the movement as a martyr. Indeed,

McVeigh was given a polygraph test by his own attorneys to assess the verity of this denial. The polygraph examiner found that McVeigh was being truthful when describing his own involvement in the bombing but exhibited evasiveness when asked about the involvement of others (see Hamm, 2002: 24; Michel and Herbeck, 2001: 296). More importantly, there is extensive evidence to suggest the involvement of others through phantom cells in which communication, though minimal, was made under the cover of the gun show circuit. McVeigh's odyssey through the gun show circuit following the Waco disaster obscured the mode of intercourse with other actors in the insurgency. In the phantom cell model of organization promoted by Louis Beam and other Patriot movement leaders, the logistics of communication were left to the enterprising efforts of the cell members. Patriots were only advised to reduce communication and employ indirect contacts if possible. The gun shows furnished an ideal conduit for infrequent contact, essentially minimizing the risk of infiltration by federal agents. McVeigh steered away from militia meetings and avoided formal affiliations with such groups for this reason. The bane of the movement was always its vulnerability to infiltration by federal agents. Beam's diatribe contained in the "Leaderless Resistance" manifesto makes this point powerfully. Veteran Patriot leaders learned from the mistakes of earlier groups by promoting silent cells and avoiding public meetings and associations.

Configuring the Insurgent Network in the Oklahoma City Bombing

The insurgent plan to bomb the Murrah Building was developed on September 13, 1994, at Elohim City and carried out by at least two phantom cells. McVeigh recruited Terry Nichols and a reluctant Michael Fortier to the cell that would construct and detonate the bomb. Within ten days of the Elohim City meeting, on September 22, McVeigh and Nichols were renting a storage shed from Mini Storage in Herington, Kansas, to store bomb-related materials. The following week, on September 30, they purchased one ton of ammonium nitrate from Mid-Kansas Co-op. Three days later, on October 2, they broke into a munitions magazine at the Hamm Rock Quarry in Marion, Kansas, and stole four cases of electric blasting caps, a partial case of Primadet, and 175 emulsion mix sticks, or Tovex "sausages," used to detonate the bomb. By October 4, McVeigh and Nichols were in Kingman, Arizona, renting another storage locker near Fortier's home and recruiting Michael Fortier to the cause. According to Lori Fortier's testimony in the Denver trial, she said McVeigh told her on October 6 that he had already decided on the Murrah Federal Building in Oklahoma City as the target for the bombing.

A second (and possibly third) cell functioned to finance the insurgency through bank robberies. Adopting the pattern of The Order in the War in '84, the Aryan Republican Army (ARA) launched a series of twenty-two bank robberies to fund the insurgency. ARA leader Peter Langan – who was ordained an Identity minister at Richard Butler's Aryan Nations compound in August 1992 and was a self-described "Aryan Warrior" – vowed to work for the revolution in the mold of Robert Mathews (Hamm, 2002: 134). Hamm's analysis of the Aryan Republican Army provides the most system-atic and compelling case to date linking the bank robberies to McVeigh and the Oklahoma City bombing. Hamm introduces new data based on inter-views with convicted ARA leader Peter Langan and a handwritten journal left behind by ARA member Richard Guthrie after his suicide that chroni-cled the gang's activities. Several key members of the ARA lived or resided at Elohim City in the months leading up to the bombing, including Mark Thomas, Kevin McCarthy, Scott Stedeford, and Michael Brescia. Brescia was Strassmeir's roommate at the compound and the man whose face bears a strong resemblance to the sketch of John Doe 2 given to federal author-ities by an eyewitness who rented the Ryder truck to McVeigh in Kansas. Hamm marshals an extensive body of supportive evidence to establish the complicity of the ARA. The new material supplied by Hamm is part of a larger cache of information emerging recently about the ARA link to the bombing.

Support for a Patriot network of insurgent involvement in the Oklahoma City bombing has been strengthened in recent years by new information from at least four major sources. In addition to Hamm's (2002) investigation of the ARA, the Oklahoma Bombing Investigation Committee (OBIC), an independent commission formed by Oklahoma congressman Charles Key, published in 2001 its *Final Report on the Bombing of the Alfred P. Murrah Federal Building April 19, 1995*. The 555-page report compiled a rich com-pendium of documents pertinent to the bombing, including court records and filings, trial testimony, sworn affidavits, independent reports, materi-als related to the Oklahoma grand jury proceedings, and more than eighty eyewitness accounts of John Doe 2, most of which never were made part of the official public record. The government's claim in the Denver trial that McVeigh and Nichols acted alone in the bombing is sharply contradicted by these accounts.

The third major source of new information arose with a 2003 Associated Press (AP) investigation that made several disturbing discoveries about federal intelligence failures prior to the bombing. The AP investigation likened the government miscues to "the intelligence failures before the Sept. 11 attacks" (Solomon, 2003a: 3A). Documents corroborating the prebombing intelligence gathered by the FBI and ATF on insurgents at Elohim City furnished significant new details in its February 12th report. It found that FBI officials in Washington were so concerned about the intentions and activities of white supremacists at Elohim City that a month *before* the bombing they questioned former CSA leader Kerry Noble, whom they knew "was familiar with an earlier plot to bomb the same Alfred P. Murrah federal building McVeigh selected" (Solomon, 2003: 3A). The government also had intelligence "suggesting that compound members had detonated a 500-pound fertilizer bomb like the one McVeigh would use and had visited Oklahoma City several times" (Solomon, 2003a: 3A). The AP investigation confirmed ATF informant Carol Howe's advanced warning to the bureau and linked it to the cancellation of a planned raid on Elohim City two months prior to the bombing. Apparently, the cancellation of the raid occurred because ATF and FBI supervisory personnel became aware for the first time that each of the agencies had an informant inside Elohim City. The AP story concluded with the unsettling observation that "[n]either law enforcement agency passed on any information or concerns to the agency that managed the federal building in Oklahoma City" (p. 3A).

A second AP story, on February 13, made further disturbing discoveries: It revealed that the FBI had evidence connecting McVeigh to the ARA bank robbers based on multiple sources, including informant reports, phone records, prisoner interviews, and even a surveillance video of an Ohio bank robbery that the FBI thought captured a picture of McVeigh. After the FBI lab found the match of McVeigh to the video to be "inconclusive," FBI investigators and prosecutors ordered the evidence destroyed, despite the fact that McVeigh and Peter Langan had legal appeals pending (Solomon, 2003b). Dan Defenbaugh, the FBI agent in charge of the Oklahoma City investigation, told the AP he was unaware of the memo ordering the destruction of the video. "Normally, all evidence is held until the completion of all appeals," Defenbaugh said (Solomon, 2003b: 1). Defenbaugh also said he was surprised to learn that federal prosecutors in the Oklahoma City bombing case in1996 made and then withdrew a plea bargain offer to Langan. Langan's attorney claimed that his client had critically important information on the bombing case. The link to the ARA was further supported by documents obtained by the AP that included an FBI teletype revealing that ARA members were familiar with explosives and had made a videotape vowing a war against the government. The teletype document also noted that two ARA members left Elohim City on April 16 for a location in Kansas near where McVeigh and Nichols had assembled the bomb.

The fourth source of new information was set into motion in pretrial filings by defense attorneys for Terry Nichols in preparation for the state trial in 2003. State prosecutors in Oklahoma sought the death penalty for Nichols by filing murder charges against him in state court (Nichols received a life sentence in the federal trial). In the discovery process, and with the renewed interest by news agencies and organizations, new documents surfaced revealing more support for the insurgent network. In January 2004, a declassified FBI memo revealed that the Southern Poverty Law Center was gathering intelligence on persons at Elohim City for the FBI in the months before the bombing (Cash, 2004a: 1). Though the memo was heavily redacted, it documented that the FBI was investigating individuals believed to be involved in two cases: the Oklahoma City bombing (OKBOMB) and the ARA bank robberies (BOMBROB). Neither Morris Dees of the SPLC nor the FBI would discuss the details of the memo for the news story. But two years before this story broke, Hamm (2002: 191) stated that Dees "has gone on record saying that his sources inside Elohim City claim McVeigh visited the religious community more than a dozen times prior to the bombing." Hamm said Dees told him personally in 1999 that "McVeigh was there [Elohim City] on numerous occasions" (2002: 191).

On February 25, 2004, in the wake of these and other published intelligence failures, the FBI ordered a formal review of the 1995 Oklahoma City bombing investigation, reopening the inquiry into the connection between McVeigh and the network of Patriot insurgents at Elohim City. As of this writing, the investigation is still under way. On March 20, approximately one month after the FBI announced it was reopening the case, ARA leader Peter Langan revealed in a news interview from prison that Arkansas gun dealer Roger Moore was robbed by Richard Guthrie, not by Nichols, as government prosecutors had contended. Langan said his claim was supported by evidence seized in Guthrie's arrest: the distinctive "pistol-grip shotgun" used in the Moore robbery (Cash, 2004b). Some of the FBI documents uncovered in the AP investigation also showed that at the time of the capture and arrest of the ARA, Richard Guthrie possessed a driver's license belonging to Roger Moore ("FBI to look into possibility of more McVeigh helpers," *Houston Chronicle*, Feb. 28, 2004).

It is noteworthy that in the light of this new evidence revealed in the state trial of Nichols in Oklahoma in 2004, the jury declined to find him guilty of murder. Instead, the jury convicted Nichols of the lesser charge of conspiracy, apparently persuaded by the evidence and arguments by defense attorneys that other conspirators were involved. After the trial ended, the jury foreman said, "The government dropped the ball. I think there are other people out there" (National Public Radio transcript, May 7, 2004).

Space does not permit a detailed recounting of all the evidence that has emerged recently to link McVeigh to the network of insurgents in the Oklahoma City bombing. Such an endeavor would require another book. Rather, my intention here is to establish the viability of the network thesis and then outline how the gun show circuit contributed to the inception and execution of the insurgency. I contend that the gun show circuit became a conduit for the formulation of the bombing and provided a cover for the communication between the cells of insurgents.

As stated previously, McVeigh's first contact with Elohim City came through Andreas Strassmeir at a Tulsa gun show in April 1993. The VPC study's assertion that gun shows served as a "gateway" to Patriot culture assumes added meaning in this context: It explicitly functioned as a gateway to the insurgency in Oklahoma City. Strassmeir invited McVeigh to Elohim City, and six months later McVeigh visited the Identity compound, where two ARA members, Kevin McCarthy and Michael Brescia, were residing. Two other ARA members, Peter Langan and Richard Guthrie, were only a short distance away, in Fayetteville, Arkansas. In Guthrie's memoirs, he alleges that he and Langan could have stayed at Elohim City that same night if they had chosen; it's likely that they were at the compound the following day. McVeigh may have already known some ARA members. Langan told Hamm in an interview that "Guthrie knew McVeigh. Guthrie met him *through the gun shows* (2002: 145; emphasis mine).

Well before the bombing plan was formulated, the principal social actors in the insurgency were in contact, expressing shared grievances and laying the groundwork for future action through the gun show network. In February 1994, Richard Guthrie met Arkansas gun dealer Roger Moore – whom he would later rob – at a gun show somewhere on the Southern circuit. McVeigh also met and befriended Moore at a Florida gun show a year earlier and then reconnected with Moore and his companion, Karen Anderson, at a gun show in Las Vegas six months later. McVeigh and Moore would subsequently have a falling out, which explains why Moore became a target of the robbery (see Michel and Herbeck, 2001: 170). The stolen weapons from Moore's Arkansas ranch were sold at gun shows to help finance the bombing. In the spring of 1994, the ARA began to develop a plan to rob banks as a form of political crime. Concomitantly, McVeigh was starting to "hear persistent rumors of impending federal raids on the homes of gun owners" on the gun show circuit (Michel and Herbeck, 2001: 152). On parallel paths, the two parties hardened their resolve to make war against the state.

In August 1994, Langan and company retreated to the safe house in Kansas and made a series of tapes called *Notes from the Underground*. Among other things, the tapes tallied the successful bank robberies the group had engineered and recommended a strategy of action for Patriot insurgency. In the recording, Langan called for an armed struggle against the government and the formation of the Aryan Republican Army under the leadership of Commander Pedro, a pseudonym taken by Langan. "The ARA's intention is to carry on with the Second Revolution that Bob Mathews started when he organized the Order in 1982," Langan declared (quoted in Hamm, 2002: 153–4). Copies of the tape were disseminated to Identity and Patriot leaders throughout the country. Many of these activists would convene in Elohim City the following month to formulate the Oklahoma City bombing plan.

In response to the call to arms by the ARA, a contingent of approximately seventy Patriot activists gathered at Elohim City on September 13, the day the assault weapons ban became law. The plan to bomb the federal building in Oklahoma City was born here. As I argued in the opening chapter, the plan was flush with Patriot meaning and signification. It resurrected a 1983 plot developed by the CSA by selecting the same federal building as its target and choosing a date that not only commemorated the ten-year anniversary of the federal raid on the CSA compound in 1985 and the two-year anniversary of the deadly federal assault on the Branch Davidians in 1993, but honored the execution date of former CSA and Elohim City resident and martyr Richard Wayne Snell, one of the original engineers of the Murrah Building bombing plan in 1983. It also called for a method that copied the blueprint of the fertilizer bomb described in *The Turner Diaries*: The bomb was constructed of ammonium nitrate and nitromethane fuel poured into fifty-five-gallon drums and loaded onto the back of a rental truck. The timing of the explosion of the federal building in Oklahoma City was planned to mirror the exact time of the eruption in *The Turner Diaries*. The rationale of the insurgent action by the Patriot cells also drew on the same rationale as Earl Turner's cell: the perceived threat of state disarmament. Indeed, as I will explain shortly, threat of an impending federal raid on Elohim City in the spring of 1995, just months before the bombing, heightened fears of the insurgents even more.

After the bombing plan was devised at Elohim City in September 1994, the silent-warrior cells sought to avoid or reduce contact and avert detection that would implicate the other group. But their paths did intersect several times in the months leading up to the bombing. On October 21, 1994, Langan and Guthrie attended a Tulsa gun show. Though McVeigh was not at this gun show, a third party with full knowledge of the bombing, Andreas Strassmeir, did attend (Hamm, 2002: 162). Strassmeir organized the September 13th conclave at Elohim City, where the bombing plan originated. If anyone could have been entrusted with passing along information to or from McVeigh, it was Strassmeir. This mode of communication comports perfectly with the phantom-cell strategy delineated by Beam.

The purpose of the Tulsa gun show contact may have been to arrange for the transfer of money from ARA bank robberies to McVeigh. A few weeks later, around November 7, 1994, McVeigh returned home to Pendleton, New York, to help settle the estate of his grandfather. During this visit, he told his sister Jennifer that he helped plan a bank robbery. According to a sworn statement made to the FBI on May 2, 1995, Jennifer said her brother had an undetermined quantity of money from a bank robbery and asked her to launder one-hundred-dollar bills (*Final Report on the Bombing of the Alfred P. Murrah Federal Building*, 2001: 306). She deposited some of the money in her bank account and gave McVeigh an equivalent amount in smaller bills.

A second intersection involving the two cells was more direct. On December 11, 1994, ARA members Langan, Kevin McCarthy, and Scott Stedeford arrived in Overland Park, Kansas, less than twenty-four hours after robbing the Middleburg Heights Bank in Cleveland, Ohio. Court records show that McCarthy and Stedeford attended the Overland Park gun show on that day. These records also show that McVeigh attended that gun show on the same day (Hamm. 2002: 178). That McVeigh and two ARA cell members were at the same gun show on the same day only four months before the Oklahoma City bombing without making contact is improbable. Kevin McCarthy was living at Elohim City, where the bombing plan originated and where McVeigh visited just three months earlier. McVeigh and McCarthy were acquainted with each other and were key actors in the Oklahoma City bombing plan. Stolen money from the Ohio bank robbery was likely passed on to McVeigh. The gun show provided an effective cover for one of the few direct contacts before the April 19 bombing.

A third intersection occurred in Arizona in February 1995. This brief episode was the only time the ARA – also known to law enforcement and the public as the "Midwest bank robbers" – ever left the Midwest or Mid-south region in the seven months between the birth and denouement of the bombing plan. In late January, McVeigh left Kansas for Arizona, checking into the Belle Art Center in Kingman on January 31. McVeigh told the motel desk clerk that he was "waiting on a package of money to be delivered" (Hamm, 2002: 197). ARA members Langan, Guthrie, McCarthy, and Stedeford also left Kansas around February 1 for Arizona, but there is no record of their whereabouts for much of a two- to three-week period. Guthrie told the FBI they were camping out in the Arizona wilderness. The manager of the Belle Art later testified that McVeigh began receiving visitors to his room around February 3, visitors who were very loud and boisterous, slinging beer cans and blasting rock music. Hamm (2002: 197) suggests that the two cells met in Kingman at McVeigh's motel room during this time. After several warnings about the noise, McVeigh was asked to leave the motel on February 8. There is no record of McVeigh's whereabouts for four days following this incident and no record of the ARA during the same time. Both surfaced on February 12: McVeigh checked into the Hill Top Motel in Kingman, while the ARA checked into a motel in Apache Junction, a suburb of Phoenix. Over the next three days, a number of phone calls were made from McVeigh's room. McVeigh claimed he was trying to reach a gun dealer in an attempt to arrange for sales tables at late-February gun shows in Tucson, Arizona, and St. George, Utah. The ARA checked out of the motel in Apache Junction on February 13, leaving only a scant record of their whereabouts for the next week. Federal prosecutors argued that McVeigh was building and testing a bomb in the Arizona desert. But McVeigh claimed he was making preparations for upcoming gun shows and retrieving guns from a storage locker in Kingman. Guthrie, a former Navy Seal with munitions training, may have been helping McVeigh build and test the bomb, for McVeigh had no munitions training. In any case, McVeigh again employed the cover of gun shows to obscure insurgent activity. Having established a continual presence on the gun show circuit in the preceding twenty-two months and still needing to sell the remainder of the guns stolen from Moore's collection, McVeigh was able to effectively disguise cell contact.

There is no evidence of contact between the cells again until a few weeks before the bombing. However, the insurgents had increased motivation to avoid contact: The ATF was planning a raid on Elohim City in March 1995. Documents obtained in the 2003 Associated Press investigation showed that the FBI agent in charge in Oklahoma at the time, Bob Ricks, cancelled the planned raid after learning that both agencies had undercover informants at Elohim City. Ricks, who was an FBI spokesman during the Branch Davidian standoff in Waco, explained his reason for canceling the federal raid in this way: "I do remember I told them I didn't want another Waco on our hands" (Solomon, 2003a: 3A). In the most peculiar of ironies, it appears that the federal impulse to avoid "another Waco" inadvertently facilitated the tragedy at Oklahoma City.

Rumors of a new round of federal gun raids had been circulating among militia, Patriot, and gun rights groups for months during the spring of 1995. The Elohim City residents were especially alarmed about the possibility of a federal raid. Strassmeir began monitoring police scanners and posting guards around the perimeter of the compound. Elohim City's founder Robert Millar complained to the local sheriff about increased overflights by helicopters. Millar's sermons assumed a more apocalyptic tone, and he warned his followers that Elohim City could become the next Waco (Hamm, 2002: 189). Aware of the rumored impending raid, the phantom cells of insurgents took extra precautions to avoid contact.

Two weeks before the bombing, on April 5, McVeigh called Elohim City and asked for Strassmeir. He was unavailable, so McVeigh left a message: "Tell Andy I'll be coming through." McVeigh could have asked to speak to ARA cell members McCarthy, Stedeford, or Brescia, who were all staying in Elohim City at this time. McVeigh likely thought direct contact with the cell was an unnecessary risk; Strassmeir was an efficient third-party channel. McVeigh left Arizona some time between April 11 and 13. Federal prosecutors argued that McVeigh left Arizona on April 13 and arrived in Junction City, Kansas, on the morning of April 14 and called Nichols from a pay phone. But this account ignores McVeigh's call to Strassmeir to say he was "coming through." Because there was no record of McVeigh's whereabouts for several days, it is possible that he went to Elohim City one last time en route to Kansas. By now, McVeigh knew Fortier had backed out of the bombing plan and Nichols was threatening to do the same. The visit to Elohim City could have been to enlist the aid of ARA members in the delivery of the bomb.

From this point forward, the bombing plan necessitated that the cells work together directly to build and deliver the bomb to its target. The active and direct participation of the two (or three) cells explains why hundreds of people in Oklahoma and Kansas saw John Doe 2 but gave different descriptions of the suspect. Two hundred and twenty-six witnesses testified in an Oklahoma grand jury proceeding that they saw McVeigh with John Doe 2, and more than eighty of these accounts are documented in the Oklahoma Bombing Investigation Committee's final report (2001: 147–69). The perpetual confusion surrounding John Doe 2 has rested on the assumption that there was only one unidentified coconspirator. The multiple sightings and descriptions of John Doe 2 are readily explained when one considers that there was a network of insurgents. Evidence suggests that there were as many as ten persons involved in the assembly and delivery of the bomb. When some of the eyewitnesses to John Doe 2 were finally allowed to testify in Nichols's state trial, they proved to be very convincing, as the jury verdict attests. FBI agents who worked on both the Oklahoma City bombing and the bank robbery cases have gone on record saying that they strongly suspected a link between the two but were stalled when ARA members produced alibis showing that they left Oklahoma three days before the bombing. However, in 2004 "[t]hat alibi . . . was contradicted by information Langan offered prosecutors and by car sales records showing the bank robbers were still in the Oklahoma area after they claimed to have left" (Solomon, 2004a). The FBI's own records showed that (1) Elohim City insurgents discussed alibis for April 19 prior to the bombing and (2) ARA members purchased a used truck on April 17, 1995, on the Oklahoma-Arkansas border and then returned to Elohim City. Langan said that the alibi claimed by ARA members was fabricated: "They didn't return to the [safe] house in Kansas until the morning of April 20," the day after the bombing, he said (Solomon, 2004a).

When Mark Thomas was indicted in January 1997 for bank robbery, he told reporters that at least one ARA member was involved in the bombing (Solomon, 2004). Thomas's ex-girlfriend, Donna Marazoff, told the FBI that shortly before Thomas traveled to Elohim City in the spring of 1995 he said that a federal building was going to be bombed. In a sworn statement to the FBI, dated April 3, 1997, she said Thomas made the following statement to her: "We are going to get them. We are going to hit one of their buildings during the middle of the day. It's going to be a federal building" (Federal Bureau of Investigation, 1997: 1).

Even the stoic and unapologetic McVeigh left a tantalizing clue behind before his execution in Terre Haute in 2001. A fellow death row inmate, David Paul Hammer, befriended McVeigh and claimed to have kept notes of conversations with the convicted bomber while awaiting execution. Hammer said McVeigh told him about the bank robbers. "He knew they were involved because he said he planned it with them," Hammer explained. "He said they were part of what he called his security detail" (Solomon, 2004a).

A Final Comment about the Insurgency in Oklahoma

In the final analysis, McVeigh was part of a Patriot insurgency that was rooted in a stream of contention by far-right challengers that developed over time. This stream of contention featured an episode or cycle of protest by an earlier cohort of Patriots – Willam Potter Gale, Richard Butler, Robert Mathews, James Ellison, and others – wherein the distinctive "war-fare" frame associated with the burgeoning Patriot movement was first constructed. The ensuing trajectory of contention was shaped by a recursive and escalating state-movement dynamic of threat attribution framed as warfare. The trajectory of contention took the form of a threat/opportunity spiral as state efforts to combat perceived threats to its interests generated yet another round of threat (and opportunity) attribution by Patriots, which in turn came to be defined as a threat by state actors, and so on.

McVeigh's motives and actions must be understood in the context of this stream of contention. Patriot identity and beliefs, the network of organizations and leaders, and their socially constructed history were part and parcel of a received culture and narrative that McVeigh encountered and adopted. None of the ideas or strategies in the Oklahoma bombing were original to McVeigh. He was a social actor in a drama of insurgency with a role to play from a script already written and directed by others. What gave this drama meaning was its triumphant reenactment of a plot that was foiled in the first episode. The insurgent motive and act were deeply rooted in the freighted meanings and collective memory of the Patriot community.

McVeigh's myopic devotion to the Patriot warfare frame blinded him to the misguided expropriation of the Branch Davidian tragedy for narrow political interest. The Branch Davidian victims and survivors whom I interviewed were horrified by the bombing in Oklahoma City and took great pains to distance their plight from McVeigh's putative motive of retaliation.

191

When I raised this point in one interview with McVeigh, he was dismissive and defensive. "I can understand why they [the Davidians] might say that publicly," he said, "but that doesn't mean anything." The strange disconnect with the victims of Waco makes sense only if we understand McVeigh's rigid adherence to the Patriot framing of the problem. It speaks to the fact that McVeigh's reading of the conflict was not an independent or particularly empathetic assessment but one that relied on a closed interpretive scheme constructed by the group with which he so strongly identified.

The perpetrator of what pre–September 11 pundits liked to call "the worst act of domestic terrorism ever on American soil" did not engineer an insurgent plan on this scale without assistance or support from others. As Mark Juergensmeyer (2002: 10–11) reminds us: "Terrorism is seldom a lone act.... [I]t takes a community of support and, in many cases, a large organizational network of support for an act of terrorism to succeed." In the 2004 Oklahoma state trial of Terry Nichols, Jennifer McVeigh testified that her brother "rarely talked about... Nichols" but referred to a "network of friends" he could count on in times of trouble (Talley, 2004). According to McVeigh's own account, Nichols backed out of the bombing plan at the end, as had Fortier a few weeks earlier. On the day the bomb exploded in front of the Murrah Federal Building in Oklahoma City, Nichols was sitting in his living room back home in Herington, Kansas, and Fortier was in Kingman, Arizona. Two hundred twenty-six eyewitnesses said they saw McVeigh with one or more persons – John Doe 2s – who were not Nichols or Fortier, many of the sightings less than twenty-four hours before the bombing. The most likely explanation is that McVeigh turned to the "network of friends" he could count on at Elohim City when he realized that Fortier and Nichols were going to back out. The April 5th call to Strassmeir at Elohim City ("Tell Andy I'm coming through"), where ARA members McCarthy, Stedeford, and Brescia were residing, was made in an effort to enlist their help in the final phase of the plan. The FBI records uncovered in the AP investigation suggest the identical reason for McVeigh's call. The FBI headquarters teletype stated that McVeigh made the April 5th call to the compound "on a day that he was believed to have been attempting to recruit a second conspirator to assist in the OKBOMB attack" (Solomon, 2004a). The new evidence suggests that the ARA insurgents agreed to help complete the mission, arranged false alibis, purchased a used truck on the Arkansas-Oklahoma border on April 17, and accompanied McVeigh to Oklahoma City as his "security detail."

The government has steadfastly maintained that McVeigh alone drove the Ryder truck to the federal building on the morning of April 19, 1995, detonated the bomb, and exited the truck, without help or accomplices, despite dozens of eyewitness accounts to the contrary. On April 19, 2004, nine years to the day after the Oklahoma City bombing, a document turned up in the AP investigation that revealed a Secret Service log entry referring to "video security" footage of the detonation – footage that investigators and prosecutors said they had never seen – and to "suspects" (plural) exiting the truck. The Secret Service document stated, "Security video tapes from the area show the truck detonation 3 minutes and 6 seconds after the *suspects* exited the truck" (Solomon, 2004b; emphasis mine). The Secret Service had an office in the Murrah Building and lost six employees in the explosion. Officials declined to comment about the security video, citing an ongoing investigation.

9

After Oklahoma City

PATRIOT DEMOBILIZATION
AND DECLINE

In this final chapter, I explore the impact of the Oklahoma City bombing on the Patriot movement and the transformation of contention between claimants and the state. The bombing set into motion a complex interplay of forces as state actors, challenging groups, and third parties all sought to seize opportunities, assign blame, attribute threat, mobilize resources, shore up alliances or form new ones, and recalibrate their respective frames. In the post–Oklahoma City political climate, the impact of the bombing on the Patriot movement remained uncertain for a period of time. It was not obvious in the short term that the bombing would have an adverse effect on the movement. Some Patriot insurgents forged ahead by committing new acts of violence, and the number of Patriot groups continued to grow well into 1996 (Southern Poverty Law Center, 1996). However, the movement also encountered an increasingly hostile political environment and well-organized opposition in the wake of the April 19 blast. Survivors and families of victims formed alliances with state actors, media, and other interest groups to effectively mobilize resources and public opinion against Patriot actors and organizations. The victim rights frame constructed in the ashes of Oklahoma City succeeded in capturing broad public support and readily trumped the Patriot war frame. Victims' rights advocacy groups, buoyed under the aegis of state and federal agencies, became a powerful political force, petitioning the courts and lobbying Congress to expand the legal rights of victims. Many Patriot movement adherents struggled to defend the insurgency in light of the "collateral damage" to children and low-level government employees in the Murrah Building. Some movement leaders condemned the bombing and sought to separate their own actions and identities from the bombers. Other Patriot actors proclaimed the bombing to be a government conspiracy contrived to justify martial law and impose a New World Order. Indeed, the bombing exposed tenuous ties among the coalition of far-right groups, revealing differences in ideology and strategy and fostering dissension and factional division. Unable to mount an effective stand against allied state and third-party actors, the dispirited Patriot campaign gradually retreated in disarray, and the movement steadily demobilized over the next several years. By examining the actions and dynamics of the parties in contention, we can gain a better understanding of how the Patriot movement lost traction and waned.

State Mobilization

In the aftermath of the bombing, the mobilized Patriot movement was met with a redoubled effort of countermobilization by the state. Federal and state leaders moved swiftly to condemn the bombing and to strategically frame the incident for the hosts of broadcast and print media descending on Oklahoma City. The perpetrators were strategically defined as "domestic terrorists." Early suspicions voiced by authorities suggested that the bombers might be Middle Eastern, adding potential nativist sentiments to the brew of reactions. President Clinton appeared on national television to denounce the bombing of innocent victims as "an act of cowardice" and promised that federal authorities would spare no expense in tracking down the terrorists to bring them to justice. The scene of the bombing in Oklahoma City was declared a national disaster area, making it eligible for federal emergency relief funds. The president pledged immediate assistance, authorizing National Guard and military support in search-and-rescue functions.

In a press conference one day after the bombing, the president also seized the opportunity to criticize right-wing Patriot radio talk show hosts for promoting hate and violence, tacitly linking these vocal opponents to the bombing. "They spread hate," he declared. "They leave the impression that, by their very words, violence is acceptable" (Fischer, 1996). The president singled out G. Gordon Liddy, the former Watergate conspirator-turned-Patriot, who had advised listeners after the Waco debacle to "shoot ATF agents in the head" if they illegally entered a home. Democratic leaders followed the president's lead and assailed Liddy and other right-wing radio demagogues – Rush Limbaugh, Oliver North, and Chuck Harder – for instigating antigovernment hostilities and encouraging Patriots like McVeigh.

House minority leader Richard Gephardt (D-MO) called Liddy's remarks "outrageous" and accused him and other like-minded radio personalities of inciting an insurrection.

From the outset of the Clinton administration, the president was a chief target of syndicated Patriot broadcasts and right-wing talk shows. The network of right-wing radio activists cultivated a significant political following and posed a formidable challenge to Clinton and the Democrats, regularly attacking them over the airwaves. By 1995, Rush Limbaugh was carried by 639 American radio stations, Chuck Harder by 300 radio stations, and G. Gordon Liddy by 225 stations (Dees and Corcoran, 1996: 117–18). High-profile figures such as Limbaugh, Liddy, and North were allied with the Republican Party and worked to frame the Clinton administration as a growing threat to conservatives and making appeals to far-right audiences. Among hard-core Patriots, Chuck Harder's People's Radio Network (PRN) was the most popular radio program. Harder coupled an above-ground program with an underground short-wave radio broadcast to reach his audience. According to IRS documents, Harder's program had revenues of more than $4 million in 1994 (Southern Poverty Law Center, 1996: 17). The aggregate effect of these airwave broadsides was believed to be a significant factor in the growth of antigovernment sentiments toward administration officials. A nationwide poll conducted by the Pew Research Center for the People and the Press (1993) revealed that 42 percent of the adult population listened to talk radio and more than 80 percent of these programs were defined in the study as "conservative." The Clinton administration sought to leverage public outrage from the bombing to quell the influence of right-wing radio firebrands and their allies.

The Clinton administration effectively used the bully pulpit to frame the tragedy while the aftershock of the bombing was still at its peak. On April 23, the national media focused on Oklahoma City. President and Mrs. Clinton attended the memorial service to honor those killed in the blast. They joined Oklahoma Governor Keating and his wife and the Reverend Billy Graham, who provided an inspirational message to the forty thousand people gathered at the state fairgrounds. Clearly articulating the perceived threat posed by the perpetrators, President Clinton echoed the moral and religious framing initiated by the Reverend Graham, casting the bombing as part of a greater Manichean struggle of good and evil:

We pledge to do all we can to help you heal the injured, to rebuild this city, and to bring to justice those who did this evil. . . . To all my fellow Americans beyond this hall, I say, one thing we owe those who have sacrificed is the duty to purge ourselves of the dark forces which gave rise to this evil. They are forces that threaten our common peace, our freedom, our way of life. Let us teach our children that the God of comfort is also the God of righteousness. Those who trouble their own house will inherit the wind. Justice will prevail. (http://www.usconstitution.com/presidentclinton'soklahomacitybombing.htm)

The president's speech was reprinted in major newspapers across the country the following day and recounted hundreds of times in broadcast news coverage. The eulogies and emotional displays of grief and loss over the tragedy expressed on this national day of mourning fused the collective sentiments that would seal the public perception of this incident.

The disaster relief effort set into motion by the president's declaration mobilized FEMA and several other government entities in the federal response plan, including the Department of Defense. Ironically, it was this kind of federal disaster response through FEMA that many Patriot movement actors feared would trigger a takeover by agents of the New World Order. A 1992 memorandum of understanding between FEMA and DOD expanded post–Cold War military support functions in emergency situations, allowing the military to have a broader role. Some provisions of the military support functions provided at Oklahoma City raised questions about the Posse Comitatus restrictions, even for military experts (Winthrop, 1997: 13–15). Just moments after the bombing, the military mobilized medical evacuation helicopters, explosive ordnance personnel, bomb detection dog teams, ambulances, and a sixty-six-person rescue team. Over the next few weeks, the military organized and coordinated a much larger relief operation. According to one official, "[T]he Secretary of the Army, through the Director of Military Support, subsequently coordinated the efforts of over 1,000 Department of Defense (DOD) personnel to perform a myriad of support functions at the height of the operation" (Winthrop, 1997: 3). Primary efforts by the DOD involved supporting FEMA's urban search-and-rescue emergency support function. "The DOD provided C-141 airlift assets to transport civilian rescue units to Oklahoma City" while the Army Corps of Engineers augmented efforts of rescuers by supplying two STOLS (Systems to Locate Survivors) teams as well as "search and structures specialists" (Winthrop, 1997: 12). Though these operations were legally prescribed in federal statutes, the close coordination of emergency relief between FEMA and the military served to reinforce the Patriot threat attribution of an NWO conspiracy.

State and federal lawmakers also responded to the bombing by mobiliz-ing an array of legislative and political resources. A week after the bombing, the Oklahoma State Senate voted unanimously to adopt a resolution "urg-ing sponsors of the G. Gordon Liddy show and other radio talk shows encouraging violence against public officials, law officers, or the private citizenry to withdraw financial sponsorship" (Fischer, 1996). On May 11, 1995, Lieutenant Governor Mary Kallin and Oklahoma City Mayor Ron Norick addressed a joint session of the state legislature to request special appropriations for relief efforts and bombing victims. Across the country, state legislatures driven by threats and other confrontations with Patriot groups began to review laws on paramilitary activity, common-law courts, and militias. By 1998, twenty-seven states had passed or considered new laws to punish or prohibit private armies and common-law courts (Levitas, 2002: 307).

Congressional leaders in Washington announced only days after the Oklahoma City bombing that they were introducing new antiterrorism legislation aimed at stiffening penalties for terrorist crimes and providing new resources for victims. One year later, on April 24, the Republican-dominated Congress passed the Antiterrorism and Effective Death Penalty Act of 1996. The act imposed a limit for all appeals relating to the right of *habeas corpus* in capital cases and reduced the length of the appeal process by sharply limiting the role of federal courts, among other things. Conser-vative Republicans in Congress, led by majority leader Newt Gingrich, had strong ties to right-wing political groups, including the gun lobby, which supported expanding capital punishment, restricting civil liberties of crim-inals, and limiting or repealing gun controls. Congressional Republicans had to perform a careful balancing act, appearing to attack terrorism while not alienating supporters and constituents.

The alignment of congressional conservatives with right-wing organiza-tions points out the complexity of the political dynamics shaping the arena of contention. Some conservative politicians were sympathetic to at least some of the ideological arguments pressed by gun rights activists and Patri-ots. In the summer of 1995, Republican leaders announced that they would hold hearings to reexamine federal law enforcement actions at Waco. My edited volume on the Branch Davidian tragedy was already in the hands of the publisher and was due out in late summer. I was contacted by a staff member of the House Subcommittee on National Security, International Affairs and Criminal Justice in June and asked if I would be willing to meet with them regarding the upcoming hearings. I agreed to meet with them and flew to Washington the following week. Over the course of the next few weeks, I gave the staff access to chapters of my book and discussed their relevance to the critical issues surrounding Waco. By the time I testified on the first day of the hearings in July, however, it was apparent to me that though conservative Republicans on the subcommittees were taking up the civil liberties side of the issue and questioning excessive law enforcement actions at Waco, they were less interested in the plight of the Davidians than in attacking the Clinton administration.

It also became evident that the gun lobby was working closely with conservative allies on the subcommittees, exploiting perceived political opportunities created by the 1994 elections that gave control of the House to Republicans. Republican subcommittee members allied with the gun lobby were able to score political points in the hearing, revealing a flawed raid plan by ATF, errors in the affidavit accompanying the warrants, miscommunication between the HRT and negotiators, and numerous errors of judgment. But "Republican credibility suffered when Democrats revealed that the majority staff had links to the NRA and that NRA staff members identified themselves as working for the committee and contacting potential witnesses" (Vizzard, 2000: 77). In the end, these revelations – in concert with allegations of Davidian child abuse, Koresh's sex with underage women, and children born of multiple wives – proved to be overwhelming, and media framing of the hearings favored the Clinton administration over Republican apologists for the gun lobby and militias.

Third-Party Interest Groups and the State

Project Heartland was created in 1995 by the Oklahoma Department of Mental Health and Substance Abuse Services (ODMHSAS) and received financial support of more than $4,000,000 from FEMA alone. Project Heartland was established as a crisis intervention community health program designed to provide immediate, short-term assistance to people affected by the bombing (Call and Pfefferbaum, 1999). It was the first state-sponsored community mental health response to a large-scale terrorist event in the United States. The program involved an extensive range of services, including crisis intervention and counseling, support groups, outreach, consultation, and education for survivors of the Oklahoma City bombing. Over a three-year period, Project Heartland provided 8,869 victims with counseling and support group services (U.S. Department of

199

Justice, 2000). This multi-institutional effort encompassing ODMHSAS, FEMA, and the U.S. Department of Justice mobilized resources for the affected families and furnished a support structure for victim rights activism. Twenty-one support groups from Project Heartland stabilized within this structure (Call and Pfefferbaum, 1999: 5), helping to create a strong victim rights advocacy network.

The DOJ's Office for Victims of Crime (OVC) played a significant role in the formation and support of the victim rights advocacy network in Oklahoma. The office of the U.S. Attorney for the Western District in Oklahoma City provided services to victims through its Victim-Witness Assistance Unit and through the appointment of an attorney liaison (U.S. Department of Justice, 2000: Ch. 3). The Victim-Witness Assistance Unit established a toll-free telephone information line to help "victims obtain assistance and initiate regular group meetings with survivors and family members" (p. 11). According to the DOJ report (2000), the Victim-Witness Assistance Unit exceeded requirements of federal laws and "organized large-scale resource coalitions and engaged in personal troubleshooting for individual victims" (p. 11). The attorney liaison served as a legal advisor and advocate for the victims, helping families to understand and exercise their legal rights and coordinating their efforts to press claims.

In March 1997, the Office for Victims of Crime awarded $234,930 to Project Heartland to fund support activities for victims groups at Safe Havens during the trials in Oklahoma City and Denver. "The Safe Havens served as places of respite for the victims' family members and survivors attending the trial proceedings in Denver or the closed-circuit television (CCTV) broadcasts of the trials in Oklahoma City" (p. 9). OVC funding of victim rights groups was made in part because FEMA guidelines did not allow funding of services outside of the federally declared disaster area. The support of bombing victims and families to attend the trials proved to be vitally important in catalyzing one victims' rights organization.

The most important victims' rights advocacy group to emerge from this effort was the Families and Survivors United. The group was founded by Marsha Kight, whose 23-year-old daughter, Frankie Merrill, was killed in the bombing. According to her autobiographical account, Kight was overwhelmed with grief and emotional pain after the loss of her daughter and struggled with depression and alcohol (Graber, 1998; Kight, 1998a). Kight became part of the victims' rights network associated with Project Heartland and benefited directly from the OVC support for victims attending the federal hearings and trials. Kight described a turning point in her involvement when the federal judge for the McVeigh case, Richard Matsch, told victims in pretrial hearings in June 1996 that if they wanted to make an impact statement during the sentencing phase, they would not be able to attend the trial. Victims and family members, some of whom had only just arrived in Denver, were given only ninety minutes to decide. Kight was outraged and said she felt revictimized by the criminal justice system. Kight decided to stay and view the trial while at the same time launching a legal fight to contend the ruling. With support of victims' rights attorneys in Washington, D.C., Kight filed an emergency petition with the Tenth Circuit Court of Appeals asking that Judge Matsch's order be rescinded. The three-judge panel on the Appeals Court refused to hear the case, ruling that the victims and their families had no legal standing. The plaintiffs then filed an *en banc* petition asking for a review by all judges on the Tenth Circuit Court. The petition was denied again.

Kight subsequently took her battle to Congress, gaining such key bipartisan allies as Senators Dianne Feinstein (D-CA) and Jon Kyl (R-AZ). Kight's dogged activism resulted in a change of law. The Victim Rights Clarification Act was passed by Congress in 1997, giving legal standing to victims. Out of this experience, Kight carved out a reputation as an ardent advocate for victims' rights. In 1998, she compiled and edited *Forever Changed*, a volume containing the accounts of eighty survivors and family members of victims in the Oklahoma City bombing. In March 1999, Kight testified before the Senate Judiciary Committee on a proposed victims' rights amendment to the Constitution, a cause she embraced with intense zeal. Using the Oklahoma City bombing as a catalyst, Kight emerged to become a prominent leader in the victims' rights movement, working with the Department of Justice and lawmakers in the U.S. House and Senate and serving as public policy assistant for the National Organization for Victim Assistance (NOVA).

The victims' rights movement gained momentum in the wake of the Oklahoma City bombing and helped to create an inhospitable political climate for Patriot and militia groups. Victims' rights groups born after the Oklahoma City tragedy labored to keep the memory of its devastation alive among legislators and the American public. These efforts effectively thwarted strategic counteractions by the gun lobby and attempts by militia and Patriot leaders to rehabilitate their image. In effect, third-party victims' rights claimants allied with powerful state actors leveraged the bombing to build broad support to defeat competing claims of gun rights by Patriot movement actors and their allies.

Movement Demobilization and Splintering

The Oklahoma City bombing exposed the tenuous ties among the coalition of far-right groups comprising the Patriot movement. Differences in ideology, strategy, and organizational culture – effectively neutralized by a common and unifying perception of threat posed by the state in the early 1990s – resurfaced in the wake of the bombing. As a result, the embattled movement faced increased disorganization, fragmentation, and splintering. Reactions to the bombing among Patriot groups disclosed their underlying divisions. Hard-core Patriot insurgents saw the bombing as an opportunity to further the revolution through more acts of violence. But the gun lobby, determined to protect its political viability and voice in the institutional arena, condemned the bombing while carefully arguing that government gun control efforts may have provoked the desperate actions of the bombers. Other Patriots turned to conspiracy theories and blamed the government for the bombing. Still others found no credible defense for the bombing and dissolved their organizational ties.

The reversal of Patriot mobilization did not occur in the immediate aftermath of Oklahoma City, however. Antigovernment hostility persisted and the number of Patriot movement organizations continued to swell, peaking in 1996. According to the Southern Poverty Law Center's monitoring project (1996), the number of Patriot groups increased from 224 in 1995 to 858 in 1996. After 1996, the movement began a steady decline, plummeting to 194 groups by the end of the decade. Figure 9.1 shows the growth and decline of Patriot organizations between 1995 and 2000, depicting a pattern of Patriot mobilization and demobilization. The SPLC data probably understate the number of groups in 1995, both because its monitoring project was just gearing up and the methods of identifying Patriot groups based on news sources and informants was limited. The data also may not have reflected rising attrition rates among existing groups in 1996 because the SPLC methodology enumerates only structures and not size or variation in groups. However, the SPLC project represents the most systematic database on Patriot groups, and the general patterns of mobilization and demobilization are supported by other sources, such as the MIPT Terrorism Knowledge Database and the ADL's Militia Watchdog project.

McVeigh's belief that the bombing might ignite a violent revolution was shared by a number of fellow insurgents comprising one faction of the Patriot movement, which continued to work toward an overthrow of the government. A survey of three databases on domestic terrorism revealed a

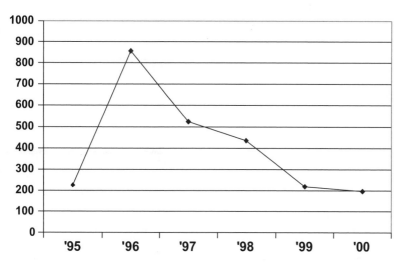

Figure 9.1 Number of Patriot Groups in the United States, 1995–2000. *Source*: Southern Poverty Law Center, 2000.

catalogue of thirty-two violent incidents involving Patriots between April 1995 and October 1996 (see Table 9.1). Some involved attempted bombings of federal buildings in the same manner as the Oklahoma City bombing, while others entailed shootouts, attacks on state and federal officers, and attempted use of biological weapons. In all but one of the thirty cases found (an Amtrak derailment), arrests were made and Patriots were charged with criminal activity. This also points up the countermobilization of the state in challenging insurgent collective action by Patriots and its effect on the trajectory of contention. A descriptive summary of selected Patriot incidents during this period provides a window into the unremitting insurgency by this segment.

In May 1995, Patriot Larry Wayne Harris was arrested for buying bubonic plague toxin by mail from a Rockville, Maryland, lab, fraudulently claiming that he supervised a microbiology lab and had approval from Ohio authorities. Police found three vials of bubonic plague bacteria in Harris's car after a traffic stop. A search of Harris's property revealed storage of freeze-dried bacteria, homemade explosive devices, hand grenade triggers, primer cord, and detonation fuses. Police also discovered a certificate stating that Harris was a lieutenant in Richard Butler's Aryan Nations. Harris told one source he was a committed Identity adherent and joined the Aryan Nations group in 1994 (Dees and Corcoran, 1996: 210; Henry, 1998; Stern,

Table 9.1. *Patriot Violence/Insurgent Acts, 1995–1996*

Month	Type of Incident	State
1995		
April		
Mark Burton	Shootout with police	Indiana
Al Hamilton	Threatened officials with gun	Montana
May		
Larry Wayne Harris	Bubonic plague/explosives	Ohio
Calvin Greenup	Threatened public officials	Montana
June		
Michael Hill	Threatened police with gun	Ohio
July		
Darwin Michael Gray	Plot to bomb federal building	Washington
Kent Allen Johnson	Theft of explosives	Idaho
Gordon Sellner	Shootout with police	Montana
September		
Charles Ray Polk	Plot to bomb federal building	Texas
Kevin Carter	Attempt to steal explosives	Utah
Fitzhugh MacCrae	Equipment theft from Army base	New Hampshire
October		
Ralph Clark	Theft/threatened officials with gun	Montana
Sons of Gestapo	Derailment of Amtrak train	Arizona
November		
Ray Willie Lampley et al. (4)	Conspiracy to bomb federal building	Oklahoma
December		
Joseph Martin Bailie	Attempted bombing of federal building	Nevada
Thomas Lavy	Possession of ricin	Arkansas
1996		
January		
Larry N. Tricket	Conspiracy to bomb federal building	Missouri
Peter Langan, Richard Guthrie	Bank robberies	Ohio
Larry Martz	Felonious assault, illegal weapons	Ohio
March		
Montana Freemen	Standoff w/federal law enforcement	Montana
Russell Fauver	Illegal weapons stockpile	New Jersey
April		
Ray Hamblin	Possession of explosives	Oregon
Robert Edward Starr	Manufacturing bombs	Georgia
William Kay	Illegal weapons and explosives	Pennsylvania

Month	Type of Incident	State
June		
Frederick Urban	Possession of explosives	Pennsylvania
July		
Arizona Vipers (12)	Conspiracy, explosives, weapons	Arizona
John Pitner et al. (8)	Conspiracy, explosives, weapons	Washington
Jose Arce	Illegal weapons and contraband	Texas
October		
Charles Barbee, Robert Berry	Bombings, bank robberies	Washington
Mountaineer Militia (7)	Conspiracy to bomb FBI facility	West Virginia
N = 30		

Sources: Anti-Defamation League's Militia Watchdog (http://www.militia-watchdog.org); Memorial Institute for the Prevention of Terrorism Knowledge Database (http://www.tkb.org/Home.jsp); Southern Poverty Law Center Intelligence Project (http://www.splcenter.org).

1996: 252). Harris was rearrested three years later while on probation for possession of military-grade anthrax with the intent to use the biological agent as a weapon. According to court documents, Harris and another man, William Job Leavitt, Jr., were attempting to develop anthrax as a biological warfare agent, possibly to release in a public facility (*U.S. v. Larry Wayne Harris, William Job Leavitt, Jr.,* 1998: 3). Harris boasted to an FBI informant that he had enough anthrax to "wipe out the city" of Las Vegas when he was arrested.

In July 1995, Patriot Darwin Michael Gray, a longtime friend of Randy Weaver, was arrested in Washington State for plotting to bomb a federal courthouse in Spokane. Gray apparently stole blueprints to the U.S. courthouse from his employer, a company that installed insulation. Gray had planned to build a fertilizer bomb, similar to the one McVeigh used in Oklahoma City, to blow up the federal courthouse building where agents who investigated the Weaver standoff were based. Gray had befriended Weaver and was Kevin Harris's stepbrother. According to court documents, he was a "visible and vocal opponent of the Federal agents at Ruby Ridge" and was linked to the Aryan Nations (Stern, 1996: 252). Also in July 1995, Kent Allen Johnson, reportedly a member of the Idaho Militia, was charged with the theft of five hundred pounds of explosives from the Lucky Friday mine in northern Idaho. Apparently, Johnson and fellow Patriots intended to sell the explosives to a Canadian group that was planning to blow up a dam (Stern, 1996: 252).

In September 1995, Patriot Charles Ray Polk was charged with the attempted use of a weapon of mass destruction, solicitation to a crime of violence, unlawful possession of a machine gun, and other violations in a failed plot to bomb IRS buildings. Polk was arrested in July in Tyler, Texas, while trying to purchase massive amounts of C-4 plastic explosives. According to court documents filed with the U.S. Fifth Circuit of Appeals, Polk told an undercover ATF agent "he was interested in purchasing two thousand pounds of plastic explosives and detonators, that he would have $150 million to spend, and that he was responsible for procuring an arsenal of weapons for an organization dedicated to restoring the United States to its 'common law roots.' This organization . . . was planning a 'massive offensive' during July 1995, an offensive that would include destroying [through the use of plastic explosives] several IRS buildings throughout the nation" (*U.S. v. Charles Ray Polk*, 1997: 2). Polk later provided photographs of the IRS building in Austin to the undercover agent. When told that the regional IRS building Polk had targeted employed more than 3,500 people, Polk replied "Doesn't hurt my feelings." Polk also produced a national map and identified at least nine other cities in which IRS buildings were located and that he wanted to bomb.

In October 1995, an Amtrak train carrying 248 passengers was derailed, killing 1 and injuring 78 people. Four cars plunged off a thirty-foot trestle after encountering damaged rail track. Two notes at the scene of the accident indicated sabotage by a group called the Sons of Gestapo. The notes were addressed to the ATF, FBI, state police, and the sheriff's office and referred to government raids at Ruby Ridge and Waco. The deadly derailment occurred about sixty miles southwest of Phoenix ("Sabotage suspected in 'terrorist' derailment," CNN, Oct. 10, 1995). No arrests were ever made.

In November 1995, Oklahoma Constitutional Militia leader Willie Ray Lampley, his wife Cecilia, John Dare Baird, and Larry Wayne Crow were arrested for conspiracy to bomb gay bars, abortion clinics, an Anti-Defamation League office in Houston, the Southern Poverty Law Center office in Montgomery, Alabama, and federal buildings. One charge in the indictment filed in the Eastern District of Oklahoma referred to defendants making "a destructive device consisting of 'homemade C-4' made of ammonium nitrate, nitromethane, aluminum powder and a detonation device" (*U.S. v. Willie Ray Lampley et al.*, 1995: 1). The plot was uncovered by an FBI informant, Richard Schrum, who told authorities that Lampley planned to test out his homemade bomb at Elohim City the day before he was arrested. Witnesses in the trial testified that Lampley believed the ADL and SPLC were part of the New World Order, designed to destroy resistance to a single world currency and government (Johnson, 1995). Lampley also met with WAR leader and part-time Elohim City resident Dennis Mahon on August 29 to recruit support for the bombing strikes. According to *The Daily Oklahoman*, the pretrial hearing was attended by Reverend Robert Millar and about one hundred Elohim City residents who "smiled and waved to the Lampleys" (Trammell, 1995).

In December 1995, Joseph Martin Bailie and Ellis Edward Hurst were arrested after a failed attempt to bomb the Internal Revenue Service building in Reno, Nevada. The two men built a one-hundred-pound bomb made of ammonium nitrate and nitromethane fuel, placed it in the back of Bailie's pickup truck, and drove to the back of the IRS building. The men unloaded the bomb, tried to detonate it, and then drove away hurriedly. However, the bomb failed to explode and was discovered by an IRS employee. The men were charged with attempted destruction of a federal building and use of a destructive device in relation to a crime of violence ("Two arrested in IRS bomb attempt," CNN, Dec. 28, 1995).

In January 1996, Larry N. Trickett of the Missouri 51st Militia was arrested after police answered a call by Trickett's wife, Patricia, alleging domestic violence. Patricia Trickett led police to the couple's basement, where they found a pipe bomb, weapons, gunpowder, and detailed diagrams of the five-story Federal Transfer Center in Oklahoma City, a hub for shipping criminals to different federal prisons. A hearing had been scheduled there for a change-of-venue motion filed by attorneys for Tim McVeigh in the Oklahoma City bombing case. The diagrams of the Federal Transfer Center were found with a memo dated May 12, 1994, suggesting that a "recon team" had infiltrated the facility and took detailed notes of the floor plan (ADL Militia Watchdog database).

In March 1996, a government standoff began near the small town of Jordan, Montana, when federal authorities arrested two leaders of the Montana Freemen, Leroy Schweitzer and Daniel Peterson, for making death threats against a judge and issuing fraudulent checks. The Montana Freeman occupied a 960-acre farm owned by Ralph and Emmett Clark, which they named "Justus Township," and declared the property free of any government jurisdiction. Invoking Posse and Identity beliefs, eleven members barricaded themselves inside the farmhouse and refused to surrender after learning of the arrests. The FBI's Hostage Rescue Team was called to the scene – the same unit that presided over Ruby Ridge and Waco – inciting Patriots across the country. Militia groups were mobilized to the site of the standoff to set up base camps and monitor government actions. The paramilitaries were determined that there would be no repeat of the assault on the Branch Davidians. Don Vos, leader of the Ohio Unorganized Militia, told a reporter: "There will not be another Waco that the government will survive. Federal agents may have that Jordan farm blocked off, but if they shoot or burn the kids inside, they will never leave Montana" (Sahagun, 1996: 18A). Keenly aware of the fallout from Waco and Ruby Ridge, the FBI kept the tactical team and the tanks far from the negotiation area, brought in third parties to consult and assist, and adhered closely to standards of crisis negotiations. Journalists on the ground observed the change; one *New York Times* reporter wrote, "Gone are the visible displays of military-style symbols and tactics that had previously defined the FBI in such faceoffs, such as black fatigues, armored personnel carriers and the deployment of snipers and other specialists" (Johnston, 1996: 2A). Showing the kind of patience they failed to exhibit in Waco, the standoff lasted eighty-one days before the barricaded Freemen surrendered without incident.

In July 1996, federal authorities arrested thirteen members of the Viper Militia in Phoenix and charged them with plotting for more than two years to bomb government buildings. The group planned to target federal buildings housing the FBI, ATF, IRS, INS, and Secret Service. Members of the Viper Militia "held training exercises in the Arizona desert in which they detonated ammonium nitrate bombs" (Macko, 1996). In an interview with the PBS *News Hour*, Undersecretary of the Treasury Raymond Kelly estimated the amount of ammonium nitrate found in the federal raid to be about one thousand pounds ("Viper Militia – Up in Arms," *Online News Hour* transcript, July 2,1996). Federal agents also found one hundred semi-automatic and automatic weapons, more than eleven thousand rounds of ammunition, and components to make rockets and grenades (Hamilton, 1996: 55). Authorities also discovered a videotape made by militia members in which the security measures of the targeted federal buildings were discussed. The video included "advice on how to collapse the buildings," suggestions to place antipersonnel devices in mailboxes near the entrance of a building housing several federal agencies, and use of a tactic to destroy a water main near the building to hamper firefighters (Macko, 1996).

An additional point of interest involving the Viper Militia is worth noting here. This group was operating in the same vicinity as both McVeigh and the Aryan Republican Army in February 1995. As I discussed in the previous chapter, the government was unable to account for the whereabouts of McVeigh and the ARA at several junctures corresponding to the time both were in Arizona. ARA member Richard Guthrie told the FBI that they were camping in the Arizona wilderness after checking out of a hotel in Apache Junction, near Phoenix, on February 12, 1995. The FBI could not account for McVeigh during this same time, but prosecutors in the federal bombing case argued that McVeigh was building and testing a bomb in the Arizona desert. That McVeigh was testing the ammonium nitrate–nitromethane bomb during the same time and in the same area that the Viper Militia "held training exercises in the Arizona desert in which they detonated ammonium nitrate bombs" (Macko, 1996) suggests yet another intersection involving McVeigh and the Patriot network that federal authorities have not addressed. After the federal raid on the Viper Militia, PBS *News Hour*'s Jim Lehrer asked Undersecretary of Treasury Raymond Kelly in an interview if there was any connection to the Oklahoma City bombing. Kelly replied, "No. There doesn't appear to be" ("Viper Militia – Up in Arms," *Online New Hour* transcript, July 2, 1996). Kelley offered no further comment or explanation.

Unlike the hard-core insurgents who sought to advance the revolution after Oklahoma City, another faction of the movement condemned the bombing and endeavored to distance itself from McVeigh while still leveling attacks on the government (Leiby, 1997). This strategy cast McVeigh and other perpetrators as misguided and/or as pawns in a government conspiracy. An alleged link between McVeigh and militia groups was vehemently denied by key movement leaders, some of whom were interviewed within days of the bombing (Chermak, 1999; Niewert, 1999). On June 15, less than two months after the Oklahoma City bombing, the Senate Judiciary Subcommittee on Terrorism, Technology and Government convened a hearing to investigate militias. A small coterie of militia leaders appeared in Washington to testify, including Norman Olsen and Robert Fletcher (Michigan Militia), Linda Thompson (Unorganized Militia of Ohio), and John Trochman (Militia of Montana). Each, in turn, defended the concept of private armies but disavowed violence. When asked by Senator Dianne Feinstein (D-CA) if there were any circumstances in which the bombing of a federal building would be justified, a unanimous chorus of activists replied "No!" However, this did not deter militia leaders from subsequently advancing theories of government conspiracy to explain the bombing. Olsen repeated the popular argument circulating in the Patriot network that a second bomb blast was detonated inside the Murrah Building by government conspirators (see Jasper, 1998). The Michigan Militia leader claimed the bombing was planned as a means to mobilize public support for expanded police powers, impose tighter gun controls, and suppress antigovernment dissent. Linda Thompson echoed Olsen's claim of conspiracy: "I definitely believe the government did the bombing. I mean, who's got a track record of killing children?" (Anti-Defamation League, 1995: 31).

The gun lobby pursued a dual strategy as well, though not adopting the most extreme Patriot version of a government conspiracy. Because gun rights organizations relied heavily on conservative allies in government, they could not afford to jeopardize these ties. Consequently, many gun rights activists adopted a different tactic: They sought to frame the Clinton White House response to the bombing as manipulative and opportunistic. The gun lobby alleged a scheme by Clinton and other Democrats to exploit the tragedy in Oklahoma City in order to further gun control initiatives. The NRA and the GOA made a concerted effort to separate McVeigh from gun control issues.

After the bombing, the NRA's Institute for Legislative Action (ILA) launched a media and letter-writing campaign encouraging gun rights supporters to "set the record straight." A May 13 NRA-ILA Fax Alert goaded activists to "[s]pread the word that from the outset the NRA condemned the malicious bombing in Oklahoma City and called for the death penalty for those responsible" (NRA-ILA Fax Network, 1995). The newsletter also proclaimed the organization was "one of the strongest supporters of this country's law enforcement officials." Yet the NRA had been one of the harshest, most vocal critics of federal enforcement of gun laws. Only days earlier, NRA Executive Vice President Wayne LaPierre was forced to defend the NRA's attack on ATF agents as "jack-booted thugs." The verbal assault prompted former president George H. W. Bush to resign his lifetime NRA membership. LaPierre and the NRA were caught in the awkward position of alleging strong support for law enforcement while castigating ATF and other federal agencies engaged in interdiction of firearms laws.

Larry Pratt's Gun Owners of America followed a similar pattern. In a June 1995 GOA newsletter, Pratt condemned the Oklahoma City bombing as "an outrage." "The person or persons proven to be involved," he declared, "should be executed. Killing innocent men, women, and children on behalf of a cause is simply barbaric" (Pratt, 1995c). However, Pratt's official denouncement of the violence against "innocent men, women, and children" rang hollow because a few years earlier he supported the bloody purge of countless villages in Guatemala by the military dictator Ríos Montt (Pratt 1990). The dual strategy readily surfaced in the June newsletter as Pratt attempted to scapegoat the Clinton administration's effort to tighten gun control laws. He attacked President Clinton and antigun activists for "exploiting this disaster to push for further gun control." Recognizing the Clinton administration's attribution of opportunity in this political climate, Pratt attacked the president and framed the executive branch response as a covert scheme. "The wanton and antagonistic outbursts from Bill Clinton in the days following the bombing," Pratt railed, "have shown that this Administration will stop at nothing to strip citizens of their Constitutional Rights" (Pratt, 1995c).

Finally, some Patriot actors became disillusioned in the aftermath of the bombing and left the movement, while others were driven away by an extensive state crackdown on militias. Chermak (2001) argues that the decline of the movement was due in part to the intense media coverage after the bombing that linked McVeigh to militias and defined all Patriots as a violent threat. Chermak searched the databases of LexisNexis and Newsbank for newspaper coverage of militia activity from 1990 to 1998 and found a sharp spike in media attention just after the Oklahoma City bombing, but virtually none before the incident. A scant eight newspaper articles were found from the combined databases on militias before 1995. But in 1995 and 1996, "nearly 300 articles were published in the newspapers indexed by Newsbank and 156 articles appeared in the *New York Times*" (Chermak, 2001: 56). The sudden wave of adverse media coverage threatened both the isolation enjoyed by some movement members and exposed the marginal commitment of others, contributing to defection. "[T]he publicity threatened the isolation of many of its members, and people started to feel pressure from friends, relatives, and members of the public who were critical of militias because of the stereotypes being created in the media. Those who left the movement were the 'weekend warriors,' who viewed their involvement as more social than political" (Chermak, 2001: 69).

In addition to negative news coverage of militia and Patriot groups, Chermak found a surge of images produced in popular culture – comics, television, and film (2001: 196–209). Movement actors depicted in made-for-TV movies and films were uniformly cast in the mold of McVeigh, threatening to bomb government buildings and bring death and destruction to densely populated cities. Drawing on portions of the Oklahoma City bombing incident and borrowing from profiles of McVeigh, Nichols, and Fortier, popular media portraits were constructed that appeared to have at least some factual basis. Chermak concluded that the fictional portrayal of militias by the entertainment industry helped to mobilize public antipathy against the movement. The net effect of media coverage "ultimately contributed to [the movement's] demise. It was never able to recover from being linked to McVeigh. Many militia members were as angry with McVeigh as they were with the media...McVeigh hoped to be a martyr; instead militia members despised him because of the negative publicity" (Chermak, 2001: 227).

News coverage surrounding McVeigh's federal trial in Denver in 1997 raised public awareness about militias and Patriots further. Federal prosecutors saw this high-profile case as an opportunity to send a message to the public about the dangers of antigovernment groups, using McVeigh to personify the threat. When the verdict was issued, the media rallied behind prosecutors and victims, celebrating the decision and lauding the criminal justice system. News reporters heralded the verdict and proclaimed that bombing victims and their families could now find "healing" and "closure" (Chermak, 2001: 171). Concomitantly, media scrutiny of Patriot groups became harsher and more critical. By the close of the federal trial, prominent leaders in the Patriot movement were making public statements to the media disassociating themselves from McVeigh, saying that he was "no martyr" and that "he stigmatized their cause" (Leiby, 1997: A8).

The state's countermobilization played a significant role as well, as federal law enforcement shifted its focus and resources to fight domestic terrorism. With the passage of the 1996 antiterrorism bill, Congress authorized more than a $1 billion over five years for various federal, state, and local programs to prevent or combat terrorism. The bill authorized $468 million specifically for FBI counterterrorism and counterintelligence efforts, giving new emphasis to enforcement of targeted Patriot movement organizations and actors. Penalties for crimes committed against federal employees and conspiracies involving explosives were increased, and terrorist crimes were now subject to a federally imposed death penalty. Armed with new, broadened powers, federal law enforcement launched a series of investigations and raids, penetrating the Patriot network and making a wave of arrests.

The FBI also pursued a strategy of cooptation by making overtures to Patriot actors and organizations to assist law enforcement in the battle against domestic terrorism. In 1996, during the Montana Freemen standoff, the FBI "turned to militia groups for help in gauging the potential threat" of the barricaded group (Johnson and Page, 1996: 3A). According to one news report, militia leaders admitted being contacted by the FBI in search of information about the Clark brothers and other Freemen. "The FBI has legitimate concerns," Militia of Montana's Bob Fletcher told journalists. FBI officials cited in the report said that the "unusual alliance is being cultivated not only to gather intelligence about the Freemen, but to assuage militia leaders who might support the group or provoke an armed confrontation" (Johnson and Page, 1996: 3A).

The cooptation strategy was articulated more systematically in the July 1997 *FBI Law Enforcement Bulletin* by James E. Duffy and Alan C. Brantley, titled "Militias: Initiating Contact." Special Agents Duffy and Brantley recommended "establishing a dialogue with militia leaders" as a way to mitigate suspicion and distrust. The FBI initiative was described as "part of a broad-based effort to establish positive contacts between law enforcement agencies and local militia groups." By making "proactive contacts" with militia leaders, the agents suggested, "relevant issues" could be broached and agents "should be in a position to arrange for future meetings, especially if a troubling issue arises or a crisis appears imminent" (p. 2). In the event of a crisis, they argued, these "contacts will keep open the avenues of communication, enhancing the opportunities for affected parties to . . . resolve trouble in a peaceful manner" (p. 2). Clearly, the goal of this effort – apart from conflict resolution – was to cultivate intelligence sources inside the movement and to develop a system of informants. The agents cited several cases in which the proactive contacts were helpful in defusing volatile incidents. As the FBI garnered increased cooperation from militia and Patriot leaders in the years after the bombing, the more violent faction of the Patriot movement was thwarted and threat attributions mutually weakened between claimants and the state.

The protracted and highly publicized federal trials of McVeigh and Nichols in 1997 kept a sustained media focus on the Patriot movement. By the time Nichols was convicted on eight counts of manslaughter in December 1997, the Patriot movement was in a state of rapid decline. Watchdog organizations, allied with federal law enforcement and state officials, continued to monitor the movement and report on the activities of Patriot groups. The news of every new arrest or unearthing of a bombing plot by Patriot insurgents was given broad coverage and seized upon by collective oppositional forces: the state, third parties, and the media. In the days before the planned federal execution of McVeigh in May 2001, the Southern Poverty Law Center released a report calling the Patriot movement "a shadow of its former self." The report cited as one of the reasons for the decline "the arrests of thousands" for criminal activity (p. 1). The impact of intensified enforcement, in turn, was fostering internal fear and suspicion in the movement: "Official crackdowns have militiamen and other Patriots in constant fear of informers" (2001: 3). The report also cited the virtual disappearance

213

of Patriot periodicals and a 41 percent drop in Patriot Web sites from the previous year as evidence of movement decline. The release of the SPLC report was timed to coincide with the execution of McVeigh. The tactic by this third-party interest group was designed to reinforce the public perception of a link between McVeigh and the Patriot movement – one that Patriot leaders were attempting to deny. John Trochman, the founder of the Militia of Montana and a prominent leader of the Patriot movement, was interviewed by *ABC News* on the eve of McVeigh's execution and asked about his response. Trochman disavowed any link to McVeigh and the bombing. "We or no one that we know of feel he is a martyr for anything," Trochman said. "Why would we want to blow up a federal building?" (Robinson, 2001). In the end, state actors and their allies were successful in making McVeigh the public face of the Patriot movement, even as movement actors vilified the insurgent in a desperate effort to distance themselves from the deadly bombing.

Three months to the exact day after McVeigh was executed (June 11) the 9/11 terrorist attack on the World Trade Center and the Pentagon dramatically shifted the nation's attention to foreign enemies. What remained of the Patriot movement's perceived war with the government dissolved as far-right warriors faced a new enemy: a foreign or surrogate enemy to replace the old communists in the post–Cold War era. The nation rallied behind the new war on terrorism that targeted al Qaeda and Muslim extremists in the wake of 9/11. New battle lines were drawn in the radically altered political environment, and the Patriot frame was divested of its meaning and resonance for right-wing audiences. Indeed, the new Bush administration would ask for and receive broad new powers to fight terrorism under the 2001 Patriot Act. Ironically, this sweeping new law, spearheaded by conservatives in the White House and Congress, expanded federal controls, enhanced roles for the military, and empowered the state to engage in heightened monitoring and surveillance of suspected groups.

Social Movement Scholarship and Right-Wing Movements

I now return to questions raised at the outset about the explanatory value of social movement theory relative to right-wing movements. As the reader is likely to surmise, the arsenal of conceptual tools and models developed by social movement scholars provides a sound analytical framework to explain the dynamics of contention in this study of the Patriot movement. While social movement research on right-wing or far-right movements has been limited, it does not appear to be a consequence of inadequate theoretical constructs or analytic programs. The three broad sets of factors that theorists generally have identified in social movement formation and growth – attribution of opportunities or threats, social appropriation of sites for mobilization, and framing – appear to have equal merit in explaining the lineaments of contention among right-wing organizations and actors. The political process approach, in particular, provides an effective lens through which to view the iterative sites of mobilization between right-wing claimants and the state. Like their counterparts on the left, right-wing challengers must constantly explore new forms in the search for tactical advantage in making claims against the state or institutional elites. Right-wing movement actors must rely on repertoires of contention and create innovative forms or strategies around their margins. Innovative collective action must also blend elements of convention with new frames of meaning.

Mobilization, whether on the right or the left, is more likely to occur when the attribution of opportunity or threat is made and seized upon by challengers. I found that key Patriot movement actors recognized and exploited opportunities and threats at critical times, taking advantage of changes in the political environment to appropriate new sites and form new alliances. Successful episodes of contention in the Patriot movement occurred when far-right actors appropriated organizational bases and brokered new alliances with farm protest and gun rights organizations, respectively. New repertoires of contention were devised (for example, the tractorade, leaderless resistance) to stimulate innovative collective action. Effective framing enabled Patriot movement actors to define the sources of problems, designate culpable agents, and devise a plan of amelioration for aggrieved groups, linking ideas to activism.

The effort to integrate intermediate, or mesolevel, dynamics into the analysis yielded important insights. I endeavored to delineate sets of factors shaping the "mutation of paths" taken in the ongoing struggle between far-right challengers and the state that eventually led to the formation of the Patriot movement. I began by examining the entire span of years during which conditions facilitative of Patriot insurgency were developing, not just the immediate premovement period. In the formation of the movement, I identified multiple sets of actors – elites, challengers, third parties – involved in an "iterative dance of stimulus-response," invoking shifting and reciprocal interpretations of reality, to help explain the trajectory of contention. I found the trajectory of contention to take the form of what has been previously described by scholars as an opportunity/threat spiral, defined as

215

a mechanism that "operates through sequences of environmental change, interpretation of that change, action and counteraction, repeated as one action alters another actor's environment" (McAdam, Tarrow, and Tilly, 2001: 243). I found this concept to be vital to the analysis and made it a centerpiece of my study. Reconfiguring and expanding elements of this construct, I attempted to show how a highly charged confluence of a "warfare" frame developed by Patriot movement and state actors engendered a kind of symbiosis, leading to an escalation of mutual threat (and opportunity) attribution. I also inverted the opportunity-threat sequence to reflect the more significant role of threat. The resulting model of a threat/opportunity spiral captured this dynamic of escalating conflict between claimants and the state quite well.

The perception and construction of threat as a primary catalyst to action is an important feature of the study and raises critical questions for future research. Clearly, the attribution of threat is more prominent in the formation and mobilization of the Patriot movement than the attribution of opportunity. The origins of the Patriot movement are rooted in the twin threats of Cold War anticommunism and racial segregation. Right-wing movements have invariably postulated a threat by liberal state and nonstate actors while invoking notions of cultural and racial superiority through coded nationalistic rhetoric. Threat attribution is crucial for far-right movement actors, who have an identity *only* in relation to a perceived enemy. Far-right movement frames are inherently conspiracy frames. Patriot conspiracy frames and claims making are predicated foremost on the attribution of an insidious threat posed by agents of a New World Order. I believe the entreaties by McAdam, Goldstone, Tilly, and others to reassess the role of threat in our models of movement origins take on added meaning, as I alluded to earlier. The modest consideration given to threat as a stimulus to collective action may well be a result of the imbalance of social movement research focusing disproportionately on progressive and left-wing movements. If right-wing organizations and politics bear a more "paranoid style," as is often asserted, then the relative inattention to threat as a catalyst to collective action by social movement scholars is certainly a reasonable explanation. In that case, a corrective course in future research incorporating more studies of right-wing movements would facilitate the goal of building threat back into models of movement formation.

Of course, there may be other explanations for scholarly inattention to threat attribution as a stimulus. In the midst of the ongoing culture wars in the United States, social movement scholars should not be lacking for evidence of threat attribution among progressive and left-wing causes. The divisive and highly politicized agenda of the Bush administration has given progressive movements in the United States ample ammunition to frame White House policies as a threat to a host of liberal-left issues. Bush-Cheney energy policies have been crafted largely by big oil and gas executives, gutting environmental protections and posing a momentous new threat to the environment. National environmental movement organizations such as the Natural Resource Defense Council, Sierra Club, and Environmental Defense have featured themes of environmental threat prominently in their efforts to mobilize members to the battle. Bush administration attacks on civil liberties since 9/11 are well documented in progressive magazines such as *The Nation, Harper's, The American Prospect,* and *The Progressive* and by civil liberties organizations such as the American Civil Liberties Union. The claim of "threats to civil liberties" has become a rallying cry for civil libertarians. Pro-choice leaders have rightly challenged Bush administration efforts to appoint right-wing judges to the federal court in a bald attempt to reverse *Roe v. Wade.* Gay and lesbian groups have been the target of an antigay campaign orchestrated by Bush and Republicans painting gays and lesbians as a threat to traditional marriage. Racial minorities and the poor have been victimized by Bush administration and Republican attacks on social programs and efforts to eviscerate the legacy of the New Deal, arousing the ire of organizations ranging from the NAACP to Americans for Democratic Action. In short, movement organizations championing progressive causes are awash in threat and have loudly said so. The question social movement scholars must confront is why our models of movement formation and mobilization fail to reflect this.

While I am still convinced that right-wing movements have exhibited a more paranoid style and have been more likely to engage in the politics of fear, clearly there is more work to be done. In the end, this is an empirical question. Certainly, it seems evident that threat attribution is an underemphasized variable in studies of progressive and liberal-left movements, but to what degree and under what conditions? As scholars reevaluate the role of threat attribution in progressive movements and, hopefully, more studies of right-wing movements accrue, a more balanced and comprehensive picture should emerge to provide us with some answers.

References

Aho, James. 1990. *The Politics of Righteousness: Idaho Christian Patriotism.* Seattle: University of Washington.

Anti-Defamation League. 1995. *Paranoia as Patriotism: Far-Right Influences on the Militia Movement.* Special Report.

Armstrong, Paula S., and Michael D. Schulman. 1990. "Financial Strain and Depression Among Farm Operators: The Role of Perceived Economic Hardship and Personal Control." *Rural Sociology* 55(4): 475–93.

Barkun, Michael. 1994. *Religion and the Racist Right.* Chapel Hill: University of North Carolina.

Barnet, Richard. 1988. "The Costs and Perils of Intervention," pp. 207–21 in Michael T. Klare and Peter Kornbluh (eds.), *Low Intensity Warfare.* New York: Pantheon.

Baumann, Robert E. 1995. "License to Steal: Take It Away." *National Review* (Feb. 20): 34–8.

Beam, Louis. 1992. "Leaderless Resistance." *The Seditionist* no. 12 (Feb.): 1–6.

Bell, Daniel. 1963. *The Radical Right.* New York: Macmillan.

Belyea, Michael J., and Linda M. Lobao. 1990. "Psychosocial Consequences of Agricultural Transformation: The Farm Crisis and Depression." *Rural Sociology* 55(1): 58–75.

Bennett, David H. 1995. *The Party of Fear.* New York: Vintage.

Berlet, Chip, and Matthew N. Lyons. 2000. *Right-Wing Populism in America.* New York: Guilford.

Bock, Alan W. 1995. *Ambush at Ruby Ridge.* Irvine, CA: Dickens Press.

Borger, Julian. 2001. "Death Row Diaries Reveal McVeigh's Goal of Martyrdom." *The Guardian* (June 9). Accessed online at http://www.guardianunlimited.co.uk/international/story/0,3604,504079,00.html.

Bovard, James. 1991. *The Farm Fiasco.* San Francisco: Institute for Contemporary Studies.

Bovard, James. 1995. *Lost Rights: The Destruction of American Liberty.* New York: Palgrave.

Boyd, David G. 1995. "On the Cutting Edge: Law Enforcement Technology." *FBI Law Enforcement Bulletin* (July). Accessed online at http://www.totse.com/en/law/justice_for_all/lawtech.html.

Bragg, Roy, and Stephanie Asin 1993. "Two Protests Fizzle." *Houston Chronicle* (April 4): 5A.

Breault, Marc, and Martin King. 1993. *Inside the Cult*. New York: Harper Regan Books.

Bromley, David G., and Edward D. Silver. 1995. "The Davidian Tradition: From Patronal Clan to Prophetic Movement," pp. 43–74 in Stuart A. Wright (ed.), *Armageddon in Waco*. Chicago: University of Chicago Press.

Broyles, J. Allen. 1964. *The John Birch Society: Anatomy of a Protest*. Boston: Beacon Press.

Bultena, Gordon, Paul Lasley, and Jack Geller. 1986. "The Farm Crisis: Patterns and Impacts of Financial Distress Among Iowa Farm Families." *Rural Sociology* 51(4): 436–48.

Call, John A., and Betty Pfefferbaum. 1999. "Lessons from the First Two Years of Project Heartland, Oklahoma's Mental Health Response to the 1995 Bombing." *Psychiatric Services* 50: 953–5.

Carter, Dan T. 1998. The Road to Oklahoma City: How Some Americans Came to Hate Their National Government." Distinguished Faculty Lecture, Emory University, March. Accessed online at http://www.emory.edu/SENATE/facultycou/fac_cmtes/dfl_carter.htm.

Cash, J. D. 2004a. "Declassified FBI memo reveals twists in probe." *McCurtain Daily Gazette* (Jan. 2). Accessed online at http://worldnetdaily.com/news/printer-friendly.asp?ARTILCE_ID=35475.

Cash, J. D. 2004b. "Withheld evidence to sink case against Nichols?" *McCurtain Daily Gazette* (March 20): 1.

Chermak, Steven M. 2002. *Searching for a Demon: The Media Construction of the Militia Movement*. Boston: Northeastern University Press.

Christenson, Jon. 1995. "Forest Service bombed in Nevada." *High Country News*, (April 17): 1A.

Cook, Phillip J., and Jens Ludwig. 1997. *Guns in America: National Survey on Private Ownership and Use of Firearms*. Washington, DC: U.S. Department of Justice, National Institute of Justice.

Corcoran, James. 1990. *Bitter Harvest: Gordon Kahl and the Posse Comitatus*. New York: Viking.

Coulson, Danny O., and Elaine Shannon. 1999. *No Heroes*. New York: Pocket Books.

Crawford, Robert, S. L. Gardiner, and Jonathan Mozzochi. 1994. "Patriot Games: Jack McLamb and Citizen Militias." Report for the Coalition for Human Dignity, Portland, OR.

Crothers, Lane. 2003. *Rage on the Right*. Lanham, MD: Rowman and Littlefield.

Cunningham, David. 2003. "State Versus Social Movement: FBI Counterintelligence Against the New Left," pp. 45–77 in Jack A. Goldstone (ed.), *States, Parties and Social Movements*. New York: Cambridge University Press.

References

Davidson, Osha Gray. 1996. *Broken Heartland: The Rise of America's Rural Ghetto*. Iowa City: University of Iowa Press.

Davidson, Osha Gray. 1998. *Under Fire: The NRA and the Struggle for Gun Control*. Expanded version. Iowa City: University of Iowa Press.

Dees, Morris, and James Corcoran. 1996. *Gathering Storm: America's Militia Threat*. New York: Harper Collins.

della Porta, Donatella, and Mario Diani. 1999. *Social Movements: An Introduction*. Malden, MA: Blackwell.

DeNardo, James. 1985. *Power in Numbers: The Political Strategy in Protest and Rebellion*. Princeton, NJ: Princeton University Press.

Diamond, Sara. 1995. *Roads to Dominion: Right-Wing Movements and Political Power in the United States*. New York: Guilford Press.

Diani, Mario. 1995. *Green Networks: A Structural Analysis of the Italian Environmental Movement*. Edinburgh: Edinburgh University Press.

Duffy, James E., and Alan C. Brantley. 1997. "Militias: Initiating Contact." *FBI Law Enforcement Bulletin* (July). Accessed online at http://www.fbi.gov/publications/leb/1997/july975.htm.

Duke, Steven B., and Albert C. Gross. 1994. *America's Longest War: Rethinking Our Tragic Crusade Against Drugs*. New York: Tarcher/Putnam.

Dunn, Timothy. 1996. *Militarization of the U.S.-Mexico Border, 1978–1992: Low Intensity Conflict Doctrine Comes Home*. Austin: University of Texas, Center for Mexican American Studies.

Dyer, Joel. 1997. *Harvest of Rage: Why Oklahoma City Is Only the Beginning*. Boulder, CO: Westview Press.

Farmer, Val. 1986. "Broken Heartland." *Psychology Today* 20(4): 54–62.

Fenster, Mark. 1999. *Conspiracy Theories: Secrecy and Power in American Culture*. Minneapolis: University of Minnesota Press.

Final Report on the Bombing of the Alfred P. Murrah Building, April 19, 1995. 2001. Oklahoma City: Oklahoma City Bombing Investigation Committee.

Fischer, Raymond L. 1996. "Hate fills the airwaves." *USA Today/Society for the Advancement of Education* (May):1–4. Accessed online at http://www.findarticles.com/p/articles/mi_m1272/is_n2612_v124/ai_18274649.

Flynn, Kevin, and Gary Gerhardt. 1989. *The Silent Brotherhood*. New York: Signet.

Forster, Arnold, and Benjamin R. Epstein. 1964. *Danger on the Right*. New York: Random House.

Fried, Arthur. 1996. *McCarthyism: The Great American Red Scare: A Documentary History*. New York: Oxford University Press.

Fyfe, James J. 1997. "Statement of James J. Fyfe." *Hearings Before the Judiciary Committee, United States Senate: The Aftermath of Waco: Changes in Federal Law Enforcement, October 31 and November 1, 1995*. Washington, DC: U.S. Government Printing Office.

Gallagher, James J. 1992. *Low Intensity Conflict: A Guide for Tactics, Techniques, and Procedures*. Harrisburg, PA: Stackpole Books.

Gallaher, Carolyn. 2003. *On the Fault-Line: Race, Class and the American Patriot Movement*. Lanham, MD: Rowman and Littlefield.

Gamson, William. 1992. "The Social Psychology of Collective," pp. 53–76 in Carol Mueller and Aldon Morris (eds.), *Frontiers of Social Movement Theory*. New Haven, CT: Yale University Press.

Gamson, William, and David Meyer. 1996. "The Framing of Political Opportunity," pp. 275–90 in Doug McAdam, John D. McCarthy, and Mayer N. Zald (eds.), *Comparative Perspectives on Social Movements: Political Opportunities, Mobilizing Structures and Cultural Framings*. Cambridge: Cambridge University Press.

Gamson, William, Bruce Fireman, and Steve Rytina. 1982. *Encounters with Unjust Authority*. Homewood, IL: Dorsey.

George, John, and Laird Wilcox. 1996. *American Extremists: Militias, Supremacists, Klansmen, Communists and Others*. Amherst, NY: Prometheus Books.

Gibson, James William. 1994. *Warrior Dreams: Paramilitary Culture in Post-Vietnam America*. New York: Hill and Wang.

Gitlin, Todd. 1993. *The Sixties: Years of Hope, Days of Rage*. New York: Bantam.

Giugni, Marco, Ruud Koopmans, Florence Passy, and Paul Stratham. 2005. "Institutional and Discursive Opportunities for Extreme Right Mobilization in Five Countries." *Mobilization* 10(1): 145–62.

Goldstone, Jack A., and Charles Tilly. 2001. "Threat (and Opportunity): Popular Action and State Response in the Dynamics of Contentious Action," pp. 179–94 in Ronald Aminzade et al. (eds.), *Silence and Voice in the Study of Contentious Politics*. New York: Cambridge University Press.

Goode, Eric. 1989. *Drugs in American Society*, 3rd ed. New York: Alfred Knopf.

Goodwin, Jeff, and James M. Jasper. 2004. *Rethinking Social Movements*. Lanham, MD: Rowman and Littlefield.

Graber, Janna. 1998. "Surviving." *Chicago Tribune* (Nov. 22). Accessed online at http://wwwjannagraber.com/surviving.htm.

Griffith, Robert, and Athan Theoharis. 1974. *The Specter: Original Essays on the Cold War and the Origins of McCarthyism*. New York: New Viewpoints.

Haggerty, Kevin D., and Richard V. Ericson. 2001. "The Military Technostructures of Policing," pp. 43-64 in Peter B. Kraska (ed.), *Militarizing the American Criminal Justice System*. Boston: Northeastern University Press.

Hall, John R. 1995. "Public Narratives and the Apocalyptic Sect: From Jonestown to Mt. Carmel," pp. 205–35 in Stuart A. Wright (ed.), *Armageddon in Waco*. Chicago: University of Chicago Press.

Hall, John R., and Mary Jo Neitz. 1993. *Culture: Sociological Perspectives*. Englewood Cliffs, NJ: Prentice-Hall.

Hall, Stuart. 1982. "The Rediscovery of Ideology: Return of the Repressed in Media Studies," pp. 56–90 in Michael Gurevitch (ed.), *Culture, Society and Media*. New York: Methuen.

Hall, Stuart, Chris Critcher, Tony Jefferson, John Clarke, and Brian Roberts. 1978. *Policing the Crisis: Mugging, the State, and Law and Order*. London: Macmillan.

Hamby, Alonzo L. 1973. *Beyond the New Deal: Harry S. Truman and American Liberalism*. New York: Columbia University Press.

Hamilton, Neil A. 1996. *Militias in America: A Reference Handbook*. Santa Barbara, CA: ABC-CLIO.

References

Hamm, Mark S. 1997. *Apocalypse in Oklahoma*. Boston: Northeastern University Press.

Hamm, Mark S. 2002. *In Bad Company: America's Terrorist Underground*. Boston: Northeastern University Press.

Hargrove, David S. 1986. "Mental Health Response to the Farm Foreclosure Crisis." *Rural Sociologist* 6(2): 88–95.

Henry, Larry. 1996. "SUN Profile: Harris' troubled past includes mail fraud, white supremacy." *Las Vegas Sun* (Feb. 23). Accessed online at http://www.lasvegassun.com/dossier/bio/harris.html.

Hoffer, Eric. 1955. *The True Believer: Thoughts on the Nature of Mass Movements*. New York: Harper.

Hofstadter, Richard. 1965. *The Paranoid Style in American Politics and Other Essays*. New York: Knopf.

Holthouse, David. 2006. "A Few Bad Men." Southern Poverty Law Center Intelligence Report (Summer). Accessed online at http://splcenter.org/intel/news/item.jsp?aid=66&printable=1

Hunt, Scott A., Robert D. Benford, and David A. Snow. 1994. "Identity Fields: Framing Processes and the Social Construction of Movement Identities," pp. 185–208 in Enrique Larana, Han Johnston, and Joseph R. Gusfield (eds.), *New Social Movements: From Ideology to Identity*.Philadelphia: Temple University Press.

Interview with Wally Kennett. 1993. Interview conducted by author on file.

Investigation into the Activities of Federal Law Enforcement Agencies Toward the Branch Davidians, Thirteenth Report by the Committee on Government Reform and Oversight Prepared in Conjunction with the Committee on the Judiciary, Aug. 2, 1996. Washington, DC: U.S. Government Printing Office.

Janson, Donald, and Bernard Eismann. 1963. *The Far Right*. New York: McGraw-Hill.

Jasper, William F. 1995. "Malicious Militia Reporting." *New American* 11(9): 1–6. Accessed online at http://www.thenewamerican.com/tna/1995/vol11no09/vol1no09_militia.htm.

Johnson, Bill. 1995. "Oklahoma Prophet Indicted in Alleged Bomb Plot." *Albion Monitor News* (Dec. 3). Accessed online at http://www.monitor.net/monitor/12-3-95/lampley.html.

Johnson, David, and Alan Booth. 1990. "Rural Economic Decline and Marital Quality: A Panel Study of Farm Marriages." *Family Relations* 39(2): 159–65.

Johnson, Kevin, and Susan Page. 1996. "Government seeking help from anti-government groups." *USA Today* (Mar. 29): 3A.

Johnston, David. 1996 "Montana standoff tests FBI director." *Houston Chronicle* (Mar. 30): 2A.

Joint Doctrine for Military Operations Other Than War. 1995. Joint Pub. 3–07. Washington, DC: U.S. Government Printing Office.

Jones, Stephen, and Peter Israel. 1998. *Others Unknown: The Oklahoma City Bombing Case and Conspiracy*. New York: Public Affairs.

Juergensmeyer, Mark. 2002. *Terror in the Mind of God.* Updated version with new preface. Berkeley: University of California Press.

Kettner, K. A., Jack Geller, R. L. Ludtke, and J. Kelly. 1988. "Economic Hardship Among Farm Operators in North Dakota: The Buffering Effect of Social Support." *Great Plains Sociologist* 1(1): 69–88.

Kight, Marsha. 1998a. *Forever Changed: Remembering Oklahoma City, April 19, 1995.* Amherst, NY: Prometheus Books.

Kight, Marsha. 1998b. "The Oklahoma City Experience." *National Center for Victims of Crime: Networks* (Winter/Spring): 14–15.

Klandermans, Bert. 1997. *The Social Psychology of Protest.* Oxford/Cambridge: Blackwell.

Klapp, Orrin. 1969. *The Collective Search for Identity.* New York: Holt, Rinehart and Winston.

Klare, Michael T. 1988. "The Interventionist Impulse: U.S. Military Doctrine for Low-Intensity Warfare," pp. 49–79 in Michael T. Klare and Peter Kornbluh (eds.), *Low Intensity Warfare: Counterinsurgency, Proinsurgency and Antiterrorism in the Eighties.* New York: Pantheon.

Klare, Michael T., and Peter Kornbluh (eds.). 1988a. *Low Intensity Warfare: Counterinsurgency, Proinsurgency and Antiterrorism in the Eighties.* New York: Pantheon.

Klare, Michael T., and Peter Kornbluh. 1988b. "The New Interventionism: Low-Intensity Warfare in the 1980s and Beyond," pp. 3–20 in Michael T. Klare and Peter Kornbluh (eds.), *Low Intensity Warfare: Counterinsurgency, Proinsurgency and Antiterrorism in the Eighties.* New York: Pantheon.

Kohl, Howard. 1988. *The Last Farmer: An American Memoir.* New York: Summit.

Koopmans, Ruud. 1997. "Dynamics of Repression and Mobilization of the German Extreme Right in the 1990s." *Mobilization* 2(2) (Sept.): 149–64.

Kopel, David B. 1995. "Knock, Knock." *National Review,* Mar. 20. Accessed online at http://www.davekopel.com/Waco/Arts/Knock-knock.htm.

Kopel, David B., and Paul H. Blackman. 1997. *No More Wacos: What's Wrong with Federal Law Enforcement and How to Fix It.* Amherst, NY: Prometheus Books.

Kornhauser, William. 1959. *The Politics of Mass Society.* Glencoe, IL: Free Press.

Kraska, Peter B. 1993. "Militarizing the Drug War: A Sign of the Times,"pp. 159–206 in Peter B. Kraska (ed.), *Altered States of Mind: Critical Observations of the Drug War.* New York: Garland.

Kraska, Peter B. 1994. "The Police and Military in the post Cold War Era: Streamlining the State's Use of Force Entities in the Drug War." *Police Forum* 4: 1–8.

Kraska. Peter B. 1996. "Enjoying Militarism: Political/Personal Dilemmas in Studying U.S. Police Paramilitary Units." *Justice Quarterly* 13: 405–29.

Kraska, Peter B. 2001a. "Crime Control as Warfare," pp. 14–25 in Peter B. Kraska (ed.), *Militarizing the American Criminal Justice System.* Boston: Northeastern University Press.

Kraska, Peter B. 2001b. *Militarizing the American Criminal Justice System.* Boston: Northeastern University Press.

References

Kraska, Peter B. 2001c. "The Military-Criminal Justice Blur," pp. 3–13 in Peter B. Kraska (ed.), *Militarizing the American Criminal Justice System*. Boston: Northeastern University Press.

Kraska, Peter B., and Louis J. Cubellis. 1997. "Militarizing Mayberry and Beyond: Making Sense of American Paramilitary Policing." *Justice Quarterly* 14 (Dec.): 607–29.

Kraska, Peter B., and Victor E. Kappeler. 1996. Militarizing American Police: The Rise and Normalization of Paramilitary Units." *Social Problems* 44(1): 1–18.

Kriesi, Hanspeter. 1996. "The Organizational Structure of New Social Movements in a Political Context," pp. 152–84 in Doug McAdam, John D. McCarthy, and Mayer N. Zald (eds.), *Comparative Perspectives on Social Movements*. Cambridge: Cambridge University Press.

Kurzman, Charles. 1996. "Structural Opportunities and Perceived Opportunities in Social-Movement Theory: Evidence from the Iranian Revolution of 1979." *American Sociological Review* 61(1) (Feb.): 153–70.

Lamy, Phillip. 1996. *Millennium Rage: Survivalists, White Supremacists, and the Doomsday Prophecy*. New York: Plenum.

Leistritz, F. Larry, and Brenda L. Ekstrom. 1988. "The Financial Characteristics of Production Units and Producers Experiencing Financial Stress," pp. 73–92 in Steve H. Murdock and F. Larry Leistritz (eds.), *The Farm Financial Crisis: Socioeconomic Dimensions and Implications for Producers and Rural Areas*. Boulder, CO: Westview Press.

Leistritz, F. Larry, and Steve H. Murdock. 1988. "Financial Characteristics of Farms and of Farm Financial Markets and Policies in the United States," pp. 112–30 in Steve H. Murdock and F. Larry Leistritz (eds.), *The Farm Financial Crisis: Socioeconomic Dimensions and Implications for Producers and Rural Areas*. Boulder, CO: Westview Press.

Levitas, Daniel. 2002. *The Terrorist Next Door: The Militia Movement and the Radical Right*. New York: Thomas Dunne Books/St. Martin's Press.

Lewis, James R. 1995. "Self-Fulfilling Stereotypes, the Anticult Movement, and the Waco Confrontation," pp. 95–110 in Stuart A. Wright (ed.), *Armageddon in Waco*. Chicago: University of Chicago Press.

Lieby, Richard. 1997. "Many Militia Groups Scale Back, Distance Themselves from McVeigh." *Washington Post* (June 14): A8.

Lincoln, C. Eric. 1974. *The Black Church Since Frazier*. New York: Schocken.

Lipset, Seymour Martin, and Earl Rabb. 1970. *The Politics of Unreason: Right-Wing Extremism in America*. New York: Harper and Row.

Luders, Joseph. 2003. "Countermovements, the State, and the Intensity of Racial Contention in the American South," pp. 27–44 in Jack A. Goldstone (ed.), *States, Parties and Social Movements*. New York: Cambridge University Press.

Macko, Steve. 1996. "Arizona Militia Group Arrested by Federal Authorities." Emergency Net News Service, July 2, vol. 2: 184. Accessed online at http://www.emergency.com/AZ-viper.htm.

Marshall, Jonathan, Peter Dale Scott, and Jane Hunter. 1987. *The Iran Contra Connection: Secret Teams and Covert Operations in the Reagan Era*. Boston: South End Press.

McAdam, Doug. 1982. *Political Process and the Development of Black Insurgency, 1930–1979*. Chicago: University of Chicago Press.

McAdam, Doug. 1988. *Freedom Summer*. New York: Oxford University Press.

McAdam, Doug. 1999. *Political Process and the Development of Black Insurgency, 1930–1970*, 2nd ed. Chicago: University of Chicago Press.

McAdam, Doug. 2003. "Beyond Structural Analysis: Toward a More Dynamic Understanding of Social Movements," pp. 281–98 in Mario Diani and Doug McAdam (eds.), *Social Movements and Networks: Relational Approaches to Collective Action*. Oxford: Oxford University Press.

McAdam, Doug. 2004. "Revisiting the U.S. Civil Rights Movement: Toward a More Synthetic Understanding of the Origins of Contention," pp. 201–32 in Jeff Goodwin and James M. Jasper (eds.), *Rethinking Social Movements*. Lanham, MD: Rowman and Littlefield.

McAdam, Doug, John D. McCarthy, and Mayer N. Zald (eds.). 1996a. *Comparative Perspectives on Social Movements: Political Opportunities, Mobilizing Structures and Cultural Framings*. Cambridge: Cambridge University Press.

McAdam, Doug, John D. McCarthy, and Mayer N. Zald. 1996b. "Introduction: Opportunities, Mobilizing Structures, and Framing Processes – Toward a Synthetic, Comparative Perspective on Social Movements," pp. 1–20 in Doug McAdam, John D. McCarthy, and Mayer N. Zald (eds.), *Comparative Perspectives on Social Movements: Political Opportunities, Mobilizing Structures and Cultural Framings*. Cambridge: Cambridge University Press.

McAdam, Doug, Sidney Tarrow, and Charles Tilly. 2001. *Dynamics of Contention*. New York: Cambridge University Press.

McAlvaney, Don. 1993. "Abuses of BATF." *McAlvaney Intelligence Advisor* (July). Accessed online at http://elfie.org/~croaker/janintel.html.

McCarthy, John D. 1996. "Constraints and Opportunities in Adopting, Adapting and Inventing," pp. 141–51 in Doug McAdam, John D. McCarthy, and Mayer N. Zald (eds.), *Comparative Perspectives on Social Movements: Political Opportunities, Mobilizing Structures and Cultural Framings*. Cambridge: Cambridge University Press.

McCarthy, John D., and Mayer N. Zald. 1973. *The Trend of Social Movements: Professionalization and Resource Mobilization*. Morristown, NJ: General Learning Press.

McCarthy, John D., and Mayer N. Zald. 1977. "Resource Mobilization and Social Movements: A Partial Theory. *American Journal of Sociology* 82(6): 1212–41.

Melucci, Alberto. 1989. *Nomads of the Present*. Philadelphia: Temple University Press.

Melucci, Alberto. 1996. *Challenging Codes*. Cambridge: Cambridge University Press.

Meyer, David. 2002. *Social Movements: Identity, Culture and the State*. New York: Oxford University Press.

Michel, Lou, and Dan Herbeck. 2000. *American Terrorist: Timothy McVeigh and the Oklahoma City Bombing*. New York: ReganBooks.

References

Miller, Richard Lawrence. 1996. *Drug Warriors and Their Prey: From Police Power to Police State*. Westport, CT: Praeger.

Moore, Carol. 1995. *The Davidian Massacre*. Franklin, TN: Legacy Communications and Springfield, VA: Gun Owners of America.

Morris, Aldon D. 1984. *The Origins of the Civil Rights Movement*. New York: Free Press.

Murdock, Steve H., Don Albrecht, Rita Hamm, F. Larry Leistritz, and Arlen G. Leholm. 1986. "The Farm Crisis in the Great Plains: Implications for Theory and Policy Development." *Rural Sociology* 51(4): 406–35.

Myrdal, Gunnar. 1944. *An American Dilemma*. New York: Harper and Brothers.

Nairn, Allan. 1981. "Reagan's Administration Links with Guatemala's Terrorist Government." *Covert Action Information Bulletin* (April): 16–21.

National Public Radio. 2004. "Analysis: Evidence of More Conspirators Involved in Bombing of the Murrah Federal Building in Oklahoma City." *All Things Considered*, with Wade Goodwyn. Transcript of May 7 broadcast.

National Rifle Association. 1994, "As Trials of Waco Survivors Open in Texas, ACLU, NRA, Others Ask Clinton to Address Federal Police Abuse." Joint Press Release with the American Civil Liberties Union, Jan. 10. Document on file with author.

Nichols, Nicole. 2003. Domestic Terrorism 101: The Kehoe Connection. Accessed online at http://www.eyeonhate.com/mcveigh/mcveigh8.html.

Niewert, David A. 1999. *In God's Country: The Patriot Movement and the Pacific Northwest*. Pullman: Washington State University Press.

Noble, Kerry. 1998. *Tabernacle of Hate*. Prescott, ON, Canada: Voyageur.

NRA-ILA FAX Network. "Media's Maligning Marches On. May 13, 1995. On file with author.

Oberschall, Anthony. 1973. *Social Conflict and Social Movements*. Englewood Cliffs, NJ: Prentice-Hall.

O'Brien, Michael. 1974. "McCarthy and McCarthyism: The Cedric Parker Case, November 1949," pp. 224–39 in Robert Griffith and Athan Theoharis (eds.), *The Specter: Original Essays on the Cold War and the Origins of McCarthyism*. New York: New Viewpoints.

O'Brien, Sean, and Donald P. Haider-Markel. 1998. "Fueling the Fire: Social and Political Correlates of Citizen Militia Activity." *Social Science Quarterly* 79(2): 456–65.

Olmstead v. United States 277 U.S. 438 [1928].

Olsen, Norman. 1994. "The Martialization of American Society. Michigan Militia Report. On file with author.

Olsen, Norman. 1997. "Citizen Militias Defend Liberty," pp. 10–18 in Charles Cozic (ed.), The Milita Movement. San Diego: Greenhaven Press.

Opp, Karl-Dieter, and Wolfgang Roehl. 1990. "Repression, Micromobilization and Political Protest." *Social Forces* 69(2): 521–47.

Palafax, Jose. 1996. "Militarizing the Border." *Covert Action Quarterly* no. 56 (Spring). Accessed online at http://mediafilter.org/MFF/caq/CAQ56border.html.

Pate, James L. 1992. "Gun Gestapo: BATF Brownshirts Terrorize Tulsa." *Soldier of Fortune* (June): 54–8.

Pate, James L. 1993a. "Gun Gestapo's Day of Infamy. *Soldier of Fortune* (June): 49–53, 62–4.

Pate, James L. 1993b. "No Longer Untouchable." *American Spectator* (Aug.): 35–6.

Pate, James L. 1993c. "Standoff in Idaho: The Randy Weaver Incident." *Soldier of Fortune* (March): 63.

Pate, James L. 1994. "Is America Becoming a Police State? *Soldier of Fortune* (Sept.): 34–7, 71–6.

Pate, James L. 1995. "Katona Gets His Guns." *Soldier of Fortune* (May): 34–5.

Pew Research Center. 1993. The Vocal Minority in American Politics. Report issued July 16, 1993. Accessed online at http://people-press.org/reports/display. php3?ReportID=19930716.

Pratt, Larry. 1990. *Armed People Victorious.* Springfield, VA: Gun Owners of America.

Pratt, Larry. 1995a. "House Throws Curve Ball to Gun Rights Supporters." Gun Owners of America News (June). Accessed online at http://www.gunowners.org/ news/nws9506.htm.

Pratt, Larry. 1995b. "Introduction: Firearms: The People's Liberty Teeth," pp. ix–xiv in Larry Pratt (ed.), *Safeguarding Liberty: The Constitution and Citizen Militias.* Franklin, TN: Legacy Communications.

Pratt, Larry. 1995c. *Safeguarding Liberty: The Constitution and Citizen Militias.* Franklin, TN: Legacy Communications.

Rand, Kristen. 1996. *Gun Shows in America: Tupperware Parties for Criminals.* Washington, DC: Violence Policy Center.

Rathge, Richard W., F. Larry Leistritz, and Gary A. Goreham. 1988. "Farmers Displaced in Economically Depressed Times." *Rural Sociology* 53(3): 346–55.

Richardson, Valerie Richardson. 1997. "McVeigh draws the maximum penalty." *Washington Times* (June 14): A5.

Ridgeway, James. 1990. *Blood in the Face: The Ku Klux Klan, Aryan Nations, Nazi Skinheads and the Rise of a New White Culture.* New York: Thunder's Mouth Press.

Robinson, Bryan. 2001. "Militias Will Not Consider McVeigh a Martyr" ABC News (June 12). Accessed online at http://www.abcnews.go.com/militias/1997/ june12.htm.

Robinson, William I. 1992. *A Faustian Bargain: U.S. Intervention in the Nicaraguan Elections and American Foreign Policy in the Post-Cold War Era.* Boulder, CO: Westview Press.

Rogin, Michael Paul. 1967. *The Intellectuals and McCarthy: The Radical Specter.* Cambridge, MA: MIT Press.

Roland, Jon. 1994. "Motivation for the modern militia." Accessed online at http://www.boogieonline.com/revolution/firearms/militia/movement.html.

Romano, Lois. 2001. "McVeigh is executed." *Washington Post* (June 12): A1.

Rome Laboratory Law Enforcement Technology Team. 1996. "Transferring Defense Technology to Law Enforcement." *New Horizon* (April):1–11. Accessed online at http://www.aci.net/kalliste/deftech.htm.

Rosenblatt, Paul C., and Linda Olsen Keller. 1983. "Economic Vulnerability and Economic Crisis in Farm Couples." *Family Relations* (Oct.): 567–73.

Sahagun, Louis. 1996. "Other groups threaten violence if agents attack Montana Freemen" *Houston Chronicle* (April 5): 18A.

References

Sahagun, Louis, and Tina Daunt. 1996. "Agents uncover guns, bombing materials in Viper home search." *Houston Chronicle* (July 2).

Saito, Theodore. 1994. "Law Enforcement Arena Ripe for Technology Transfer." International Society for Optical Engineering, OE Reports (Dec.): 1–2. Accessed online at http://www.spie.org/app/Publications/magazines/oearchive/december/law_enf.html.

Sherwood, Samuel. 1992. *The Guarantee of the Second Amendment*. Blackfoot, ID: Founders Press.

Sherwood, Samuel. 1995. *Establishing an Independent Militia in the United States*. Blackfoot, ID: Founders Press.

Sklar, Holly. 1988. *Washington's War on Nicaragua*. Boston: South End Press.

Skolnick, Jerome H., and James J. Fyfe. 1993. *Above the Law: Police and the Excessive Use of Force*. New York: Free Press.

Smelser, Neil. 1962. *The Theory of Collective Behavior*. London: Routledge and Kegan Paul.

Smith, Brent. 1994. *Terrorism in America: Pipe Bombs and Pipe Dreams*. Albany: State University of New York Press.

Snow, David A., and Robert D. Benford. 1992. "Master Frames and Cycles of Protest," pp.133-55 in Aldon D. Morris and Carol McClurg Mueller (eds.), *Frontiers in Social Movements*. New Haven, CT: Yale University Press.

Snow, David A., Burke E. Rochford, Steven Worden, and Robert Benford. 1986. "Frame Alignment Process, Micromobilization, and Movement Participation." *American Sociological Review* 51(4): 464–81.

Solomon, John. 2003a. "Agencies sat on data before attack." *Houston Chronicle* (Feb. 12): 3A.

Solomon, John. 2003b. "FBI Linked McVeigh to Group After Bombing." Associated Press (Feb.12). Accessed online at http://www.okcbombing.org/News%20articles/fbi_linked_mcveigh.htm.

Solomon, John. 2004a. "Document: Oklahoma City Bombing Was Taped." Associated Press (April 20). Accessed online at http://news.yahoo.com/news?tmpl=story&cid=542^u=/ap/20040419/

Solomon, John. 2004b. "FBI Tried, and Failed, to Interview McVeigh on Death Row." Associated Press (May 4). Accessed online at http://www.capitolhillblue.com/cgi-bin/artman/exec/view.cgi?/archive=29&num=4170&print.htm.

Sonnet, Neal R. 1990. "War on Drugs – or the Constitution?" *Trial* (April): 24–30.

Southern Poverty Law Center. 1996. *False Patriots: The Threat of Antigovernment Extremists*. Montgomery, AL: SPLC.

Southern Poverty Law Center. 2001. "The Rise and Decline of the Patriots." Intelligence Report. Accessed online at http://www.splcenter.org/intel/intelreport/article.jsp?aid_195&printable=1.

Spitzer, Robert J. 1995. *The Politics of Gun Control*. Chatham, NJ: Chatham House.

Sterling, Eric. 1990. "Is the Bill of Rights a Casualty of the War on Drugs?" Address delivered to the Colorado Bar Association, Sept. 14.

Stern, Kenneth S. 1996. *A Force upon the Plain*. New York: Simon & Schuster.

Stock, Catherine M. 1996. *Rural Radicals: Righteous Rage in the American Grain*. Ithaca: Cornell University Press.

Stouffer, Samuel. 1955. *Communism, Conformity and Civil Liberties: A Cross-Section of the Nation Speak[s] Its Mind*. Garden City, NY: Doubleday.

Sugarman, Josh. 1992. *NRA: Money, Firepower and Fear*. Washington, DC: National Press Books.

Talley, Tim, 2004. "Sister: McVeigh rarely spoke of Nichols." *Daily Oklahoman* (May 15): 1.

Tanner, William, and Robert Griffith. 1974. "Legislative Politics and 'McCarthyism': The Internal Security Act of 1950," pp. 172–89 in Robert Griffith and Athan Theoharis (eds.), *The Specter: Original Essays on the Cold War and the Origins of McCarthyism*. New York: New Viewpoints.

Tarrow, Sidney. 1989. *Democracy and Disorder: Protest and Politics in Italy, 1965–1974*. Oxford: Oxford University Press.

Tarrow, Sidney. 1994. *Power in Movement*. Cambridge: Cambridge University Press.

Tarrow, Sidney. 1995. "Cycles of Collective Action: Between Moments of Madness and the Repertoire of Contention," pp. 89–115 in Mark Traugott (ed.), *Repertoires and Cycles of Collective Action*. Durham, NC: Duke University Press.

Taylor, Verta. 1989. "Social Movement Continuity: The Women's Movement in Abeyance." *American Sociological Review* 54: 761–75.

Thibodeau, David, and Leon Whiteson. 1999. *A Place Called Waco: A Survivor's Story*. New York: Public Affairs.

Thomas, Jo. 1997. "McVeigh Speaks at Last, Fleetingly and Obscurely." *New York Times* (Aug. 15): 1A.

Tilly, Charles. 1978. *From Mobilization to Revolution*. Reading, MA: Addison-Wesley.

Tilly, Charles. 1986. *The Contentious French*. Cambridge, MA: Harvard University Press.

Trammell, Robby. 1998. "Self-Proclaimed Prophet Admits Building Bomb." *Daily Oklahoman* (Nov.14): 1.

Turner, Ralph, and Lewis Killian. 1962. *Collective Behavior*. Englewood Cliffs, NJ: Prentice-Hall.

Uekert, Brenda K. 1995. *Rivers of Blood: A Comparative Study of Government Massacres*. New York : Praeger.

U.S. Department of Justice. 1994. Department of Justice Ruby Ridge Report. Unpublished report accessed online at http://www.prostar.com/web/amerika/Ruby005.htm.

U.S. Department of Justice. 2000. *Responding to Terrorism Victims: Oklahoma City and Beyond*. Report by Office for Victims of Crime. Washington, DC: U.S. Government Printing Office.

U.S. Department of the Treasury. 1993. *Report of the Department of Treasury on the Bureau of Alcohol, Tobacco, and Firearms Investigation of Vernon Wayne Howell, Also Known as David Koresh*. Washington, DC: U.S. Government Printing Office.

U.S. Department of the Treasury. 2000. *Commerce in Firearms in the United States*. Washington, DC: U.S. Government Printing Office.

References

U.S. District Court, Western District of Texas. Application and Affidavit for Search Warrant, W93–15M, filed Feb. 26, 1993, Waco, TX.

U.S. Government Accounting Office. 1993. *Small Arms Parts: Poor Controls Invite Widespread Theft*. Report Number NSIAD-94-21. Washington, DC: U.S. GAO.

United States of America v. Charles Ray Polk, U.S. Court of Appeals for the 5th District, Appeal from the U.S. District Court for the Eastern District of Texas, Case no. 96–40836, 1997.

United States of America v. Larry Wayne Harris, William Job Leavitt, Jr., U.S. District Court, District of Nevada, Case no. MAG-98-2042-M-RLH, 1998.

United States of America v. Willie Ray Lampley, Cecilia Lampley, Larry Wayne Crow and John Dare Baird, U.S. District Court for the Eastern District of Oklahoma, No. CR-95-63-S, 1995.

Vaughn, Ed. 1992. "National Guard Involvement in the Drug War." *Justicia* (Dec.): 1–4.

Vizzard, William J. 2000. *Shots in the Dark: The Policy, Politics and Symbolism of Gun Control*. Lanham, MD: Rowman and Littlefield.

Wagoner-Pacifici, Robin. 1994. *Discourse and Destruction*. Chicago: University of Chicago Press.

Walter, Jess. 1995. *Every Knee Shall Bow*. New York: Harper.

Warren, Donald I. 1976. *The Radical Center: Middle Americans and the Politics of Alienation*. Notre Dame, IN: University of Notre Dame Press.

Wattenberg, Ben. 1993. "Gunning for Koresh." *American Spectator* (Aug.): 31–40.

Welch, Robert. 1966. "Two Revolutions at Once," p. 203, reprinted in *The New Americanism—And Other Speeches and Essays*. Boston and Los Angeles: Western Island Publishers.

Westcott, Kathryn. 2001. "Militias in Retreat." BBC News Online (May 11). Accessed online at http://news.bbc.co.uk/1/low/world/americas/1325330stm.

Westin, Alan F. 1963. "The John Birch Society," pp. 201–28 in Daniel Bell (ed.), *The Radical Right*. New York: Doubleday.

White, Robert W. 1989. "From Peaceful Protest to Guerrilla War: Micromobilization of the Provisional Irish Republican Army." *American Journal of Sociology* 94(6): 1277–302.

Whittier, Nancy. 1995. *Feminist Generations: The Persistence of the Radical Women's Movement*. Philadelphia: Temple University Press.

Whittier, Nancy. 1997. "Political Generation, Micro-Cohorts, and the Transformation of Social Movements." *American Sociological Review* 62(5) (Oct.): 760–78.

Winthrop, Jim. 1997. "The Oklahoma City Bombing: Immediate Response Authority and Other Military Assistance to Civil Authority (MACA)." *Army Law* (July): 3–15.

Wirpsa, Leslie. 1995. "Rural Despair Feeds Militia Growth." *National Catholic Reporter* (June 30): 10.

Wisotsky, Steven. 1990. *Beyond the War on Drugs*. New York: Prometheus Books.

Wright, Stuart A. 1995a. *Armageddon in Waco: Critical Perspectives on the Branch Davidian Conflict*. Chicago: University of Chicago Press.

Wright, Stuart A. 1995b. "Construction and Escalation of a Cult Threat: Dissecting Moral Panic and Official Reaction to the Branch Davidians," pp. 75–94 in Stuart A. Wright (ed.), *Armageddon in Waco*. Chicago: University of Chicago Press.

Wright, Stuart A. 1999. "Anatomy of a Government Massacre: Abuses of Hostage-Barricade Protocols During the Waco Standoff." *Terrorism and Political Violence* 11(2): 39–68.

Wright, Stuart A. 2001. "Field Notes: Isabel Andrade et al. v. U.S." *Nova Religio* 4(2): 157–64.

Wright, Stuart A. 2003. "A Decade after Waco: Reassessing Crisis Negotiations at Mt. Carmel in Light of New Government Disclosures." *Nova Religio* 7(2): 101–10.

Wright, Stuart A. 2005. "Explaining Militarization at Waco: Construction and Convergence of a Warfare Narrative," pp. 75–97 in James R. Lewis (ed.), *Controversial New Religions*. New York: Oxford University Press.

Zeskind, Leonard. 1987. *The Christian Identity Movement*. Atlanta: Center for Democratic Renewal; New York: National Council of Churches, Division of Church and Society.

Zhao, Dingxin. 1989. "Prodemocracy Movement in Beijing." *American Journal of Sociology* 103(6): 1493–529.

Index

233

Index

Horiuchi, Lon, 147, 148
Hostage Rescue Team, 89, 92, 146, 162, 207
Howarth, Chuck, 142
Howe, Carol, 12, 13, 180, 183

intrinsic narrative, 143, 155

John Birch Society, 33, 54, 60, 67, 81, 85, 169
Jones, Stephen, 1–3, 9, 12–14

Kahl, Gordon, 4, 20, 84–7, 89, 98, 143, 144, 160, 164
Kennett, Wally, 156–8
Kight, Marsha, 200, 201
Kindred, George Lee, 65–8
Kirk, Arthur, 20, 82, 98, 149
Koresh, David, 5, 86, 152, 153, 155–62, 176, 199
Kraska, Peter, 105–8, 114, 127, 137
Ku Klux Klan, 24, 61

Lampley, Willie Ray, 204, 206, 207
Langan, Peter, 182–8, 190, 204
LaPierre, Wayne, 139, 210
LaRouche, Lyndon, 77, 82, 98
leaderless resistance, 87, 150, 151, 181, 215
Levitas, Daniel, 62, 63, 65, 66, 68, 73, 80–2
Liberty Lobby, 33, 61, 81
Low-intensity conflict, 100
Luders, Joseph, 31, 32

Mahon, Dennis, 12, 180, 207
Mathews, Robert, 4, 88, 89, 92, 94, 95, 98, 133, 140, 142, 143, 164, 182, 186, 191
McAdam, Doug, 26, 28–30, 32, 34–6, 39, 41, 44, 45, 49, 53, 93, 97, 216
McCarthy, John D., 41
McCarthy, Joseph, 48, 49
McCarthy, Kevin, 187–9, 192

McLamb, Jack, 147, 148
McVeigh, Timothy, 1–19, 21, 38, 75, 85, 86, 91, 113, 129, 133, 137, 163, 164, 173–93, 195, 201, 202, 205, 207–14
Metzger, Tom, 88, 133, 140
Michigan Militia, 173, 209
militarization, 14, 19, 38, 99, 101, 106, 107, 112, 113, 127, 137, 167
military model, 19, 105, 109, 128, 139
militia, 11, 37, 38, 45, 92, 105, 116, 117, 124–6, 138, 147, 150, 162, 168–76, 181, 189, 199, 201, 205, 208, 209, 211–13
Militia Correspondence Committee, 172
Militia of Montana, 142, 170, 174, 212, 214
Millar, Robert, 85, 90, 179, 189, 207
Minutemen, 58–61, 65
mobilization, 20, 25–9, 31, 32, 34–41, 44, 53, 68, 96, 97, 105, 107, 114, 116, 140, 155, 167, 170, 173, 175, 202, 215–17
Montana Freemen, 204, 207, 212
Mountaineer Militia, 205
Mt. Carmel, 7, 152, 153, 156–8, 161–4, 171
Murrah Building

National Alliance, 88, 127, 140, 162
National Rifle Association, 115, 119–23, 126, 130–2, 134, 135, 139, 199, 210
network, 19, 20, 27, 28, 33, 37–9, 56, 58, 61, 62, 66, 68, 70, 81, 110, 113, 114, 116, 122, 129, 138, 140, 141, 143, 150, 159, 167, 170, 171, 175–7, 180, 182, 184, 185, 190–2, 196, 200, 209, 212
New World Order, 4, 34, 38, 70, 81, 113, 126, 149, 167, 168, 171, 172, 176, 177, 195, 197, 207, 216
Nichols, James, 75

Index